MODERN
BABY NAMES FOR A NEW INDIA

Radhika Dogra Swarup spent a nomadic childhood in India, Italy, Qatar, Pakistan, Romania and England. She studied at Cambridge University and worked in finance before turning to writing. Her work has been published in India and the UK. The birth of her baby was her inspiration for much of her current work. She lives in London with her husband and her young son.

MODERN

BABY NAMES FOR A NEW INDIA

Radhika Dogra Swarup

RUPA

Published by
Rupa Publications India Pvt. Ltd 2011
7/16, Ansari Road, Daryaganj
New Delhi 110002

Sales centres:
Allahabad Bengaluru Chennai
Hyderabad Jaipur Kathmandu
Kolkata Mumbai

ISBN: 978-81-291-1868-4

10 9 8 7 6 5 4 3 2

The moral right of the author has been asserted.

Printed at Yash Printographics, Noida

~

For *Maanas*,
who has brought meaning
to our words as he has to our lives

~

For *Maanas*,
who has brought meaning
to our words as he has to our lives

Contents

Acknowledgements

My hearfelt thanks go to those with unforgettable names across the world – whether they be a Delight or a Wisdum in Zambia, a Rambo or a Bravo in Italy, a Seksi or a Burberry in England, or nearer home, a Twinkle, Dolly, Lovely or Sundari. If it wasn't for you, my search for my baby's name would have been filled with tedium.

Thanks naturally follow to my parents for giving me access to the Rambos and the Seksis of this world. I am also grateful to them for taking me to countries where Radhika – which is an inoffensive enough name in India – came at times to resemble the most impenetrable phonetic maze.

I reserve my biggest thanks for the last. These go to my son Maanas, whose name this book celebrates, and to my husband Amarendra, whose name it can't. Amarendra has kept me company at crazy hours of the morning – which invariably is the best time to work around a sleeping infant – has taken over weekend nappy changes and walks so I can concentrate on this book, and in a Herculean effort, has pored endlessly through Sanskrit and Hindi dictionaries in search of names thousands of years of civilization haven't unearthed.

How to Use the Book

1. The name is followed by its phonetic pronunciation in *italics*.

2. The gender of the name is denoted (M) for male names and (F) for female names. Where there is a name that can be used or adapted for use by both genders, they are listed separately with their individual phonetic pronunciations.

3. Origins of the name marked by (S) for Sanskrit, (A) for Arabic, (P) for Persian, (H) for Hindi, and (O) for Other. In the case of 'Other', further explanatory notes are provided.

4. Meaning of the name.

5. Ease of pronunciation has been rated through a three star system. As a rule I have listed names that are international, but still, ease of use varies. A single star (*) means some integrity of the sound is lost, two stars (**) show that the name is taken up fairly easily by foreign tongues, and three stars (***) mean that the name is articulated in its completeness by international users.

Guide to Phonetics

The list below details the manner in which the book handles the phonetics of each name.

As with most names, a degree of personalisation is natural. Names that begin with 'i' can easily be spelt with two 'e's instead. Similarly, names in the book that begin with 'q' could also be spelt with 'k', and those with 'b' could as easily start with 'v'. Names which feature the long 'a' can be spelt with two 'a's or with one 'a'. To maintain consistency, where the first syllable of a name contains a long 'a', the book spells it with two 'a's, all further syllables are spelt with a single 'a'. For instance, the name Aakanksha only has its first syllable spelt with two 'a's even though each 'a' is pronounced with a long 'a' sound.

Ae –   A as in *a*ngel

Ah –   Long a, as in *Aa*rt

Ai –   i as in hide

Uh –   Short *a*, as in *a*ttention

D –   Softly accented *d*, as in the Hindi pronunciation for *D*illi

Dd –   Strongly accented *d*, as in the English pronunciation for *D*elhi

Ee –   Long *i*, as in Ind*i*a

Eh –   E as in *e*lle

Ih –   Soft *i*, as in *I*ndia

Oa –   *o* as in *o*ak

Oh –   *o* as in *o*n

Oo –   long o / u sound as in t*oo*l

T –   Softly accented *t*, as in the Hindi pronunciation for *t*amanna

Tt –   Strongly accented *t*, as in *t*omorrow

U –   short *u*, as in An*u*j

Introduction

Becoming a parent is a momentous occasion – one filled with hope and worries. Your life changes forever, as do your relationships and responsibilities. The decisions to be taken have consequences that will resonate for years – does one of you decide to give up work, does a grandparent take on a bigger role in your lives, do you bring in a full-time carer? There are fears to go with the excitement, particularly for first-time parents. A baby – tiny as it is – and facing its own traumatic entry into a new and noisy world, turns your own upside down. Everything is in a state of flux – finances, relationships between partners, even the much treasured staple of 'me time'.

And of course, as you near your due-date, it seems as if the to-do list is never ending. Amidst all the mood swings and endless shopping trips and advice sought (and often unsought!) from elders and friends with children, there is the child's name to think of.

Every culture has its unique baby-naming customs. In some Western civilisations, babies are named after a deceased relative in the hope that the newborn will imbibe some of the qualities of their namesake. On the other hand, the Ashkenazic Jewish tradition stipulates that babies are not named after a living person for fear that the Angel of Death will mistake the child for the older person! In Italy, babies may be named after their grandparents – favouring the paternal side first – but not after the parents for it is considered arrogant to name your child after yourself. In many Catholic cultures, children are named after saints. And fittingly for a country with a great population, the Chinese put a great many factors into play when deciding a child's name: astrological principles, the birth date and time, the five key elements (metal, wood, water, fire and earth), the written form, the pronunciation, and the meaning of the name.

A lot of this resonates with our own customs. Historically, parents waited until the child was born to consult astrological charts based on the baby's birth date and time. A Sanskrit letter was chosen as lucky for the newborn which would form the first letter of the baby's name. Then, at an elaborate *Namkaran* ceremony at least ten days after the birth, the child would be named, with the father typically whispering the name four times into the baby's right ear.

Today, these traditions tend not to be followed to the letter. Besides, as several priests have told me, people can put too much emphasis on an astrologically auspicious letter when choosing a child's name. If the letter was all that mattered, would two such divergent personalities like Krishna and Kans have names that begin with the same letter? A mere coincidence, you say? Well, what about Raavan and Raam? Both their names began with the letter R, but their characters and ultimate destinies couldn't have been more different.

It is only natural, then, that Indians put extra care into the choice of name – we don't simply consider the most auspicious letter, nor do we limit ourselves to thinking of the sound or the popularity of a name. We consult friends and relatives, study books and religious texts, browse countless parenting websites, and more. Once we have a viable shortlist, we ponder on meanings and look into the histories of famous holders of our preferred names, and often take into account the numerological implications of our choice, all in the attempt to find a name that will complement the person we hope our child will be.

Of course, in a country like India, with its many languages and cultures, and with the numerous religious and cultural influences that have coloured the nation's psyche, the choices are truly overwhelming. And in today's era of globalisation, this task is made more difficult than ever before. The child may well travel abroad – whether for education or work – and even at home, it is prudent to consider a name that is easy to pronounce. There is increasing exposure to the West through call centres and through the ever-growing reliance of Europe and North America on Indian service industries, and it is safe to assume that a new generation of Indians will be well-served by names that sit well with foreign pronunciations.

Interestingly, in this time of great change, our tastes in names are evolving too. Gone are the days when classrooms were filled with dozens of Nehas or Rahuls, and equally, no caring parent today would dream of naming a poor, defenceless child with a tongue twister like Kirpanarayan or Charulata. Instead, people are turning to more unique names such as Moksh and Tiara, and in an imaginative and romantic twist, are combining the names of each parent to form the most individual declaration of belonging. So a Rakesh and an Ayesha could name their child Rayesha, though given how many endless combinations such couplings can provide, I have refrained from including these more personal derivatives in this book.

My sympathy for the quandary of choosing the most appropriate name grew as I began to research names for

3

my own child. There is a plethora of source material in the form of baby name books and websites, but they often left me feeling overwhelmed. The books, though excellent foundations – and some of them are positively encyclopaedic in their comprehensiveness – seem out of date. A lot of inappropriate names of demons and anti-heroes have to be trawled through, and many of the genuinely good names are missed in a cursory read. The websites, on the other hand, are excellent sources of ideas, but are often lacking in complete information on the meanings and origins of names. And importantly, both seem to miss out the international angle. A name like Aaryan, for instance, replete as it is with history and legend, brings up connotations of the Nazi era in the West. And my own name, Radhika, only seems understood by international friends when I tell them to omit the letter 'l' from the word 'radical'!

Ultimately, though, names are a very personal choice. My endeavour in this book has been to include names that capture the beauty of the Indian cadence for a new generation of Indians. These are primarily Hindu names, but as the influences on the Indian subcontinent have been manifold, I have included Arabic, Persian and Western names where they have come into Indian use.

Much like the India and the Indians taking shape today, the names in this book have an anchor in the past, but also pay heed to the future our children are growing up in – one where there is no restraint on their individuality, nor on their ability to achieve or to travel.

A

Aabad, *Ahb-ahd*, (M), (P), inhabited, happy, prosperous, ★★

Aabha, *Ahbh-ah*, (F), (S), brilliance, light, beauty, reflection, ★★

Aabhas, *Ahbh-ahs*, (M), (S), brilliance, light, reflection, premonition, feeling, ★★

Aabhat, *Ahbh-aht*, (M), (S), brilliant, ★

Aacharya, *Ahch-ahr-yah*, (M), (S), teacher, ★★

Aadarsh, *Ahd-uhrsh*, (M), (S), principle, belief, excellence, ★

Aadesh, *Ahd-aesh*, (M), (S), command, counsel, ★

Aadi, *Ah-dee*, (M), (S), first, unequalled, perfect, ★★

Aadia, *Ahdd-yah*, (F), (S), first, unequalled, perfect, the earth, another name for Durga, (O) – Swahili / African, gift, Hebrew, god's ornament, ★★★

Aadil, *Ah-dihl*, (M), (A), just, righteous, ★★

Aadim, *Ahd-ihm*, (M), (S), first, foundation, original, ★★

Aadish, *Ahd-eesh*, (M), (S), commanded, counselled, ★★

Aadit, *Ahd-iht*, (M), (S), first, the sun, ★★

Aadita, *Ahd-iht-ah*, (F), (S), first, original, ★★

Aaditey, *Ahd-iht-ey*, (M), (S), Aditi's son, the sun, ★

Aaditya, *Ahd-iht-yah*, (M), (S), Aditi's son, ★

Aadya, *Ahd-yah*, (F), (S), first, unequalled, perfect, the earth, another name for Durga, (O) – Swahili / African, gift, Hebrew, god's ornament, ★★

Aadyot, *Ahd-yoht*, (M), (S), brilliant, ★

Aafreen, *Ahf-reen*, (F), (P), praise, blessing, ★★★

Aaftab, *Ahf-tahb*, (M), (P), sun, brilliance, ★★

Aagam, *Ahg-uhm*, (M), (S), insight, intelligence, wisdom, ★★★

Aagha, *Ahgh-ah*, (M), (O) – Turkish, master, chief, elder brother, another name for god, ★★★

Aahna, *Ah-huh-nah*, (F), (S), day, to exist, eternal, ★★★

Aaina, *Ah-een-ah*, (F), (O) – Urdu, mirror, reflective, ★★★

Aakampan, *Ahk-uhmp-uhn*, (M), (S), calm, determined, ★★

Aakanksh, *Ahk-ahnksh*, (M), (S), desire, hope, ★★

Aakanksha, *Ahk-ahnk-shah*, (F), (S), desire, hope, ★★

Aakar, Ahk–uhr, (M), (S), treasure, rare, ★★★

Aakar, *Ahk-ahr*, (M), (S), form, shape, ★★★

Aakarshan, *Ahk-uhr-shuhn*, (M), (S), attraction, charm, ★★★

Aakash, *Ahk-ahsh*, (M), (S), sky, open mindedness, ★★★

Aakashi, *Ahk-ahsh-ee*, (M), (S), universal, atmosphere, ★★★

Aakriti, *Ahk-riht-ee*, (F), (S), form, figure, appearance, ★★

Aalakshya, *Ahl-uhk-shyuh*, (M), (S), visible, ★★

Aalamb, *Ahl-uhmb*, (M), (S), support, sanctuary, ★★★

Aalap, *Ahl-ahp*, (M), (H), conversation, musical prelude, ★★★

Aalay, *Ah-luhy*, (M), (S), home, refuge, ★★★

Aalaya, *Ah-luhy-ah*, (F), (S), home, refuge, ★★★

Aalisha, *Ahl-ihsh-ah*, (F), (S), protected by god, ★★★

Aalok, *Ahl-oak*, (M), (S), vision, light, brilliance, ★★★

Aalop, *Ahl-oap*, (M), (S), small, ★★★

Aamara, *Ahm-ahr-ah*, (F), (O) – Old Greek, unfading flower, ★★★

Aamish, *Ahm-ihsh*, (M), (S), pleasing, ★★★

Aamisha, *Ahm-ihsh-ah*, (F), (S), pleasing, ★★★

Aamod, *Ahm-oahd*, (M), (S), pleasure, serenity, fragrance, ★★

Aamodin, *Ahm-oahd-ihn*, (M), (S), fragrant, celebrated, ★★

Aamodini, *Ahm-oahd-ihn-ee*, (F), (S), fragrant, celebrated, ★★

Aanamra, *Ahn-uhm-rah*, (F), (S), modest, yielding, ★★★

Aanand, *Ahn-uhnd*, (M), (S), delight, pleasure, ★★

Aanandit, *Ahn-uhnd-iht*, (M), (S), happy, pleased, ★

Aanantya, *Ahn-uhnt-yuh*, (M), (S), undying, divine, ★

Aanavi, *Ahn-uh-vee*, (F), (S), kind, ★★★

Aanaya, *Ahn-ahy-ah*, (F), (O) – Hebrew, god has shown favour, ★★★

Aanchal, *Ahnch-uhl*, (F), (S), the decorative end of a sari, shelter, ★★★

Aantika, *Ahn-tihk-ah*, (F), (S), older sister, ★★

Aantya, *Ahnt-yuh*, (M), (S), successful, accomplished, ★★

Aapt, *Ahpt*, (M), (S), successful, logical, reliable, ★★

Aapti, *Ahp-tee*, (F), (S), success, completion, ★★

Aapu, *Ahp-ooh*, (M), (S), faultless, virtuous, divine, ★★★

Aaradhana, *Ahr-ahdh-uhn-ah*, (F), (S), worship, adoration, ★

Aaradhita, *Ahr-ahdh-iht-ah*, (F), (S), worshipped, ★

Aarav, *Ahr-uhv*, (M), (S), sound, shout, ★★★

Aaria, *Ahr-yah*, (F), (S), honoured, noble, worshipped, (P), friend,
    faithful, (O) – Latin, melody, air, tune, ★★★

Aarit, *Ahr-iht*, (M), (S), honoured, admired, ★★

Aarjav, *Ahr-juhv*, (M), (S), honest, sincere, ★★★

Aarksh, *Ahrk-sh*, (M), (S), celestial, of the stars, ★★★

Aarochan, *Ahr-oach-uhn*, (M), (S), brilliant, ★★★

Aarohi, *Ahr-oa-hee*, (F), (S), progressive, evolving, ★★★

Aaron, *Aer-uhn*, (M), (O) – Hebrew, enlightened, lofty, powerful
    mountain, ★★★

Aarti, *Ahr-tee*, (F), (S), singing of hymns in praise of god, ★★

Aarya, *Ahr-yah*, (F), (S), honoured, noble, (P), friend, faithful,
    (O) – Latin, Aaria is Latin for melody, air, tune, ★★★

Aarya, *Ahr-yuh*, (M), (S), honoured, noble, wise, benevolent, auspicious, (P) – friend, faithful, ★★★

Aaryak, *Ahr-yuhk*, (M), (S), honourable, noble, wise, kind, ★★★

Aryaki, *Ahr-yuhk-ee*, (F), (S), respected, another name for Durga, ★★★

Aaryaman, *Ahr-yuhm-uhn*, (M), (S), noble, belonging to the sun, (O) – Pahlavi, noble, ★★★

Aaryamani, *Ahr-yuhm-uhn-ee*, (F), (S), the noblest of nobles, belonging to the sun, ★★★

Aaryamik, *Ahr-yuhm-ihk*, (M), (S), noble, ★★★

Aaryan, *Ahr-yuhn*, (M), (S), best, noble, (O) – Avestan, that which is beyond anyone's strength, ★★★

Aaryana, *Ahr-yuhn-ah*, (F), (S), best, noble, ★★★

Aaryik, *Ahr-yihk*, (M), (S), masterful, respected, ★★★

Aasav, *Ahs-uhv*, (M), (S), essence, distilled, wine, liquor, ★★★

Aasha, *Ah-shah*, (F), (S), wish, hope, ★★★

Aashali, *Ah-shuhl-ee*, (F), (S), amenable, popular, ★★★

Aashang, *Ahsh-uhng*, (M), (S), affectionate, loyal, ★★★

Aashi, *Ahsh-ee*, (F), (S), blessing, ★★★

Aashim, *Ahsh-ihm*, (M), (S), limitless, ★★★

Aashima, *Ahsh-ihm-ah*, (F), (S), limitless, ★★★

Aashish, *Ahsh-eesh*, (M), (S), blessing, blessed, ★★★

Aashisha, *Ahsh-eesh-ah*, (F), (S), wish, blessed, ★★★

Aashman, *Ahsh-muhn*, (M), (S), gem, ★★★

Aashna, *Ahsh-nah*, (F), (P), friend, ★★★

Aashrut, *Ahsh-rut*, (M), (S), famous, ★★

Aashu, *Ahsh-ooh*, (M), (S), fast, active, ★★★

Aashumat, *Ahsh-um-uht*, (M), (S), quick-witted, ★★

Aashutosh, *Ahsh-ut-oash*, (M), (S), content, happy, another name for Shiva, ★

Aasit, *Ah-siht*, (M), (S), calm, self-possessed, ★★

Aasman, *Ahs-mahn*, (M), (P), heaven, ★★★

Aasmani, *Ahs-mahn-ee*, (F), (P), celestial, azure, ★★★

Aastha, *Ahs-thah*, (F), (S), hope, regard, support, ★★

Aastik, *Ahs-tihk*, (M), (S), believing in existence and god, ★★

Aatish, *Aht-ihsh*, (M), (S), fire, sacred, purifying, (P), fire, brilliance, strength, ★★

Aatmaj, *Aht-muhj*, (M), (S), born of the soul, ★★

Aatmaja, *Aht-muhj-ah*, (F), (S), born of the soul, another name for Paarvati, ★★

Aatman, *Aht-muhn*, (M), (S), soul, another name for Krishna, ★★

Aatmay, *Aht-muhy*, (M), (S), long-lived, ★★

Aatrey, *Aht-raey*, (M), (S), glorious, able to cross the three worlds, ★★

Aatreyi, *Aht-raey-ee*, (F), (S), glorious, able to cross the three worlds, ★★

Aavantika, *Ahv-uhnt-ihk-ah*, (F), (S), modest, ★

Aayati, *Ahy-uht-ee*, (F), (S), majesty, dignity, ★★

Aayesha, *Ah-yeesh-ah*, (F), (A), life, lively, daughter of the Prophet, (P), beautiful, ★★★

Aayod, *Ahy-oad*, (M), (S), giver of life, ★★

Aayus, *Ah-yus*, (M), (S), age, man, life, ★★★

Aayush, *Ah-yush*, (M), (S), long-lived, age, duration of life, ★★★

Aayushi, *Ah-yush-ee*, (F), (S), long-lived, ★★★

Aayushman, *Ah-yush-mahn*, (M), (S), long-lived, ★★★

Abadhya, *Uhb-ahdh-yuh*, (M), (S), invincible, ★

Abhay, *Uhb-hey*, (M), (S), fearless, ★★

Abhi, *Uhb-hee*, (M), (S), fearless, ★★

Abhijan, *Uhb-hee-juhn*, (M), (S), noble, pride of a family, ★★

Abhijat, *Uhb-hee-jaht*, (M), (S), wise, handsome, noble, ★

Abhijay, *Uhb-hee-juhy*, (M), (S), victory, ★★

Abhijit, *Uhb-hee-jeeht*, (M), (S), victorious, ★

Abhijiti, *Uhb-hee-jeeht-ee*, (F), (S), victory, ★

Abhik, *Uhb-hee-k*, (M), (S), fearless, ★★

Abhilash, *Uhb-hee-lah-sh*, (M), (S), desire, affection, ★★

Abhilasha, *Uhb-hee-lah-shah*, (F), (S), desire, affection, ★★

Abhim, *Uhb-heem*, (M), (S), destroyer of fear, another name for
  Vishnu, ★★

Abhimanyu, *Uhb-hee-muhn-yoo*, (M), (S), heroic, passionate, proud, ★

Abhinav, *Uhb-hee-nuhv*, (M), (S), young, modern, ★★

Abhiraj, *Uhb-hee-rahj*, (M), (S), regal, bright, ★★

Abhiram, *Uhb-hee-rahm*, (M), (S), wonderful, handsome, another
  name for Shiva, ★★

Abhishek, *Uhb-hee-shey-k*, (M), (S), to anoint, ★★

Abhishri, *Uhb-hee-shree*, (F), (S), brilliant, powerful, ★★

Abhishri, *Uhb-hee-shree*, (M), (S), brilliant, ★★

Abhram, *Uhb-ruhm*, (M), (S), steady, purposeful, ★★

Abhu, *Uhb-hoo*, (M), (S), unearthly, another name for Vishnu, ★★

Abir, *Uhb-eer*, (M), (S), auspicious red powder traditionally applied
  during the festival of Holi, (O) – Hebrew, strong, ★★★

Abira, *Uhb-eer-ah*, (F), (O) – Hebrew, strong, brave, ★★★

Abja, *Uhb-jah*, (F), (S), water born, ★★★

Abjit, *Uhb-jiht*, (M), (S), one who has conquered water, ★★

Achal, *Uhch-uhl*, (M), (S), constant, ★★★

Achala, *Uhch-uhl-ah*, (F), (S), constant, the earth, ★★★

Achira, *Uhch-eer-ah*, (F), (S), quick, agile, ★★★

Adhrit, *Uhdh-riht*, (M), (S), independent, supportive, ★★

Adhrita, *Uhdh-riht-ah*, (F), (S), independent, supportive, ★★

Adhya, *Uhdh-yah*, (F), (S), great, beyond perception, ★★

Adin, *Uhd-een*, (M), (S), noble of spirit, ★★

Aditi, *Uhd-iht-ee*, (F), (S), liberty, perfection, creativity, ★★

Adrika, *Uhd-rihk-ah*, (F), (S), hill, an apsara or celestial nymph, ★★

Advait, *Uhd-vaeht*, (M), (S), unique, another name for Brahma and
      Vishnu, ★

Advaita, *Uhd-vaeht-ah*, (F), (S), unique, ★

Advay, *Uhd-vaeh*, (M), (S), with no duplicate, unique, ★★

Advaya, *Uhd-vaeh-ah*, (F), (S), with no duplicate, unique, ★★

Advik, *Uhd-vihk*, (M), (S), unique, ★★

Advika, *Uhd-vihk-ah*, (F), (S), unique, ★★

Agaja, *Uhg-uhj-ah*, (F), (S), born on a mountain, another name for
      Paarvati, ★★

Agarv, *Uhg-uhrv*, (M), (S), not arrogant, balanced, ★★

Agastya, *Uhg-uhst-yah*, (M), (S), a sage, one who humbles even the
      mountain, ★

Agraj, *Uhg-ruhj*, (M), (S), first born, ★★★

Agraja, *Uhg-ruhj-ah*, (F), (S), first born, ★★★

Agrim, *Uhg-rihm*, (M), (S), first, leader, ★★★

Agrima, *Uhg-rihm-ah*, (F), (S), leadership, ★★

Ah, *Uh*, (M), (S), affirmation, ★★★

Ahalya, *Uh-uhl-yah*, (F), (S), pleasant, first woman created by
      Brahma, ★★★

Ahan, *Uh-huhn*, (M), (S), dawn, ★★★

Ahana, *Uh-huhn-ah*, (F), (S), immortal, born during the day, ★★★

Ahankar, *Uh-huhn,kahr.*, (M), (S), the sun, (O) – Gurmukhi, pride, ego, ★★★

Ahanti, *Uh-huhn-tee*, (F), (S), eternal, indestructible, ★★

Ahar, *Uh-huhr*, (M), (S), protector, ★★★

Ahi, *Uh-hee*, (M), (S), the sun, cloud, water, eight, ★★★

Ahi, *Uh-hee*, (F), (S), the meeting of earth and heaven, ★★★

Ahim, *Uh-hihm*, (M), (S), one who travels, cloud, water, ★★★

Ahimsa, *Uh-hihm-sah*, (F), (S), nonviolence, ★★★

Ahin, *Uh-heen*, (M), (S), complete, snake, ★★★

Ahlad, *Aeh-lahd*, (M), (S), pleasing, ★★

Ahladita, *Aeh-lahd-iht-ah*, (F), (S), happy, ★

Ail, *Ay-l*, (M), (S), originating from the intellect, ★★★

Aisha, *AE-shah*, (F), (S), desire, regal, best, ★★★

Aishi, *Eh-shee*, (F), (S), belonging to Shiva, ★★★

Aishwarya, *Aeh-sh-vuhr-yah*, (F), (S), success, fame, wealth, ★

Aj, *Uhj*, (M), (S), eternal, leader, ★★★

Aja, *Uhj-ah*, (F), (S), eternal, ★★★

Ajala, *Uhj-ahl-ah*, (F), (S), eternal, the earth, ★★★

Ajan, *Uhj-uhn*, (M), (S), leader, another name for Brahma, ★★★

Ajanta, *Uhj-uhn-tah*, (F), (S), a famous Buddhist cave, ★★

Ajara, *Uhj-uhr-ah*, (F), (S), youthful, ★★★

Ajat, *Uhj-aht*, eternal, a god, ★★

Ajay, *Uhj-uhy*, invincible, ★★★

Ajaya, *Uhj-uhy-ah*, invincible, ★★★

Ajir, *Uhj-ihr*, nimble, quick, ★★★

Ajira, *Uhj-ihr-ah*, nimble, quick, another name for Durga, ★★★

Ajish, *Uhj-eesh*, another name for Shiva, ★★★

Ajit, *Uhj-eet*, victorious, indestructible, ★★

Akalka, *Uhk-uhl-kah*, (F), (S), pure, moonlight, ★★★

Akalp, *Uhk-uhlp*, (M), (S), jewel, ornament, ★★★

Akaam, *Uhk-ahm*, (M), (S), virtuous, pious, ★★★

Akampit, *Uhk-uhm-piht*, (M), (S), peaceful, determined, a Jain or
    Buddhist saint, ★★

Akhand, *Uhk-huhn-dd*, (M), (S), imperishable, divine, ★

Akhil, *Uhk-hihl*, (M), (S), entire, complete, ★★

Akhila, *Uhk-hihl-ah*, (F), (S), entire, complete, ★★

Akhilesh, *Uhk-hihl-aesh*, (M), (S), omnipresent, divine, ★★

Akop, *Uhk-oap*, (M), (S), calm, ★★★

Akrant, *Uhk-rahnt*, (M), (S), first, undefeated, ★★

Akrur, *Uhk-roohr*, (M), (S), gentle, ★★★

Aksh, *Uhk-sh*, knowledge, the five senses, soul, sky, earth, ★★★

Akshaj, *Uhk-sh-uhj*, diamond, knowledge, another name for
    Vishnu, ★★★

Akshak, *Uhk-sh-uhk*, sensual, ★★★

Akshar, *Uhk-sh-uhr*, letter, eternal, indestructible, another name for
    Brahma, Vishnu, Shiva, Om, ★★

Akshat, *Uhk-sh-uht*, complete, another name for Shiva, ★★

Akshata, *Uhk-sh-uht-ah*, complete, holy grain of rice, ★★

Akshay, *Uhk-sh-ehy,* (M), (S), eternal, indestructible,
    the Supreme spirit, ★★

Akshaya, *Uhk-sh-ehy-ah,* (F), (S), eternal, ★★

Akshi, *Uhk-shee*, (F), (S), home, life, eye, ★★★

Akshin, *Uhk-shihn*, (M), (S), permanent, unfailing, ★★★

Akshina, *Uhk-shihn-ah*, (F), (S), permanent, unfailing, ★★★

Akshit, *Uhk-shiht*, (M), (S), permanent, ★★

Akshita, *Uhk-shiht-ah*, (F), (S), permanent, goddess of the earth, ★★

Akshiti, *Uhk-shiht-ee*, (F), (S), eternal, ★★

Akul, *Uhk-ul*, (M), (S), divine, superlative, another name for
    Shiva, ★★★

Alaka, *Uhl-uhk-ah*, (F), (S), girl, curl of hair, ★★★

Alana, *Uhl-ahn-ah*, (F), (O) – Gaelic, fair, beautiful, ★★★

Alay, *Uhl-aey*, (M), (S), attacker, warrior, another name for Indra, ★★

Aleeza, *Uhl-eez-ah*, (F), (O) – Hebrew, joy, ★★★

Alesh, *Uhl-aesh*, (M), (S), large, ★★

Alessa, *Uhl-ehs-sah*, (F), (O) – Old Greek, helper, defender of men, ★★★

Alin, *Uhl-ihn*, (M), (S), one who stings, the zodiac sign of Scorpio, ★★★

Alisah, *Ael-ee-sah*, (F), (O) – Hebrew, joy, German, noble, ★★★

Alisha, *Uhl-eesh-ah*, (F), (S), majestic, (O) – German noble, ★★★

Aliya, *Uhl-ee-yah*, (F), (A), lofty, sublime, (O) – Hebrew, to ascend,
    rise up, ★★★

Alka, *Uhl-kah*, (F), (S), long haired, defender of men, the capital city
    of Kubera, ★★★

Alpana, *Uhl-puhn-ah*, (F), (S), beautiful, delighted, ★★★

Alpesh, *Uhl-paesh*, (M), (S), another name for Krishna, ★★

Alyssa, *Uhl-ihss-ah*, (F), (O) – Hebrew, joy, German, noble, ★★★

Amad, *Uhm-uhd*, (M), (S), somber, ★★

Amadhya, *Uhm-uhdh-yah*, (M), (S), kind, affectionate, ★

Amal, *Uhm-ahl*, (M), (A), hope, expectation, (O) – Hebrew,
    hardworking, optimistic, Germanic, Latin, work, ★★★

Amal, *Uhm-uhl*, (M), (S), pure, brilliant, another name for
Narayana, ★★★

Amala, *Uhm-uhl-ah*, (F), (S), pure, brilliant, another name for
Lakshmi, ★★★

Amalia, *Uhm-ahl- yah*, (F), (O) – Hebrew, work of the Lord,
Germanic, Latin, work, effort, ★★★

Amam, *Uhm-uhm*, (M), (S), modest, ★★★

Aman, *Uhm-uhn*, (M), (S), peace, ★★★

Amani, *Uhm-uhn-ee*, (F), (S), leader, insightful, ★★★

Amar, *Uhm-uhr*, (M), (S), immortal, a god, ★★★

Amari, *Uhm-uhr-ee*, (F), (S), immortal, ★★★

Amarta, *Uhm-uhrt-ah*, (F), (S), immortality, ★★

Amartya, *Uhm-uhrt-yah*, (M), (S), eternal, divine, ★★

Amati, *Uhm-uht-ee*, (F), (S), time, beyond intellect, splendour, ★★

Amav, *Uhm-uhv*, (M), (S), powerful, undefeated, ★★★

Amaay, *Uhm-ahy*, (M), (S), honest, artless, ★★★

Amay, *Uhm-aey*, (M), (S), immeasurable, without limit, ★★★

Amaya, *Uhm-aey-ah*, (F), (S), immeasurable, without limit, night
rain, ★★★

Amba, *Uhm-bah*, (F), (S), mother, worthy woman, ★★★

Ambak, *Uhm-buhk*, (M), (S), eye, ★★★

Ambala, *Uhm-bah-lah*, (F), (S), mother, affectionate, kind, ★★★

Ambali, *Uhm-bahl-ee*, (F), (S), mother, affectionate, kind, ★★★

Ambalika, *Uhm-bahl-ihk-ah*, (F), (S), mother, insightful, ★★★

Ambar, *Uhm-buhr*, (M), (S), sky, ★★★

Ambav, *Uhm-buhv*, (M), (S), like water, ★★★

Ambaya, *Uhm-buh-yah*, (F), (S), mother, ★★★

Amber, *Uhm-buhr*, (M), (S), sky, ★★★

Ambhini, *Uhm-bhihn-ee*, (F), (S), water born, ★★

Ambhoj, *Uhm-bh-oaj*, (M), (S), water born, lotus, ★★

Ambi, *Uhm-bee*, (F), (S), mother, affectionate, kind, ★★★

Ambika, *Uhm-bihk-ah*, (F), (S), mother, affectionate, kind, a worthy woman, another name for Paarvati, ★★★

Ambikeya, *Uhm-bihk-ehy-ah*, (M), (S), mountain, another name for Ganesha, ★★

Ambu, *Uhm-bu*, (M), (S), water, ★★★

Ambuj, *Uhm-bu-j*, (M), (S), water born, Indra's thunderbolt, lotus, ★★★

Amelia, *Uhm-eel-yah*, (F), (O) – Latin, German, work, ★★★

Amil, *Uhm-eel*, inaccessible, exalted, invaluable, ★★★

Amish, *Uhm-eesh*, (M), (S), truthful, ★★★

Amisha, *Uhm-eesh-ah*, (F), (S), truthful, guileless, ★★★

Amit, *Uhm-iht*, (M), (S), great, infinite, ★★

Amita, *Uhm-iht-ah*, (F), (S), great, infinite, ★★

Amitabh, *Uhm-iht-ahbh*, (M), (S), incomparable, glorious, ★

Amitay, *Uhm-iht-ehy*, (M), (S), infinite, ★

Amitesh, *Uhm-iht-ehsh*, (M), (S), master of the infinite, ★

Amiti, *Uhm-iht-ee*, (F), (S), infinite, divine, ★★

Amitosh, *Uhm-iht-oash*, (M), (S), happy, ★

Amiya, *Uhm-ee-yuh*, (F), (S), delight, nectar, ★★★

Amlan, *Uhm-lahn*, (M), (S), brilliant, fresh, clear, ★★★

Amoh, *Uhm-oah*, (M), (S), unblemished, clear, ★★★

Amol, *Uhm-oal*, (M), (S), priceless, precious, ★★★

Amrit, *Uhm-riht*, (M), (S), nectar, eternal, ★★

Amrita, *Uhm-riht-ah*, (F), (S), nectar, eternal, splendid, gold, the sun's ray, the Supreme Spirit, ★★

Amul, *Uhm-oohl*, (M), (S), eternal, unsurpassed, ★★★

Amulya, *Uhm-oohl-yuh*, (M), (S), priceless, ★★

Anabhra, *Uhn-uhbh-rah*, (F), (S), clear headed, ★★

Anadi, *Uhn-ah-dee*, (M), (S), eternal, godly, another name for Shiva
    and Krishna, ★★

Anadya, *Uhn-ahd-yuh*, (M), (S), eternal, godly, another name for
    Krishna, ★

Anadya, *Uhn-ahd-yah*, (F), (S), eternal, godly, ★

Anagh, *Uhn-uhgh*, (M), (S), perfect, pure, sinless, ★★

Anagha, *Uhn-uhgh-ah*, (F), (S), perfect, pure, sinless, ★★

Anahat, *Uhn-ah-huht*, (F), (S), new, uninjured, ★

Anahita, *Uhn-ah-eet-ah*, (F), (O) – Pahlavi, undefiled, stainless,
    immaculate, ★

Anais, *Uhn-aey*, (F), (P), a variation of Anaitis, the Persian goddess of
    love, (O) – Hebrew, god has shown favour, ★★★

Anaita, *Uhn-iy-iht-ah*, (F), (P), angel, variation of Anaitis, the Persian
    goddess of love, ★★★

Aanaia, *Uhn-ahy-ah*, (F), (O) – Hebrew, god has shown favour, ★★★

Anak, *Uhn-uhk*, (M), (S), strong, cloud, ★★★

Anal, *Uhn-uhl*, (M), (S), wind, fire, ★★★

Anala, *Uhn-uhl-ah*, (F), (S), perfect, fiery, ★★★

Anam *Uhn-uhm*, (M), (S), one who blesses, ★★★

Anamika, *Uhn-ahm-ihk-ah*, (F), (S), virtuous, free of the limitations
    imposed by a name, ★★★

Ananmay, *Uhn-uhn-mehy*, (M), (S), indestructible, healthy, another
    name for Vishnu, ★★

Anant, *Uhn-uhnt*, (M), (S), eternal, godly, the earth, another name
    for Brahma, Vishnu, Shiva, ★★

Ananta, *Uhn-uhnt-ah*, (F), (S), eternal, godly, the earth, another name
    for Paarvati, ★★

Anantya, *Uhn-uhnt-yah*, (F), (S), eternal, godly, ★

Ananya, *Uhn-uhn-yah*, (F), (S), unique, without match, ★★★

Anarv, *Uhn-uhr-v*, (M), (S), charming, irresistible, ★★★

Anash, *Uhn-ahsh*, (M), (S), indestructible, the sky, Brahman or the
    Supreme Spirit, ★★★

Anashay, *Uhn-ahsh-ehy*, (M), (S), unselfish, ★★

Anashin, *Uhn-ahsh-ihn*, (M), (S), eternal, indestructible, ★★★

Anasuya, *Uhn-uh-soo-yah*, (F), (S), full of goodwill, not resentful, ★★★

Anashya, *Uhn-uhsh-yuh*, (M), (S), eternal, indestructible, ★★

Anav, *Uhn-uhv*, (M), (S), generous, kind, ★★★

Anavi, *Uhn-uhv-ee*, (F), (S), generous, kind, ★★★

Anay, *Uh-naey*, (M), (S), without a superior, another name for
    Vishnu, ★★★

Anaya, *Uh-naey-ah*, (F), (S), without a superior, ★★★

Andaz, *Uhn-dahz*, (M), (P), purpose, guess, measure, opinion, ★★

Aneesa, *Uhn-ees-ah*, (F), (A), friendly, ★★★

Aneeta, *Uhn-eet-ah*, (F), (S), guileless, leader, ★★

Aneeta, *Uhn-eett-ah*, (F), (A), friendly, (O) – Greek, flower, Hebrew,
    god has shown favour, ★★

Angad, *Uhn-guhd*, (M), (S), warrior, beautifully formed, ★★

Angaj, *Uhn-guhj*, (M), (S), a son, corporeal, earthly love, another
    name for the love god Kaama, ★★★

Angaja, *Uhn-guhj-ah*, (F), (S), a daughter, corporeal, ★★★

Angam, *Uhng-uhm*, (M), (S), impenetrable, strong, morally
    upright, ★★★

Angana, *Uhng-uhn-ah*, (F), (S), beautiful, with a beautiful form, zodiac sign of Virgo, ★★★

Angarika, *Uhn-guhr-ihk-ah*, (F), (H), flame coloured flower, ★★

Anhati, *Uhn-huht-ee*, (F), (S), gift, ★★

Anhiti, *Uhn-hiht-ee*, (F), (S), gift, ★★

Anik, *Uhn-eek*, (M), (S), light, army, face, ★★★

Aniket, *Uhn-ihk-eht*, (M), (S), worldly, at ease across the world, ★

Anil, *Uhn-eel*, (M), (S), fair, ★★★

Anil, *Uhn-ihl*, (M), (S), the god of wind, another name for Vishnu and Shiva, ★★★

Animan, *Uhn-ihm-ahn*, (M), (S), omnipresent, divine, ★★★

Animesh, *Uhn-ihm-aesh*, (M), (S), omnipresent, omniscient, divine, ★★★

Aninda, *Uhn-ihn-dah*, (F), (S), perfect, blameless, ★★

Anindini, *Uhn-ihn-dihn-ee*, (F), (S), irreproachable, full of goodwill, ★★

Anindita, *Uhn-ihn-diht-ah*, (F), (S), honoured, irreproachable, virtuous, ★

Anindya, *Uhn-ihn-dyah*, (F), (S), irreproachable, ★★

Anirban, *Uhn-ihr-bahn*, (M), (S), immortal, divine, ★★

Anirudh, *Uhn-ihr-udh*, (M), (S), unopposed, victorious, an incarnation of Brahma and Vishnu, ★

Anirudha, *Uhn-ihr-udh-ah*, (F), (S), unopposed, victorious, ★

Anirvan, *Uhn-ihr-vuhn*, (M), (S), undying, progressive, ★★

Anirved, *Uhn-ihr-vaed*, (M), (S), positive, courageous, resilient, independent, ★

Anirveda, *Uhn-ihr-vaed-ah*, (F), (S), positive, courageous, resilient, independent, ★

Anirvin, *Uhn-ihr-vihn*, (M), (S), active, cheerful, another name for Vishnu, ★★

Anisa, *Uhn-ees-ah*, (F), (A), friendly, ★★★

Anish, *Uhn-eesh*, (M), (S), best, supreme, another name for Vishnu, (P), small garden, ★★★

Anisha, *Uhn-eesh-ah*, (F), (S), without darkness, light, unceasing, ★★★

Anit, *Uhn-iht*, (M), (S), simple, artless, leader, ★★

Anita, *Uhn-iht-ah*, (F), (S), simple, artless, leader, ★★

Anjak, *Uhn-juhk*, (M), (S), anointed, ★★★

Anjali, *Uhn-juhl-ee*, (F), (S), one who joins both hands together in prayer, respectful, ★★★

Anjan, *Uhn-juhn*, (M), (S), dusky, ★★★

Anjana, *Uhn-juhn-ah*, (F), (S), dusky, mother of Hanuman, ★★★

Anjas, *Uhn-juhs*, (M), (S), honest, morally upstanding, ★★★

Anjasi, *Uhn-juhs-ee*, (F), (S), honest, morally upstanding, ★★★

Anji, *Uhn-jee*, (F), (S), one who blesses, blessing, ★★★

Anjik, *Uhn-jihk*, (M), (S), blessed, dusky, ★★★

Anjini, *Uhn-jihn-ee*, (F), (S), blessed, ★★★

Anju, *Uhn-ju*, (F), (S), beloved, ★★★

Anjum, *Uhn-jum*, (F), (A), stars, ★★★

Anjuman, *Uhn-jum-uhn*, (M), (P), gathering, society, ★★★

Ankit, *Uhn-kiht*, (M), (S), distinguished, marked out, ★★

Ankita, *Uhn-kiht-ah*, (F), (S), distinguished, marked out, ★★

Ankolika, *Uhnk-oal-ihk-ah*, (F), (S), the embodiment of love, respect, ★★★

Ankolit, *Uhnk-oal-iht*, (M), (S), loved, respected, ★★

Ankur, *Uhnk-ur*, (M), (S), sapling, offshoot, newborn, ★★★

Ankura, *Uhnk-ur-ah*, (F), (S), sapling, offshoot, newborn, ★★★

Ankush, *Uhn-kush*, (M), (S), control, possession, a hook used to drive elephants, ★★★

Ankushi, *Uhn-kuhsh-ee*, (F), (S), self-possessed, a Jaina goddess, ★★★

Anmol, *Uhn-moal*, (M), (S), invaluable, precious, ★★★

Anokhi, *Uhn-oakh-ee*, (F), (S), unique, ★★

Anoma, *Uhn-oam-ah*, (F), (S), illustrious, ★★★

Anram, *Uhn-ruhm*, (M), (S), continuous, constant, ★★★

Ansal, *Uhn-suhl*, (M), (S), strong, passionate, ★★★

Ansh, *Uhn-sh*, (M), (S), portion, day, ★★★

Anshak, *Uhn-sh-uhk*, (M), (S), heir, ★★★

Anshal, *Uhn-sh-uhl*, (M), (S), heir, ★★★

Anshin, *Uhn-sh-ihn*, (M), (S), heir, ★★★

Anshu, *Uhn-shu*, (M), (S), sunbeam, splendour, speed, ★★★

Anshuk, *Uhn-shuk*, (M), (S), sunbeam, gentle, brilliant, ★★★

Anshuka, *Uhn-shuk-ah*, (F), (S), sunbeam, gentle, brilliant, ★★★

Anshul, *Uhn-shul*, (M), (S), brilliant, ★★★

Anshula, *Uhn-shul-ah*, (F), (S), brilliant, ★★★

Anshuman, *Uhn-shu-muhn*, (M), (S), the sun, the moon, brilliant, ★★★

Anshumat, *Uhn-shu-muht*, (M), (S), brilliant, ★★

Anshumati, *Uhn-shu-muht-ee*, (F), (S), brilliant, wise, ★★

Antam, *Uhn-tuhm*, (M), (S), bright, intimate, ★★

Antar, *Uhn-tuhr*, (M), (S), intimate, security, soul, heart, ★★

Antara, *Uhn-tuhr-ah*, (F), (H), second note in Hindustani classical music, ★★

Anu, *Uhn-u*, (M), (S), an atom, celestial, another name for Shiva, ★★★

Anubha, *Uhn-ubh-ah*, (F), (S), ambitious, seeking glory, ★★

Anubhaj, *Uhn-ubh-uhj*, (M), (S), worshipper, spiritual, ★★

Anubhav, *Uhn-ubh-uhv*, (M), (S), insight, experience, ★★

Anubodh, *Uhn-ub-oadh*, (M), (S), memory, ★★

Anuchan, *Uhn-ooh-ch-ahn*, (M), (S), lover of knowledge, conscientious, an apsara or celestial nymph, ★★

Anuchana, *Uhn-ooh-ch-ahn-ah*, (M), (S), lover of knowledge, conscientious, ★★

Anuh, *Uhn-u*, (M), (S), calm, without desire, content, ★★★

Anuj, *Uhn-uj*, (M), (S), younger brother, ★★★

Anuja, *Uhn-uj-ah*, (F), (S), younger sister, ★★★

Anuka, *Uhn-uk-ah*, (F), (S), attuned to nature, passionate, an apsara or celestial nymph, ★★★

Anukanksha, *Uhn-uk-ahnk-shah*, (F), (S), desire, hope, ★★★

Anukash, *Uhn-uk-ahsh*, (M), (S), reflection, ★★★

Anukul, *Uhn-uk-ool*, (M), (S), pleasant, ★★★

Anumit, *Ahn-um-iht*, (M), (S), analytical, logical, ★★

Anumita, *Ahn-um-iht-ah*, (F), (S), analytical, logical, ★★

Anup, *Uhn-oop*, (M), (S), unique, full of water, ★★★

Anupam, *Uhn-up-uhm*, (M), (S), precious, unique, ★★★

Anupama, *Uhn-up-uhm-ah*, (F), (S), precious, incomparable, ★★★

Anurag, *Uhn-ur-ahg*, (M), (S), love, affection, ★★★

Anuraj, *Uhn-ur-ahj*, (M), (S), brilliant, ★★★

Anurima, *Uhn-ur-ihm-ah*, (F), (S), affectionate, ★★★

Anushka, *Uhn-ush-kah*, (F), (O) – Hebrew, god has shown favour, Russian, a term of endearment, ★★★

Anushna, *Uhn-ush-nah*, (F), (S), cool, calming, ★★★

Anushri, *Uhn-ush-ree*, (F), (S), glorious, celebrated, good looking, another name for Lakshmi, ★★★

Anutosh, *Uhn-ut-oash*, (M), (S), relief, satisfaction, ★★

Anvita, *Uhn-viht-ah*, (F), (S) reasoned, understood, ★★

Anya, *Uhn-yah*, (F), (S), limitless, ★★★

Anya, *Aen-yah*, (F), (O) – Hebrew, god has shown favour, Greek, resurrection, ★★★

Anyang, *Uhn-yuhng*, (M), (S), godly, perfect, virtuous, ★★★

Apara, *Uhp-ahr-ah*, (F), (S), limitless, unique, godly, ★★★

Aparajit, *Uhp-uhr-ahj-iht*, (M), (S), undefeated, another name for Vishnu and Shiva, ★

Aparajita, *Uhp-uhr-ahj-iht-ah*, (F), (S), undefeated, another name for Durga, ★

Aparna, *Uhp-uhr-nah*, (F), (S), another name for Paarvati, ★★★

Apasyu, *Uhp-uhs-yoo*, (M), (S), energetic, talented, ★★

Apij, *Uhp-ihj*, (M), (S), brother, ★★★

Apsara, *Uhp-suhr-ah*, (F), (S), a celestial nymph, ★★★

Apurv, *Uhp-oohrv*, (M), (S), unique, unmatched, new, Brahman or the Supreme Spirit, ★★★

Apurva, *Uhp-oohr-vah*, (F), (S), unique, unmatched, new, ★★

Aradhya, *Uhr-uhdh-yuh*, (M), (S), to be worshipped, ★

Aran, *Uhr-uhn*, (M), (S), heaven, ★★★

Aran, *Eh-ruhn*, (M), (O) – Hebrew, exalted, enlightened, ★★★

Aravind, *Uhr-uhv-ihnd*, (M), (S), lotus, auspicious, handsome, ★

Archan, *Uhr-chuhn*, (M), (S), worship, respected, ★★★

Archana, *Uhr-chuhn-ah*, (F), (S), worship, respected, ★★★

Archat, *Uhr-chuht*, (M), (S), admired, brilliant, ★★

Archin, *Uhr-chihn*, (M), (S), brilliant, pious, ★★★

Archit, *Uhr-chiht*, (M), (S), revered, ★★

Arhan, *Uhr-hahn*, (M), (S), worship, homage, respect, ★★★

Arhan, *Uhr-huhn*, (M), (S), revered, ★★

Arhana, *Uhr-huhn-ah*, (F), (S), revered, ★★

Arhant, *Uhr-huhnt*, (M), (S), calm, benevolent, another name for
    Shiva, ★★

Arhat, *Uhr-huht*, (M), (S), worthy, honourable, ★★

Arin, *Uhr-ihn*, (M), (S), discus, ★★★

Arja, *Uhr-jah*, (F), (S), pure, godly, ★★★

Arjan, *Uhr-juhn*, (M), (S), victor, conqueror, ★★★

Arjit, *Uhr-jiht*, (M), (S), earned, won, ★★

Arjun, *Uhr-jun*, (M), (S), fair, open minded, pure, brilliant, a Pandava
    prince, ★★★

Ark, *Uhrk*, (M), (S), the sun, lightening, fire, hymn, a sage, another
    name for Indra, ★★★

Arkaj, *Uhr-kuhj*, (M), (S), born of the sun, ★★★

Arkash, *Uhr-kuhsh*, (M), (S), enlightened by the sun, ★★★

Arkin, *Uhr-kihn*, (M), (S), brilliant, venerated, ★★★

Armaan, *Uhr-mahn*, (M), (P), wish, hope, ambition, ★★★

Arnav, *Uhr-nuhv*, (M), (S), ocean, air, sun, ★★★

Arpan, *Uhr-puhn*, (M), (S), devotional offering, auspicious, ★★★

Arpana, *Uhr-puhn-ah*, (F), (S), devotional offering, auspicious, ★★★

Arpit, *Uhr-piht*, (M), (S), offered, dedicated, ★★

Arpita, *Uhr-piht-ah*, (F), (S), offered, dedicated, ★★

Arsh, *Uhrsh*, (M), (S), worshipped, divine, (P), gift,
    compensation, ★★★

Arshad, *Uhr-shahd*, (M), (S), pious, ★★

Arshad, *Uhr-shuhd*, (M), (S), (H), (O) – Urdu, devoted, pious, ★★

Arshya, *Uhrsh-yuh*, (M), (S), heavenly, sacred, ★★

Artham, *Uhr-thuhm*, (M), (S), fortune, ★★

Arthana, *Uhr-thuhn-ah*, (F), (S), request, supplication, ★★

Artika, *Uhr-tihk-ah*, (F), (S), elder sister, ★★

Aru, *Uhr-u*, (M), (S), the sun, ★★★

Aruj, *Uhr-uj*, (M), (S), born of the sun, ★★★

Aruja, *Uhr-uj-ah*, (F), (S), born of the sun, healthy, ★★★

Arujas, *Uhr-uj-uhs*, (M), (S), healthy, active, happy, ★★★

Arukshita, *Uhr-oohk-shiht-ah*, (F), (S), young, gentle, ★

Arukshna, *Uhr-oohk-shuhn-ah*, (F), (S), young, gentle, ★★

Arul, *Uhr-ul*, (M), (S), brilliant, shining, ★★★

Arun, *Uhr-un*, (M), (S), the red glow of the rising sun, mythical charioteer of the sun, dawn, passionate, ★★★

Aruna, *Uhr-un-ah*, (F), (S), red, passionate, fertile, ★★★

Arunabha, *Uhr-un-ah-bhhah*, (F), (S), the sun's glow, passionate, fertile, ★★★

Arundhati, *Uhr-un-dhuht-ee*, (F), (S), faithful, devoted, ★

Arunesh, *Uhr-un-aeyh*, (M), (S), the sun god, another name for Surya, ★★

Aruni, *Uhr-un-ee*, (F), (S), dawn, passionate, precious, illuminating, sacred, ★★★

Arunika, *Uhr-un-ihk-ah*, (F), (S), red, passionate, fertile, illuminating, ★★★

Arunima, *Uhr-un-ihm-ah*, (F), (S), the glow of dawn, ★★★

Arupa, *Uhr-oohp-ah*, (F), (S), without the limitations of form, divine, ★★★

Arush, *Uhr-ush*, (M), (S), calm, red, brilliant, another name for the sun, ★★★

Arushi, *Uhr-ush-ee*, (F), (S), the dawn, flame, bright, life giving, ★★★

Arv, *Uhrv*, (M), (S), horse, speedy, ★★★

Arvan, *Uhr-vuhn*, (M), (S), speedy, another name for Indra, ★★★

Aryam, *Uhr-yuhm*, (M), (S), kind, benevolent, ★★★

Aryaman, *Uhr-yuhm-uhn*, (M), (S), friend, the sun, ★★

Ashan, *Uhsh-uhn*, (M), (S), rock, strong, ★★★

Ashank, *Uhsh-uhnk*, (M), (S), fearless, without hesitation or doubt, ★★★

Ashankit, *Uhsh-uhnk-iht*, (M), (S), fearless, positive, without hesitation or doubt, ★★★

Ashesh, *Uhsh-aesh*, (M), (S), perfect, complete, godly, ★★★

Ashim, *Uhsh-ihm*, (M), (S), limitless, ★★★

Ashima, *Uhsh-ihm-ah*, (F), (S), limitless, ★★★

Ashit, *Uh-shiht*, (M), (S), hot, the planet Saturn, ★★

Ashm, *Uhshm*, (M), (S), stone, hard, ★★★

Ashmak, *Uhsh-muhk*, (M), (S), rock, gem, ★★★

Ashmaki, *Uhsh-muhk-ee*, (F), (S), rocklike, strong, ★★★

Ashmit, *Uhsh-miht*, (M), (S), hard, strong, ★★

Ashan, *Uhsh-uhn*, (M), (S), to pervade, to eat, food, ★★★

Ashna, *Uhsh-nah*, (F), (S), pervading, insatiable, ★★★

Ashni, *Uhsh-nee*, (F), (S), thunderbolt, lightning, ★★★

Ashok, *Uhsh-oak*, (M), (S), happy, content, one who knows no sorrow, a king of the Mauryan dynasty, ★★★

Ashoka, *Uhsh-oak-ah*, (F), (S), happy, content, one who knows no sorrow, a Jaina goddess, ★★★

Ashpan, *Ush-puhn*, (M), (S), another name for Brahman or the Supreme Spirit, ★★★

Ashraf, *Uhsh-ruhf*, (M), (A), honourable, noble, ★★★

Ashrav, *Uhsh-ruhv*, (M), (S), obedient, amenable, ★★★

Ashravya, *Uhsh-ruhv-yuh*, (M), (S), well-known, a highly regarded mentor and advisor, a sage, ★★

Ashul, *Uhsh-ool*, (M), (S), one who meets no obstacles, calm, happy, ★★★

Ashva, *Uhsh-vuh*, (M), (S), horse, strong, quick, fortunate, ★★★

Ashvarya *Uhsh-vuhr-yuh*, (M), (S), extraordinary, ★★

Ashvin, *Uhsh-vihn*, (M), (S), one who owns horses, the name of the group of divine physicians, ★★★

Ashvini, *Uhsh-vihn-ee*, (M), (S), wealthy, quick, ★★★

Ashvini, *Uhsh-vihn-ee*, (F), (S), wealthy, quick, ★★★

Asim, *Uhs-eem*, (M), (S), infinite, boundless, ★★★

Asima, *Uhs-eem-ah*, (F), (S), infinite, boundless, ★★★

Asir, *Uhs-eer*, (M), (S), devout, active, ★★★

Asit, *Uh-siht*, (M), (S), limitless, dark, ★★

Asita, *Uh-siht-ah*, (F), (S), limitless, night, dark, ★★

Asmi, *Uhs-mee*, (M), (S), nature, pride, self-respect, ★★★

Asmi, *Uhs-mee*, (F), (S), nature, pride, self-respect, ★★★

Asmita, *Uhs-miht-ah*, (F), (S), nature, pride, self-respect, ★★

Asta, *Uhs-tah*, (F), (S), arrow, weapon, ★★

Asti, *Uhs-tee*, (F), (S), existence, eminence, ★★

Astrit, *Uhs-triht*, (M), (S), unconquerable, gold, ★

Astriti, *Uhs-triht-ee*, (F), (S), invincibility, ★

Atal, *Uhtt-uhl*, (M), (S), firm, unshakeable, constant, ★★★

Atas, *Uht-uhs*, (M), (S), the soul, divine, ★★

Atharv, *Uhth-uhrv*, (M), (S), a Vedic text, ★

Atim, *Uht-ihm*, (M), (S), proud, self-respecting, ★★

Atul, *Uht-ul*, (M), (S), unique, without match, ★★

Atulya, *Uht-ul-yuh*, (M), (S), unique, without match, ★★

Avabha, *Uhv-uhbh-ah*, (F), (S), brilliant, ★★★

Avadh, *Uhv-uhdh*, (M), (S), strong, firm, invincible, ★★

Avani, *Uhv-uhn-ee*, (F), (S), the earth, a river, ★★★

Avanish, *Uhv-uhn-eesh*, (M), (S), lord of the earth, ruler, ★★★

Avanti, *Uhv-uhn-tee*, (F), (S), infinite, humble, the sacred city of
    Ujjain, ★★

Avantika, *Uhv-uhn-tihk-ah*, (F), (S), princess, of the sacred city of
    Ujjain, ★★

Avara, *Uhv-uhr-ah*, (F), (S), youngest, another name for Paarvati, ★★★

Avaraj, *Uhv-uhr-uhj*, (M), (S), younger brother, ★★★

Avaraja, *Uhv-uhr-uhj-ah*, (F), (S), younger sister, ★★★

Avas, *Uhv-uhs*, (M), (S), joy, protection, ★★★

Avash, *Uhv-uhsh*, (M), (S), free, independent, ★★★

Avatar, *Uhv-uht-ahr*, (M), (S), incarnation of a god, ★★

Avi, *Uhv-ee*, (M), (S), favourite, guardian, master, air, another name
    for the sun, ★★★

Avijit, *Uhv-ee-jeet*, (M), (S), victorious, undefeated, ★★

Avik, Uhv-ihk, (M), (S), hard, strong, diamond, ★★★

Avika, Uhv–ihk-ah, (F), (S), strong, diamond, ★★★

Avinash, *Uhv-ee-nashsh*, (M), (S), invincible, indestructible, ★★★

Avish, *Uhv-ihsh*, (M), (S), ruler, sky, ocean, nectar, life giving, ★★★

Avishi, *Uhv-ihsh-ee*, (F), (S), heaven, earth, river, like nectar, life giving, ★★★

Avishya, *Uhv-ihsh-yah*, (F), (S), desire, passionate, ★★★

Avit, *Uhv-iht*, (M), (S), guarded, protected, ★★

Avkash, *Uhv-kahsh*, (M), (S), space, opportunity, leisure, ★★★

Avya, *Uhv-yah*, (F), (S), eternal, unchanging, ★★

Avya, *Uhv-yuh*, (M), (S), eternal, unchanging, Brahman or the Supreme Spirit, another name for Shiva and Vishnu, ★★

Avyay, *Uhv-yuhy*, (M), (S), unchanging, eternal, ★★

Ayan, *Uh-yuhn*, (M), (S), path, walking, the sun's course from one solstice to another, refuge, ★★★

Ayodhika, *Uhy-oadh-ihk-ah*, (F), (S), calm, peaceful, ★

Ayodhya, *Uhy-oadh-yah*, (M), (S), peaceful, irresistible, the sacred city of the Raamayana and seat of King Raam, ★

Ayuj, *Uh-yuj*, (M), (S), unequalled, unique, ★★★

Ayut, *Uh-yut*, (M), (S), unhindered, limitless, ★★

B

Baadal, *Bah-duhl*, (M), (S), cloud, ★★

Baahu, *Bah-ooh*, (M), (S), arm, ★★★

Baahuk, *Bah-huk*, (M), (S), arm, reliant, ★★★

Baal, *Bahl*, (M), (S), pure, youthful, another name for the sun, ★★★

Baala, *Bah-lah*, (F), (S), youthful, jasmine, (A), height, ★★★

Baali, *Bah-lee*, (M), (S), strong, ★★★

Bamya, *Bahm-yah*, (F), (O) – Avestan, brilliant, ★★★

Baan, *Bahn*, (M), (S), arrow, wit, intellect, ★★★

Baani, *Bahn-ee*, (F), (S), speech, eloquent, ★★★

Baani, *Bahn-ee*, (M), (S), an orator, eloquent, ★★★

Baano, *Bahn-oh*, (F), (P), noblewoman, ★★★

Baanu, *Bahn-u*, (F), (P), noblewoman, (O) – Avestan, lady, a ray of light, ★★★

Baansuri, *Bahn-sur-ee*, (F), flute, ★★

Baasav, *Bahs-uhv*, (M), (S), manly, bull, strong, ★★★

Babita, *Buhb-iht-ah*, (F), (S), astrological term referring to someone born in the early morning, (O) – Greek, foreign, a stranger, ★★

Bachil, *Buhch-ihl*, (M), (S), eloquent, an orator, ★★★

Bahaar,*Buh-hahr*, (F), (P), spring, glory, elegance, beauty, ★★★

Bahul, *Buh-hul*, (M), (S), large, plentiful, ★★★

Bahula, *Buh-hul-ah*, (F), (S), large, plentiful, ★★★

Bahuli, *Buh-hul-ee*, (F), (S), multifaceted, adaptable, ★★★

Bahuli, *Buh-hul-ee*, (M), (S), multifaceted, adaptable, ★★★

Bahulika, *Buh-hul-ihk-ah*, (F), (S), multifaceted, adaptable, ★★

Bahumanya, *Buh-hu-mahn-yuh*, (M), (S), universally respected and valued, ★★

Bair, *Baehr*, (M), (S), brave, ★★★

Baksh, *Buhksh*, (M), (P), fortune, donor, ★★★

Bakul, *Buh-kul*, (M), (S), clever, patient, circumspect, attentive, another name for Shiva, ★★★

Bakula, *Buh-kul-ah*, (F), (S), clever, patient, circumspect, attentive, ★★★

Bakur, *Buh-kur*, (M), (S), war horn, thunderbolt, lightning, brilliant, ★★★

Bal, *Buhl*, (M), (S), strength, vigour, (P), bridge, victory, ★★★

Bala, *Buhl-ah*, (F), (S), strength, vigour, ★★★

Balaj, *Buhl-uhj*, (M), (S), grain, born of strength, (A), glitter, shine, ★★★

Balaja, *Buhl-uhj-ah*, (F), (S), jasmine, beautiful, born of strength, the earth, ★★★

Balar, *Buhl-uhr*, (M), (S), strength, power, army, ★★★

Bali, *Buh-lee*, (M), (S), offering, powerful, ★★★

Balin, *Buh-lihn*, (M), (S), strong, ★★★

Balini, *Buh-lihn-ee*, (F), (S), powerful, strong, ★★★

Bandan, *Buhn-duhn*, (M), (S), prayer, sacred, unworldly, ★★

Bandana, *Buhn-duhn-ah*, (F), (S), prayer, sacred, unworldly, ★★

Bandhini, *Buhn-dhihn-ee*, (F), (S), a bond, one who glues together, is bound, ★

Bandin, *Buhn-dihn*, (M), (S), one who honours, poet, ★★

Bankim, *Buhn-kihm*, (M), (S), crescent, ★★★

Banshik, *Buhn-shihk*, (M), (S), lion, ★★★

Barhan, *Buhr-huhn*, (M), (S), strong, vigorous, swift, dazzling, ★★★

Barkha, *Buhr-khah*, (F), (S), rain, life giving, ★★

Barsaat, *Buhr-saht*, (F), (H), rain, ★★

Baru, *Buhr-ooh*, (M), (S), noble, ★★★

Barun, *Buhr-un*, (M), (S), lord of the water, ★★★

Basant, *Buhs-uhnt*, (M), (S), one who bestows wishes, spring, ★★

Basanta, *Buhs-uhnt-ah*, (F), (S), spring, ★★

Basu, *Buhs-ooh*, (M), (S), prosperous, ★★★

Bedar, *Baed-ahr*, (M), (P), awake, alert, ★★

Beg, *Baeg*, (M), (O) – Turkish, noble, prince, ★★★

Bekuri, *Baeh-kur-ee*, (F), (S), one with musical leanings, an apsara or celestial nymph, ★★★

Bela, *Bael-ah*, (F), (S), a vine, the jasmine creeper, ★★★

Bella, *Behl-lah*, (F), (O) – Italian, beautiful, ★★★

Bhaagya, *Bhah-gyah*, (F), (S), fate, happiness, ★★

Bhaakosh, *Bhah-koash*, (M), (S), treasure of light, another name for the sun, ★★

Bhaam, *Bhahm*, (M), (S), light, brilliance, ★★

Bhaama, *Bhah-mah*, (F), (S), charming, beautiful, famous, passionate, brilliance, ★★

Bhaamini, *Bhah-mihn-ee*, (F), (S), brilliant, beautiful, passionate, ★★

Bhaanavi, *Bhah-nuhv-ee*, (F), (S), descendent of the sun, brilliant, sacred, ★★

Bhaanu, *Bhah-nooh*, (F), (S), brilliant, virtuous, beautiful, ★★

Bhaanu, *Bhah-nu*, (M), (S), ruler, brilliance, eminence, ★★

Bhaanuj, *Bhah-nuj*, (M), (S), born of the sun, ★★

Bhaanuja, *Bhah-nuj-ah*, (F), (S), born of the sun, another name for the river Yamuna★★

Bhaarat, *Bhahr-uht*, (M), (S), descended from Bharat, India, ★★

Bhaarati, *Bhahr-uht-ee*, (F), (S), descended from Bharat, Indian, well-groomed, eloquent, ★★

Bhaarav, *Bhahr-uhv*, (M), (S), bowstring, ★★

Bhaarava, *Bhahr-uhv-ah*, (M), (S), pleasant, adaptable, the Tulsi plant, ★★

Bhaargav, *Bhahr-guhv*, (M), (S), archer, brilliant, ★★

Bhaargavi, *Bhahr-guhv-ee*, (F), (S), beautiful, pleasant, brilliant,
another name for the goddesses Lakshmi and Paarvati, ★★

Bhaasin, *Bhahs-ihn*, (M), (S), brilliant, ★★

Bhaaskar, *Bhahs-kuhr*, (M), (S), sun, fire, gold, brilliant, ★★

Bhaasu, *Bhah-su*, (M), (S), the sun, ★★

Bhaasur, *Bhah-sur*, (M), (S), hero, the shining god, brilliant, holy, ★★

Bhaasvan, *Bhahs-vahn*, (M), (S), brilliant, another name for the sun
god Surya, ★★

Bhaasvar, *Bhahs-vuhr*, (M), (S), brilliant, ★★

Bhaavan, *Bhah-vuhn*, (M), (S), creator, solicitous, charming, brilliant,
another name for Krishna, ★★

Bhaavana, *Bhah-vuhn-ah*, (F), (S), feelings, imagination,
contemplation, ★★

Bhaaviki, *Bhah-vihk-ee*, (F), (S), natural, emotional, ★★

Bhaavini, *Bhah-vihn-ee*, (F), (S), beautiful, eminent, emotional,
caring, noble, ★★

Bhadra, *Bhuhd-rah*, (F), (S), fair complexioned, attractive, worthy,
wealthy, successful, happy, another name for the river Ganges, ★★

Bhadra, *Bhuhd-ruh*, (M), (S), fair complexioned, attractive, worthy,
wealthy, successful, happy, blessed, ★★

Bhadrak, *Bhuhd-ruhk*, (M), (S), handsome, brave, worthy, ★★

Bhadrik, *Bhuhd-rihk*, (M), (S), noble, ★★

Bhadrika, *Bhuhd-rihk-ah*, (F), (S), noble, beautiful, worthy,
propitious, ★★

Bhagan, *Bhuhg-uhn*, (M), (S), happy, ★★

Bhagat, *Bhuhg-uht*, (M), (S), disciple, ★★

Bhairav, *Bhae-ruhv*, (M), (S), one who vanquishes fear, formidable, another name for Shiva, ★★

Bhairavi, *Bhae-ruhv-ee*, (F), (S), formidable, a form of Goddess Kali, ★★

Bhajan, *Bhuhj-uhn*, (M), (S), prayer, devotional song, ★★

Bhakt, *Bhukt*, (M), (S), disciple, loyal, ★

Bhakti, *Bhukt-ee*, (F), (S), devotion, ★

Bharani, *Bhuhr-uhn-ee*, (F), (S), accomplished, high achiever, ★★

Bharat, *Bhuhr-uht*, (M), (S), fire, race, actor, one who fulfills all desires, a demigod and brother of Raam, ★★

Bharata, *Bhuhr-uht-ah*, (F), (S), pleasure-seeking, well-groomed, a celestial nymph, ★★

Bharg, *Bhuhrg*, (M), (S), satisfied, brilliance, ★★

Bharu, *Bhuh-ru*, (M), (S), leader, responsible, gold, ocean, ★★

Bharuk, *Bhuh-ruk*, (M), (S), responsible, ★★

Bhaumik, *Bhau-mihk*, (M), (S), lord of the earth, earthly, ★

Bhav, *Bhuhv*, (M), (S), sentiment, real, ★★

Bhavad, *Bhuhv-uhd*, (M), (S), real, life giving, ★★

Bhavada, *Bhuhv-uhd-ah*, (F), (S), real, life giving, ★★

Bhavesh, *Bhuhv-aesh*, (M), (S), lord of existence, lord of sentiment, another name for Shiva, ★★

Bhavik, *Bhuhv-ihk*, (M), (S), devout, worthy, happy, ★★

Bhavika, *Bhuh-vihk-ah*, (F), (S), well-behaved, worthy, ★★

Bhavin, *Bhuhv-ihn*, (M), (S), man, ★★

Bhavya, *Bhuhv-yah*, (F), (S), beautiful, brilliant, virtuous, composed, another name for Paarvati, ★★

Bhavya, *Bhuhv-yuh*, (M), (S), handsome, brilliant, virtuous, excellent, devout, ★★

Bhoj, *Bhoaj*, (M), (S), generous, an open-minded king, ★★

Bhoja, *Bhoaj-ah*, (F), (S), generous, open-minded, ★★

Bhoomi, *Bhoo-mee*, (F), (S), earth, ★★

Bhoomika, *Bhoo-mihk-ah*, (F), (S), earth, (H), introduction, ★★

Bhrami, *Bhruhm-ee*, (F), (S) powerful, whirlwind, ★★

Bhuman, *Bhoo-muhn*, (M), (S), all-encompassing, the earth, ★★

Bhumat, *Bhu-muht*, (M), (S), ruler, one who possesses the earth, ★

Bhumi, *Bhoo-mee*, (F), (S), earth, ★★

Bhuv, *Bhuv*, (M), (S), earth, world, another name for Agni, ★★

Bhuva, *Bhuv-ah*, (F), (S), fire, earth, world, ★★

Bhuvan, *Bhuv-uhn*, (M), (S), world, home, human, ★★

Bhuvana, *Bhuv-uhn-ah*, (F), (S), all-pervading, world, home, ★★

Bhuvas, *Bhuv-uhs*, (M), (S), heaven, air, atmosphere, ★★

Bidisha, *Bihd-eesh-ah*, (F), (S), a river, ★★

Bina, *Been-ah*, (F), (S), lute, melodious, (P), perceptive, wise, ★★★

Bindu, *Bihn-du*, (F), (S), decorative dot worn on the forehead by women in India, drop, ★★

Binita, *Bihn-eet-ah*, (F), (S), modest, ★★

Bipasha, *Bihp-ahsh-ah*, (F), (S), limitless, a river now known as the Beas, ★★★

Bipin, *Bihp-ihn*, (M), (S), forest, glorious, providing refuge, ★★★

Biipul, *Bihp-uhl*, (M), (S), abundance, powerful, ★★★

Bir, *Beer*, (M), (S), warrior, (H), strong, (P), lightning, thunder, ★★★

Birbal, *Beer-buhl*, (M), (S), a powerful warrior, ★★★

Bisala, *Bihs-ahl-ah*, (F), (S), bud, young, ★★★

Bishakh, *Bihsh-ahkh*, (M), (S), with many branches, another name for Shiva, ★★

Bishakha, *Bihsh-ahkh-ah*, (F), (S), with many branches, stars, a Nakshatra or constellation, ★★

Bodh, *Boadh*, (M), (S), knowledge, intelligence, enlightenment, ★★

Bodhi, *Boadh-ee*, (F), (S), knowledge, wisdom, enlightenment, ★★

Bonnie, *Bawn-nee*, (F), (O) − Scottish, Spanish, good, pretty, ★★★

Bonita, *Bawn-eett-ah*, (F), (O) − Spanish, good, pretty, ★★★

Brahma, *Bruhm-ah*, (M), (S), creator of the universe, the first of the holy Hindu trinity, progress, prayer, ★★★

Brahmi, *Bruhm-ee*, (F), (S), sacred, the feminine spirit of Brahma embodied as Sakti, ★★★

Brihat, *Brih-huht*, (M), (S), loud, powerful, clear, ★★

Brihati, *Brih-huht-ee*, (F), (S), speech, powerful, heaven and earth, ★★

Brihit, *Brih-hiht*, (M), (S), nourished, loved, ★★

Brinda, *Brihn-dah*, (F), (S), popular, accompanied by many, the holy Tulsi plant, ★★

Buddha, *Buddh-ah*, (M), (S), enlightened, the title first used for Prince Gautam who was the founder of the Buddhist religion, ★★

Bulbul, *Bul-bul*, (F), (P), nightingale, lover, ★★★

C

Caara, *Caa-rah*, (F), (O) – Celtic, friend, Italian, dear, Vietnamese, diamond, ★★★

Caarina, *Caah-ree-nah*, (F), (O) – Celtic, friend, Italian, dear, Vietnamese, diamond, ★★★

Chaah, *Chaa-huh*, (M), (S), wish, longing, desired, ★★★

Chaahana, *Chaa-hanah*, (F), (S), longing, desired, ★★★

Chaanakya, *Chaan-uhk-yuh*, (M), (S), renowned Mauryan writer and politician, author of the *Arthashastra*, ★★★

Chaand, *Chah-nd*, (M), (S), the moon, to shine, ★★

Chaandani, *Ch-ahn-duh-nee*, (F), (S), moonlight, cool, fair, luminous, ★

Chaaran, *Chaa-r-uhn*, (M), (S), one who chants praises, bard, ★★★

Chaarani, *Chaa-r-uhn-ee*, (F), (S), nomad, bird, ★★★

Chaaya, *Chch-aa-yah*, (F), (S), shade, reflection, ★★

Chaayan, *Chch-aa-yuhn*, (M), (S), moon, ★★

Chaaru, *Chaa-ruh*, (M), (S), pleasant, beautiful, loved, cherished, ★★★

Chaaru, *Chaa-ruh*, (F), (S), pleasant, beautiful, ★★★

Chaaruvi, *Chaa-ruh-vee*, (F), (S), light, brilliant, ★★★

Chahel, *Cheh-hehl*, (M), (H), good cheer, ★★

Chaidya, *Chay-d-yuh*, (M), (S), wise, ruler, king of Chedi, ★

Chaitali, *Chay-tuhl-i*, (F), (S), of the mind, blessed with a good memory, ★

Chaitan, *Chay-tuhn*, (M), (S), perception, intelligence, life, vigour, ★

Chaitana, *Chay-tuhn-ah*, (F), (S), perception, intelligence, life, vigour, ★

Chaitanya, *Chay-tuhn-yuh*, (M), (S), intelligence, soul, intellect, ★

Chaitri, *Chay-tri*, (F), (S), born in spring, fresh, beautiful, happy, ★

Chaitya, *Chay-t-yuh*, (M), (S), of the mind, spirit, a stupa, ★★

Chak, *Ch-uhk*, (M), (S), happy, sated, brilliant, ★★★

Chakrik, *Ch-uhk-rik*, (M), (S), one with a discus, ★★★

Chakrin, *Ch-uhk-rin*, (M), (S), one with a discus, another name for
   Krishna and Shiva, ★★★

Chakshan, *Ch-uhk-shun*, (M), (S), good looking, ★★★

Chakshani, *Ch-uhk-shun-ee*, (F), (S), good looking, brilliant, ★★★

Chakshas, *Ch-uhk-shus*, (M), (S), guide, vision, brilliance, another
   name for Brihaspati, the teacher of the gods, ★★★

Chaman, *Ch-uhm-uhn*, (M), (P), flower garden, ★★★

Chanak, *Ch-uhn-uhk*, (M), (S), the father of Chaanakya, ★★★

Chanasyaa, *Ch-uhn-uhs-yah*, (F), (S), pleasant, wonderful, ★★★

Chanchal, *Ch-uhn-ch-uhl*, (M), (S), lively, mischievous, agile, ★★★

Chanchala, *Ch-uhn-ch-uhl-ah*, (F), (S), playful, moving constantly,
   lightening, ★★★

Chandak, *Chuhn-duhk*, (M), (S), moonlit, brilliant, ★★

Chandan, *Chuhn-duhn*, (M), (S), sandalwood, perfumed, auspicious,
   (P), sandalwood, ★★

Chandana, *Chuhn-duhn-ah*, (F), (S), sandalwood, perfumed,
   auspicious, ★★

Chann, *Ch-uhn*, (M), (S), famous, ★★★

Charak, *Ch-uhr-uhk*, (M), (S), nomadic religious student, ★★★

Charita, *Ch-uhr-iht-ah*, (F), (S), warm hearted, ★

Chavi, *Chchc-uhv-ee*, (F), (S), reflection, ray of light, ★★

Chedi, *Cheh-dee*, (M), (S), leader, charming, wise, king and founder
   of the Chedi dynasty, ★

Chelana, *Cheh-luhn-ah*, (F), (S), consciousness, ★★★

Chetak, *Cheh-tuhk*, (M), (S), pensive, ★

Chetaki, *Cheh-tuhk-ii*, (F), (S), conscious, ★

Chetan, *Cheh-tuhn*, (M), (S), perception, intelligence, life, vigour, ★

Chetana, *Cheh-tuhn-ah*, (F), (S), perception, intelligence, life, vigour, ★

Chetas, *Cheh-tuhs*, (M), (S), perception, intelligence, brilliance, ★

Cheera, *Ch-eehr-ah*, (F), (O) – Greek, face, warm expression, ★★★

Chiara, *Kee-ah-rah*, (F), (O) – Italian, light, ★★★

Chidaksha, *Chee-dahk-shuh*, (M), (S), the ultimate consciousness, Brahman or the Supreme Spirit, ★

Chidambar, *Chee-dahm-buhr*, (M), (S), generous, big hearted, ★

Chikit, *Chihk-eet*, (M), (S), wise, liberal, ★★

Chiman, *Ch-ihm-uhn*, (M), (S), inquisitive, ★★★

Chinmay, *Ch-ihn-meh*, (M), (S), supreme consciousness, ★★

Chinmayi, *Ch-ihn-muh-yee*, (F), (S), supreme consciousness, ★★

Chintan, *Ch-ihn-tuhn*, (M), (S), contemplation, thought, mind, ★

Chintana, *Ch-ihn-tuhn-ah*, (F), (S), contemplation, thought, mind, ★

Chintya, *Ch-ihn-t-yuh*, (M), (S), thought provoking, ★

Chir, *Ch-eehr*, (M), (P), brave, victor, ★★★

Chirag, *Ch-ihr-aahg*, (M), (P), lamp, brilliance, ★★★

Chirah, *Ch-eehr-ah*, (M), (P), articulate, wise, brave, powerful, (O) – Hebrew, this Biblical name is derived from Hirah and means a noble race, ★★★

Chirayu, *Ch-ihr-aa-yoo*, (M), (S), blessed with a long life, ★★★

Chirayus, *Ch-ihr-aa-yoohs*, (M), (S), blessed with a long life, ★★

Chitayu, *Ch-iht-aa-yoo*, (M), (S), the mind, born of the intellect, ★

Chitra, *Ch-iht-rah*, (F), (S), picture, worldly illusion, attractive, heaven, ★

Chitra, *Ch-iht-ruh*, (M), (S), picture, brilliant, illustrious, excellent, ★

Chitra, *Ch-iht-ruh*, (F), (S), picture, brilliant, illustrious, excellent, ★

Chitrai, *Ch-iht-ruh-ee*, (F), (O) – Tamil, spring, ★

Chitrak, *Ch-iht-ruhk*, (M), (S), tiger, handsome, brilliant, brave, ★

Chitral, *Chiht-ruhl*, (M), (S), colourful, ★

Chitrali, *Ch-iht-rahl-ee*, (F), (S), wonderful, with unusual tastes, ★

Chitrani, *Chiht-rahn-ee*, (F), (S), varied, many pictures, ★★

Chitramayi, *Ch-iht-ruh-muh-yee*, (F), (S), like a picture, wonderful, ★

Chitresh, *Ch-iht-rehsh*, (M), (S), master of all that is wonderful, ★

Chitrini, *Ch-iht-rihn-ee*, (F), (S), talented, multifaceted, ★

Chitrish, *Ch-iht-reesh*, (M), (S), master of all that is wonderful, ★

Chitt, *Ch-iht*, (M), (S), knowledge, consciousness, another name for Brahma, ★

Chittaj, *Ch-iht-ahj*, (M), (S), produced in the heart, another name for the love god Kaama, ★

Chitti, *Ch-iht-ee*, (F), (S), devotion, contemplation, knowledge, ★★

Chittin, *Ch-iht-in*, (M), (S), philosopher, intelligent, ★★

Chitvan, *Ch-iht-vuhn*, (M), (S), look, glance, ★

Chitvat, *Ch-iht-vuht*, (M), (S), wise, clear, rational, ★

Choksha, *Choh-ksh-uh*, (M), (S), pure, charming, ★★★

Choksha, *Choh-ksh-ah*, (F), (S), pure, charming, ★★★

Chumba, *Ch-uhm-bah*, (F), (S), kiss, amiable, ★★★

Chumban, *Ch-uhm-bahn*, (F), (S), kiss, amiable, ★★★

Ciara, *Kee-ah-rah*, (F), (O) – Celtic, brunette, ★★★

D

Daadar, *Dah-duhr*, (M), (P), brother, dear friend, another name for god, ★★

Daakshi, *Dahksh-ee*, (M), (S), golden, son, son of Daksh, ★★

Daam, *Dahm*, (M), (O) – Pahlavi, creature, creation, ★★

Daama, *Dahm-ah*, (F), (S), prosperous, self-possessed, (A), river, ocean, ★★

Daaman, *Dahm-uhn*, (M), (S), rope, ★★

Daamini, *Dahm-ihn-ee*, (F), (S), lightning, ★★

Daana, *Dahn-ah*, (F), (P), learned, intelligent, another name for god, (H), grain, ★★

Daanish, *Dahn-ihsh*, (M), (P), knowledge, intelligence, consciousness, ★★

Daar, *Dahr*, (M), (P), owner, master, another name for god, ★★

Daaria, *Ddahr-ee-ah*, (F), (P), (O) – Greek, wealthy, sea, ★★★

Daav, *Dahv*, (M), (S), uncontrollable, fire, another name for Agni, ★★

Daivat, *Deh-vuht*, (M), (S), divinity, heart of the gods, ★★

Daivik, *Deh-vihk*, (M), (S), divine, relating to the gods, ★★

Daivya, *Deh-vyuh*, (M), (S), heavenly, wonderful, ★★

Daksh, *Duhksh.*, (M), (S), fire, gold, talented, excellent, vigorous, ★★

Daksha, *Duhksh-ah.*, (F), (S), the earth, another name for Paarvati, ★★

Dakshin, *Duhksh-ihn*, (M), (S), clever, competent, talented, sincere, with a southern orientation, ★★

Dakshina, *Duhk-shihn-ah*, (F), (S), donation, competent, talented, with a southern orientation, ★★

Dal, *Duhl*, (M), (S), group, petal, particle, ★★

Daler, *Duhl-aer*, (M), (P), brave, daring, fearless, bold, ★★

Dam, *Duhm*, (M), (S), wealth, residence, self-control, to conquer, ★★

Daman, *Duhm-uhn*, (M), (S), conquering, taming, self-controlled, ★★

Damin, *Duhm-ihn*, (M), (S), conquering, self-controlled, ★★

Damini, *Duhm-ihn-ee*, (F), (S), conquering, self-controlled, ★★

Darpak, (M), (S), pride, another name for the love god Kaama, ★★

Darpan, (M), (S), mirror, ★★

Darpana, (F), (S), mirror, ★★

Darsh, *Duhrsh*, (M), (S), sight, handsome, when the moon just becomes visible, ★★

Darshan, *Duhrsh-uhn*, (M), (S), vision, knowledge, observation, doctrine, philosophy, ★★

Darshana, *Duhrsh-uhn-ah*, (F), (S), vision, knowledge, observation, doctrine, philosophy, ★★

Darshani, *Duhrsh-uhn-ee*, (F), (S), beautiful, another name for Goddess Durga, ★★

Darshat, *Duhr-shuht*, (M), (S), radiant, handsome, discernable, ★

Dasha, *Duhsh-ah*, (F), (S), circumstance, period of life, wick, (H), condition, degree, ★★

Daya, *Duh-yah*, (F), (S), mercy, favour, compassion, ★★

Deeba, *Deeb-ah*, (F), (P), silk, eye of a mistress, ★★

Deeksha, *Deek-shah*, (F), (S), sacrifice, preparation for ceremony or sacrifice, ★★

Deekshin, *Deek-shihn*, (M), (S), prepared, initiated, ★★

Deekshit, *Deek-shiht*, (M), (S), prepared, initiated, ★★

Deekshita, *Deek-shiht-ah*, (F), (S), prepared, initiated, ★★

Deena, *Deen-ah*, (F), (P), decree, judge, ★★

Deep, *Deep*, (M), (S), lamp, light, brilliance, ★★

Deepa, *Deep-ah*, (F), (S), brilliant, that which blazes, ★★

Deepak, *Deep-uhk*, (M), (S), lamp, light, brilliant, ★★

Deepakshi, *Deep-ahk-shee*, (F), (S), one with bright eyes, ★★

Deepali, *Deep-ahl-ee*, (F), (S), row of lamps, ★★

Deepan, *Deep-uhn*, (M), (S), brilliant, invigorating, passion, ★★

Deepavali, *Deep-ah-vuh-lee*, (F), (S), row of lamps, Hindu festival, ★

Deepika, *Deep-ihk-ah*, (F), (S), a small lamp, light, ★★

Deepit, *Deep-iht*, (M), (S), inflamed, passionate, made visible, ★★

Deepti, *Deep-tee*, (F), (S), brilliance, beauty, ★★

Deeta, *Deet-ah*, (F), (S), answer of prayers, another name for
Lakshmi, ★★

Deetya, *Deet-yah*, (F), (S), answer of prayers, another name for
Lakshmi, ★★

Deshak, *Dae-shuhk*, (M), (S), one who governs, ruler, showing,
pointing out, ★★

Deshna, *Daesh-nah*, (F), (S), gift, instruction, ★★

Dev, *Daev*, (M), (S), light, heavenly, cloud, god, ★★

Devaj, *Daev-uhj*, (M), (S), born of the gods, ★★

Devak, *Daev-uhk*, (M), (S), divine, ★★

Devaki, *Daev-uhk-ee*, (F), (S), heavenly, devout, wonderous, mother
of Krishna, ★★

Deval, *Daev-uhl*, (M), (S), dedicated to the gods, ★★

Devala, *Daev-uhl-ah*, (F), (S), dedicated to the gods, the
personification of music, ★★

Devamani, *Daev-uhm-uhn-ee*, (F), (S), jewel of the gods, ★★

Devamayi, *Daev-uhm-ah-yee*, (F), (S), divine illusion, ★★

Devan, *Daev-ahnn*, (M), (S), food offered to the gods, holy, ★★

Devang, *Daev-uhng*, (M), (S), like a god, ★★

Devangi, *Daev-uhng-ee*, (F), (S), like a goddess, ★★

Devansh, *Daev-ahnsh*, (M), (S), demigod, ★★

Devanshi, *Daev-ahnsh-ee*, (F), (S), divine, ★★

Deven, *Daev-aen*, (M), (S), king of the gods, another name for Indra, ★★

Devesh, *Daev-aesh*, (M), (S), king of the gods, another name for Indra, ★★

Devin, *Ddehv-ihn*, (M), (O) – Celtic, poet, fawn, ★★★

Devi, *Daev-ee*, (F), (S), holy, goddess, queen, noblewoman, ★★

Devika, *Daev-ihk-ah*, (F), (S), minor goddess, a river in the Himalayas, ★★

Deviki, *Daev-ihk-ee*, (F), (S), from the goddess, ★★

Devin, *Daev-ihn*, (M), (S), one who takes chances, resembling a god, ★★

Devina, *Daev-ihn-ah*, (F), (S), resembling a goddess, ★★

Devish, *Daev-eesh*, (M), (S), king of the gods, another name for Brahma, Vishnu, Shiva and Indra, ★★

Devishi, *Daev-eesh-ee*, (F), (S), queen of the goddesses, another name for Durga and Devaki, ★★

Devya, *Daev-yuh*, (M), (S), divine power, ★★

Devyan, *Daev-yahn*, (M), (S), serving the gods, chariot of the gods, ★★

Devyani, *Daev-yahn-ee*, (F), (S), serving the gods, chariot of the gods, one invested with divine power, ★★

Devyosha, *Daev-yoash-ah*, (F), (S), the wife of a god, ★★

Dhaaran, *Dhah-ruhn*, (M), (S), keeping, protecting, ★★

Dhaarani, *Dhah-ruhn-ee*, (F), (S), keeping, protecting, ★★

Dhaavak, *Dhah-vuhk*, (M), (S), runner, swift, a poet in the Harsha dynasty, ★★

Dhaavit, *Dhah-viht*, (M), (S), cleaned, purified, ★★

Dhairya, *Dhaer-yuh*, (M), (S), courage, ★★

Dham, *Dhahm*, (M), (S), light, power, place of pilgrimage, ★★

Dhaman, *Dhahm-uhn*, (M), (S), light, power, majesty, home, ★★

Dhanya, *Dhuhn-yah*, (F), (S), worthy, fortunate, auspicious, happy, ★★

Dhar, *Dhuhr*, (M), (S), mountain, holding, sustaining, the earth, ★★

Dhara, *Dhuhr-ah*, (F), (S), one who holds, one who sustains, the earth, gold, ★★

Dharm, *Dhuhrm*, (M), (S), path of life, custom, duty, order, law, justice, merit, vitue, nature, religion, ★★

Dharman, *Dhuhrm-uhn*, (M), (S), supporter of Dharma, observer of the right path, ★★

Dhaarmik, *Dhahrm-ihk*, (M), (S), virtuous, righteous, pious, holy, ★★

Dharmini, *Dhuhrm-ihn-ee*, (F), (S), religious, just, pious, ★★

Dharun, *Dhuhr-un*, (M), (S), upholding, supporting, another name for Brahma, ★★

Dhaval, *Dhuh-vuhl*, (M), (S), dazzling, handsome, ★★

Dheeman, *Dheem-ahn*, (M), (S), wise, prudent, learned, ★

Dheemant, *Dheem-uhnt*, (M), (S), wise, prudent, learned, ★

Dheemat, *Dheem-uht*, (M), (S), wise, learned, prudent, ★

Dheer, *Dheer*, (M), (S), patient, clever, calm, resolute, firm, wise, skilful, ★★

Dheeraj, *Dheer-uhj*, (M), (S), tolerant, born of tolerance, clever, calm, resolute, firm, ★★

Dheeshana, *Dheesh-uhn-ah*, (F), (S), knowledge, wisdom, speech, hymn, goddess, ★★

Dheeti, *Dheet-ee*, (F), (S), thought, wisdom, prayer, ★★

Dheetik, *Dheet-ihk*, (M), (S), considerate, clever, ★★

Dhiran, *Dhihr-uhn*, (M), (S), devoted, ★★

Dhishan, *Dheesh-uhn*, (M), (S), wise, another name for Brihaspati, the god of speech★★

Dhrit, *Dhriht*, (M), (S), pledged, ★★

Dhriti, *Dhriht-ee*, (F), (S), steadiness, command, pleasure, ★★

Dhriti, *Dhriht-ee*, (M), (S), determination, steadiness, patience, virtue, ★★

Dhruv, *Dhruv*, (M), (S), steady, immovable, eternal, firm, the pole star, ★★

Dhruvak, *Dhruv-uhk*, (M), (S), firm, eternal, a tone in music, ★★

Dhyaan, *Dhyahn*, (M), (S), meditation, reflection, ★★

Diler, *Dihl-aer*, (M), (P), brave, bold, ★★

Dilip, *Dihl-ihp*, (M), (S), defender, protector, big-hearted, a generous king, ★★

Dillon, *Ddihl-uhn*, (F), (O) – Welsh, sea, ★★★

Dillon, *Ddihl-uhn*, (M), (O) – Welsh, sea, ★★★

Dina, *Ddeen-ah*, (F), (O) – Hebrew, vindicated, ★★★

Dinar, *Dihn-ahr*, (M), (A), gold coin, ★★

Dinesh, *Dihn-aesh*, (M), (S), the sun, ★★

Dipra, *Dihp-rah*, (F), (S), brilliant, ★★

Disha, *Dihsh-ah*, (F), (S), direction, ★★

Disht, *Dihsh-tt*, (M), (S), ordered, shown, appointed, ★★

Dishti, *Dihsh-tt-ee*, (F), (S), command, direction, destiny, an
    auspicious event, happiness, ★★

Diti, *Diht-ee*, (F), (S), radiance, brilliance, beauty, ★★

Div, *Dihv*, (M), (S), sky, heaven, day, light, ★★

Diva, *Dihv-ah*, (F), (S), through heaven, daytime, ★★

Divakar, *Dihv-ahk-uhr*, (M), (S), the sun, ★

Divij, *Dihv-ihj*, (M), (S), heaven born, divine, ★★

Divija, *Dihv-ihj-ah*, (F), (S), heaven born, divine, ★★

Divit, *Dihv-iht*, (M), (S), immortal, ★★

Divoj, *Dihv-oaj*, (M), (S), heaven born, ★★

Divya, *Dihv-yah*, (F), (S), charming, beautiful, divine, ★★

Divyanshi, *Dihv-yahn-shee*, (F), (S), with divine power, ★

Divyanshu, *Dihv-yahn-shu*, (M), (S), the sun, ★

Drav, *Druhv*, (M), (S), play, sport, essence, practical, wealthy, ★★

Dravid, *Druhv-ihdd*, (M), (S), landlord, wealthy, ★★

Dhridh, *Dhrih-dh*, (M), (S), firm, resolute, solid, strong, persevering, ★

Dhridha, *Dhrih-dhah*, (F), (S), firm, fortress, a Buddhist goddess, ★

Drishti, *Drihsh-ttee*, (F), (S), sight, ★★

Dron, *Droan*, (M), (S), guide, saviour, learned sage and teacher from
    the Mahabharata, ★★

Drona, *Droan-ah*, (F), (S), guide, saviour, ★★

Dulal, *Duhl-ahl*, (M), (S), lovable, young, ★★

Durg, *Durg*, (M), (S), fort, inpenetrable, ★★

Durga, *Durg-ah*, (F), (S), inpenetrable, the terrifying goddess, ★★

Durva, *Door-vah*, (F), (S), sacred grass, ★★

Dushal, *Dush-uhl*, (M), (S), firm, resolute, ★★

Dushtar, *Dush-ttuhr*, (M), (S), irresistible, inpenetrable,
    unconquerable, excellent, ★★
Dylan, *Ddihl-uhn*, (F), (O) – Welsh, sea, ★★★
Dylan, *Ddihl-uhn*, (M), (O) – Welsh, sea, ★★★

E

Edha, *Aedh-ah*, (F), (S), wealth, strength, happiness, ★★

Edhas, *Aedh-uhs*, (M), (S), sacred fuel, happiness, ★★

Edhit, *Aed-hiht*, (M), (S), developed, strengthened, ★★

Edi, *Aedd-ee*, (M), (S), healer, ★★

Ednit, *Aed-niht*, (M), (S), developed, evolved, ★

Ednita, *Aed-niht-ah*, (F), (S), developed, evolved, ★

Eh, *Aeh*, (M), (S), longing, cherished, desired, another name for Vishnu, ★★★

Eha, *Aeh-ah*, (F), (S), longing, cherished, desired, ★★★

Ehimay, *Ae-hee-mahy*, (M), (S), all-pervading intelligence, ★

Ek, *Aek*, (M), (S), the best, chief, excellent, first, one, unique, ★★★

Eka, *Aek-ah*, (F), (S), the best, chief, excellent, first, one, unique, ★★★

Ekada, *Aek-uhd-ah*, (M), (S), first, Brahman or the Supreme Spirit, leader, spiritual guide, ★

Ekada, *Aek-uhd-ah*, (F), (S), first, Brahman or the Supreme Spirit, leader, spiritual guide, ★

Ekadyu, *Aek-uhd-yoo*, (M), (S), sky, best, a scholar in the *Rig Veda*, ★

Ekaj, *Aek-uhj*, (M), (S), the only child, ★★

Ekaja, *Aek-uhj-ah*, (F), (S), the only child, ★★

Ekam, *Aek-uhm*, (M), (S), unmatched, Brahman or the Supreme Spirit, ★★★

Ekansh, *Aek-ahn-sh*, (M), (S), complete, one, ★★★

Ekansha, *Aek-ahn-sh-ah*, (F), (S), complete, one, ★★★

Ekanta, *Aek-ahn-tah*, (F), (S), beautiful, exclusive, devoted to one, ★

Ekantika, *Aek-ahn-tihk-ah*, (F), (S), focused, single-minded, ★

Ekbal, *Aek-bahl*, (M), (S), (A), dignity, ★★★

Ekesh, *Aek-aesh*, (M), (S), Brahman or the Supreme Spirit, ★★

Ekish, *Aek-eeh-sh*, (M), (S), Brahman or the Supreme Spirit, ★★★

Ekisha, *Aek-eeh-sh-ah*, (F), (S), the one goddess, ★★★

Ekshika, *Aek-shih-kah*, (F), (S), the eye, ★★★

Ekta, *Aek-tah*, (F), (S), harmony, unity, ★★

Ela, *Ael-ah*, (F), (S), the earth, cardamom, (O) – Turkish, halo, moonlight, Hebrew, oak tree, turpentine tree, terebinth tree, ★★★

Elena, *Ehl-aen-ah*, (F), (O) – Greek, brilliant, champion, defender of men, ★★★

Eleni, *Ehl-aen-ee*, (F), (O) – Greek, brilliant, sun's ray, ★★★

Elina, *Ehl-een-ah*, (F), (A), god is my light, (O) – Greek, brilliant, ★★★

Ella, *Ehl-ah*, (F), (O) – Greek, brilliant, shining, Gothic, complete, ★★★

Enakshi, *Aen-ahk-shee*, (F), (S), doe–eyed, ★★★

Eni, *Ae-nee*, (F), (S), a deer, marked, a brook, ★★★

Esh, *Aesh*, (M), (S), attractive, desired, another name for Vishnu, ★★★

Esha, *Aesh-ah*, (F), (S), attractive, desire, ★★★

Eshan, *Aesh-uhn*, (M), (S), wish, impulse, aim, ★★★

Eshana, *Aesh-uhn-ah*, (F), (S), aim, impulse, ★★

Eshanika, *Aesh-uhn-ihk-ah*, (F), (S), satisfying, ★★

Eshika, *Aesh-ihk-ah*, (F), (S), an arrow, one who achieves, ★★★

Eshit, *Aesh-iht*, (M), (S), desired, sought, ★

Eshita, *Aesh-iht-ah*, (F), (S), one who seeks, desirous, ★

Etash, *Aet-ah-sh*, (M), (S), brilliant, ★★

Eva, *Aev-ah*, (F), (O) – Hebrew, alive, Greek, auspicious news, ★★★

Eva, *Eev-ah*, (F), (O) – Hebrew, alive, Greek, auspicious news, ★★★
Evani, *Ehv-uhn-ee*, (F), (S), the earth, (O) – Hebrew, alive, ★★★
Evyavan, *Aev-yahv-ahn*, (M), (S), fast, agile, another name for
    Vishnu, ★

F

Faalguni, *Fahl-gun-ee*, (F), (S), the day of the full moon in the
Hindu month of Phaalgun (which falls between February
and March), ★★

Faiz, *Faez*, (M), (A), liberality, favour, abundance, affluence, ★★★

Falak, *Fuhl-uhk*, (M), (S), sky, ★★★

Farah, *Fuhr-ah*, (F), (A), happiness, joy, ★★★

Faranah, *Fuhr-ahn-ah*, (F), (P), wonderous, ★★★

Farhan, *Fuhr- hahn*, (M), (A), happy, ★★★

Farhat, *Fuhr-huht*, (M), (A), pleasure, delight, (P), decency,
majesty, ★★

Farman, *Fuhr-mahn*, (M), (P), instruction, command, ★★★

Farnad, *Fuhr-nahd*, (M), (P), strength, ★★

Farsad, *Fuhr-sahd*, (M), (P), wise, learned, ★★

Fateh, *Fuht-aeh*, (M), (H), (O) – Urdu, triumph, victory, ★★

Faye, *Faeh*, (F), (O) – Old English, fairy, faith, ★★★

Faza, *Fuhz-ah*, (F), (A), youth, bloom, ★★★

Firoz, *Fihr-oaz*, (M), (A), (O) – Urdu, victorious, to vanquish, ★★★

Fiza, *Fihz-ah*, (F), (P), developed, grown, ★★★

Freeya, *Free-yah*, (F), (A), beloved, ★★★

Freya, *Frae-yah*, (F), (O) – Norse, noble, lady, ★★★

Frieda, *Free-ddah*, (F), (O) – Germanic, peace, protection, ★★★

G

Gaalav, *Gah-luhv*, (M), (S), ebony, strong, to worship, a sage, ★★★

Gaangi, *Gahn-gee*, (F), (S), sacred, pure, comparable to the Ganges, another name for Durga, ★★★

Gaangika, *Gahn-gihk-ah*, (F), (S), sacred, pure, comparable to the Ganges, another name for Durga, ★★★

Gaayatri, *Gah-yuht-ree*, (F), (S), a Vedic mantra praising the sun, ★

Gagan, *Guhg-uhn*, (M), (S), sky, heaven, atmosphere, ★★★

Gaj, *Guhj*, (M), (S), origin, aim, elephant, ★★★

Gajra, *Guhj-rah*, (F), (S), garland of flowers, ★★★

Gambhir, *Guhm-bheer*, (M), (S), profound, tolerant, sensitive, powerful, influential, ★★

Ganak, *Guhn-uhk*, (M), (S), mathematician, astrologer, ★★★

Gandhali, *Guhn-dhah-lee*, (F), (S), fragrant, sweet smelling, ★★

Gandhalika, *Guhn-dhah-lihk-ah*, (F), (S), fragrant, sweet smelling, another name for Paarvati, ★★

Gandharika, *Guhn-dhahr-ihk-ah*, (F), (S), one who prepares perfume, ★

Gandharin, *Guhn-dhahr-ihn*, (M), (S), sweet smelling, another name for Shiva, ★

Gandharv, *Guhn-dhuhrv*, (M), (S), singer, divine musician, another name for Surya, ★★

Gandhik, *Guhn-dhihk*, (M), (S), fragrance, aroma, perfume seller, ★★

Ganesh, *Guhn-aesh*, (M), (S), the god of auspicious beginnings, one who removes all obstacles, the son of the gods Shiva and Paarvati with the head of an elephant, ★★

Gangah, *Guhn-gah*, (F), (S), fast, free flowing, the holy and purifying river Ganges, ★★★

Gangaj, *Guhn-guhj*, (M), (S), son of Gangah, ★★★

Ganika, *Guhn-ihk-ah*, (F), (S), Jasmine flower, conscious, ★★★

Ganin, *Guhn-ihn*, (M), (S), with many followers, ★★★

Ganit, *Guhn-iht*, (M), (S), numerate, honoured, mathematics, ★★

Ganjan, *Guhn-juhn*, (F), (S), first, excelling, winning, vanquishing, ★★★

Ganjan, *Guhn-juhn*, (M), (S), first, excelling, winning, vanquishing, ★★★

Gannika, *Guhn-ihk-ah*, (F), (S), valuable, cherished, the Jasmine blossom, ★★★

Garg, *Guhrg*, (M), (S), bull, a sage, ★★★

Garima, *Guhr-ihm-ah*, (F), (S), grace, holiness, dignity, power, one of the eight siddhis of the science of yoga, ★★★

Gariman, *Guhr-ihm-uhn*, (M), (S), weighty, profound, ★★★

Garul, *Guhr-ul*, (M), (S), facilitator, one who carries the great, another name for the bird Garuda, the vehicle of the gods, ★★★

Gati, *Guht-ee*, (F), (S), gait, speed, path, obedience, success, power of understanding, ★★

Gatik, *Guht-ihk*, (M), (S), fast, progressive, ★★

Gaur, *Gaur*, (M), (S), white, beautiful ★★

Gaura, *Gaur-ah*, (F), (S), white, beautiful ★★

Gaurang, *Gaur-ahng*, (M), (S), fair complexioned, another name for Vishnu, Krishna, and Shiva, ★★

Gaurav, *Gaur-uhv*, (M), (S), importance, glory, dignity, honour, ★★

Gauri, *Gaur-ee*, (F), (S), white, fair, beautiful, brilliant, another name for the earth and Paarvati, ★★

Gaurika, *Gaur-ihk-ah*, (F), (S), fair, a young girl, beautiful, ★★

Gautam, *Gaut-uhm*, (M), (S), one who enlightens, one who removes darkness, Gautam Buddha and the founder of the Buddhist religion, ★

Gautami, *Gaut-uhm-ee*, (F), (S), one who enlightens, one who removes darkness, another name for Durga, ★

Gavah, *Guhv-ah*, (F), (S), stars, ★★★

Gayan, *Guh-yuhn*, (M), (S), sky, ★★★

Ghalib, *Ghah-lihb*, (M), (A), first, predominant, victorious, another name for god, ★★★

Ghazal, *Ghuhz-uhl*, (F), (A), lyric poem, words of love, ★★★

Ghosha, *Ghoash-ah*, (F), (S), resounding, a proclamation, noise, fame, ★★

Ghoshini, *Ghoash-ihn-ee*, (F), (S), famed, proclaimed, noisy, ★★

Gia, *Jih-yah*, (F), (H), heart, (O) – Hebrew, god is merciful, Greek, earth, Chinese, good, beautiful, ★★★

Giri, *Gihr-ee*, (M), (S), mountain, hill, rock, cloud, title given to sages, ★★★

Girija, *Gihr-ihj-ah*, (F), (S), daughter of Himalaya, another name for Paarvati, ★★★

Girik, *Gihr-ihk*, (M), (S), the heart of the gods, epithet of Shiva, ★★★

Girika, *Gihr-ihk-ah*, (F), (S), mountain peak, ★★★

Girisa, *Gihr-his-ah*, (F), (S), one belonging to the mountains, another name for Paarvati, ★★★

Girish, *Gihr-eesh*, (M), (S), lord of speech, lord of the mountain, epithet of Shiva, ★★★

Girish, *Gihr-ihsh*, (M), (S), lord of speech, lord of the mountain, epithet of Shiva, ★★★

Girishma, *Gihr-eesh-mah*, (F), (S), summer, ★★★

Git, *Gee-t*, (M), (S), song, poem, chant, ★★

Gita, *Gee-tah*, (F), (S), song, poem, the Bhagvad Gita, the renowned Hindu religious treatise on philosophy and morality, ★★

Gitali, *Gee-tah-lee*, (F), (S), musical, one who appreciates song, ★★

Gitanjali, *Gee-than-juhl-ee*, (F), (S), devotional offering of musical praise, ★

Gitika, *Gee-tihk-ah*, (F), (S), a short song, ★★

Godavari, *Goad-ahv-uhr-ee*, (F), (S), largest and longest river in South India, one who bestows water and wealth, ★

Gogan, *Goag-uhn*, (M), (S), many rays, ★★★

Goja, *Goaj-ah*, (F), (S), born among rays, created of milk, rooted in the earth, ★★★

Gopal, *Goap-ahl*, (M), (S), cowherd, another name for Krishna, ★★★

Gopika, *Goap-ihk-ah*, (F), (S), defender, one who protects cows, another name for Raadha, ★★★

Goral, *Goar-uhl*, (M), (S), lovable, charming, ★★★

Gotam, *Goat-uhm*, (M), (S), best, the wisest, ★★

Goya, *Goah-yah*, (F), (P), articulate, ★★★

Graamani, *Grah-muhn-ee*, (F), (S), belonging to the village, attending to Surya and Shiva, ★★★

Grahin, *Gruh-hihn*, (M), (S), pertaining to the planets, ★★★

Gul, *Gul*, (F), (P), rose, red, precious, fortune, ★★

Gulika, *Gul-ihk-ah*, (F), (S), circular, a shot, a pearl, ★★★

Gunaj, *Gun-uhj*, (M), (S), born of virtue, ★★★

Gunaja, *Gun-uhj-ah*, (F), (S), born of virtue, ★★★

Gunin, *Gun-ihn*, (M), (S), with all the virtues, ★★★

Gunit, *Gun-iht*, (M), (S), excellent, virtuous, talented, ★★

Gunita, *Gun-iht-ah*, (F), (S), excellent, virtuous, talented, ★★

Gunj, *Gunj*, (M), (S), cohesive, well-woven, ★★

Gunjan, *Gunj-uhn*, (F), (S), humming, blossoms, ★★

Gunjik, *Gun-jihk*, (M), (S), humming, meditation, ★★

Gunnika, *Gunn-ihk-ah*, (F), (S), cohesive, a garland, ★★

Guptak, *Gup-tuhk*, (M), (S), guarded, defended, ★★

Gyaan, *Gyahn*, (M), (S), knowledge, consciousness, ★★★

Gyaanav, *Gyahn-uhv*, (M), (S), wise, learned, knowledgeable, ★★★

H

Haardik, *Hahr-dihk*, (M), (H), heartfelt, affectionate, cordial, ★★

Haarij, *Hahr-ihj*, (M), (S), the horizon, ★★★

Haarit, *Hahr-iht*, (M), (S), green, ★★★

Haasini, *Hahs-ihn-ee*, (F), (S), pleasant, wonderful, an apsara or celestial nymph, ★★★

Haim, *Haeh-m*, (M), (S), snow, made of gold, the Himalaya mountain range, another name for Shiva, ★★

Haima, *Haeh-mah*, (F), (S), of the snow, made of gold, another name for Paarvati and the river Ganges, an apsara or celestial nymph, ★★

Haimi, *Haeh-mee*, (F), (S), golden, ★★

Halik, *Huhl-ihk*, (M), (S), ploughman, ★★★

Halin, *Huhl-ihn*, (M), (S), ploughman, a sage, ★★★

Hans, *Huhns*, (M), (S), swan, mountain, pure, soul, Brahman or the Supreme Soul, another name for Surya, Shiva and Vishnu, ★★★

Hansi, *Huhn-see*, (F), (S), swan, soul, pure, ★★★

Hansika, *Huhn-sihk-ah*, (F), (S), swan, ★★★

Hansin, *Huhn-sihn*, (M), (S), containing Brahman or the Supreme Soul, another name for Krishna, ★★★

Hansini, *Huhn-sihn-ee*, (F), (S), swan, ★★

Haresh, *Huhr-aesh*, (M), (S), Shiva and Vishnu united, another name for Krishna, ★★★

Hari, *Huhr-ee*, (M), (S), man, green, light, sun, moon, lion, fire, another name for Indra, Brahma, Vishnu and Shiva, ★★★

Harish, *Huhr-eesh*, (M), (S), Shiva and Vishnu united, another name for Krishna, ★★★

Harit, *Huhr-iht*, (M), (S), green, lion, sun, gold, ★★

Harita, *Huhr-iht-ah*, (F), (S), green, gold, ★★

Harsh, *Huhrsh*, (M), (S), joy, excitement, ★★★

Harsha, *Huhrsh-ah*, (F), (S), joy, excitement, ★★★

Harshad, *Huhrsh-uhd*, (M), (S), delighted, ★★

Harshada, *Huhrsh-uhd-ah*, (F), (S), delighted, ★★

Harshak, *Huhrsh-uhk*, (M), (S), delightful, ★★

Harshal, *Huhr-shuhl*, (M), (S), delighted, a lover, ★★★

Harshala, *Huhr-shuhl-ah*, (F), (S), delighted, ★★★

Harshan, *Huhr-shuhn*, (M), (S), delightful, ★★★

Harshil, *Huhr-shihl*, (M), (S), delighted, ★★★

Harshit, *Huhr-shiht*, (M), (S), happy, cheerful, ★★

Harshita, *Huhr-shiht-ah*, (F), (S), happy, cheerful, ★★

Harshul, *Huhr-shul*, (M), (S), gregarious, funny, cheerful, lover, deer, Buddha, ★★★

Hasan, *Huhs-uhn*, (M), (S), laughing, (A), handsome, grandson of Prophet Mohammed, ★★★

Hasik, *Huhs-ihk*, (M), (S), smiling, gregarious, funny, delightful, ★★★

Hasika, *Huhs-ihk-ah*, (F), (S), smiling, gregarious, funny, delightful, ★★★

Hasit, *Huhs-iht*, (M), (S), laughing, happy, delightful, ★★

Hasita, *Huhs-iht-ah*, (F), (S), laughing, happy, delightful, ★★

Hatish, *Huht-ihsh*, (M), (S), simple, not greedy, ★★

Havan, *Huhv-uhn*, (M), (S), offering, sacrifice, another name for Agni, ★★★

Havish, *Huhv-ihsh*, (M), (S), sacrifice, one who gives offerings to god, another name for Shiva, ★★★

Havya, *Huhv-yuh*, (M), (S), to be invoked, ★★★

Hayley, *Haeh-lee*, (F), (O) – Old English, from the hay meadow, Norse, hero, ★★★

Heem, *Heem*, (M), (S), snow, winter, ★★★

Heema, *Heem-ah*, (F), (S), snow, winter, an apsara or celestial nymph, ★★★

Hela, *Hae-lah*, (F), (S), moonlight, comfort, passion, ★★★

Hem, *Haem*, (M), (S), gold, golden, a Buddha, ★★★

Hema, *Hae-mah*, (F), (S), gold, golden, beautiful, an apsara or celestial nymph, ★★★

Hemal, *Haem-uhl*, (M), (S), goldsmith, ★★★

Heman, *Hae-muhn*, (M), (S), gold, golden, water, ★★★

Hemang, *Hae-mahng*, (M), (S), with a golden body, lion, Brahmin, another name for Garuda, Vishnu, Brahma, and Mount Meru, ★★

Hemangi, *Haem-ahng-ee*, (F), (S), with a golden body, ★★

Hemani, *Hae-mahn-ee*, (F), (S), golden, precious, another name for Paarvati, ★★★

Hemant, *Hae-muhnt*, (M), (S), winter, cold, ★★

Hemanti, *Hae-muhnt-ee*, (F), (S), of winter, ★★

Hemesh, *Haem-aesh*, (M), (S), master of gold, ★★★

Hemish, *Haem-ihsh*, (M), (S), master of gold, ★★★

Herak, *Haer-uhk*, (M), (S), spy, follower of Shiva, ★★★

Hida, *Hihd-ah*, (F), (A), gift, ★★

Him, *Hihm*, (M), (S), snow, night, frost, ice, sandalwood tree, ★★★

Hima, *Hihm-ah*, (F), (S), snow, night, ice, frost, an apsara or celestial nymph, ★★★

Himachal, *Hihm-ahch-uhl*, (M), (S), where snow abounds, the Himalaya mountain range, ★★★

Himani, *Hihm-ahn-ee*, (F), (S), glacier, snow, another name for Paarvati, ★★★

Himanshu, *Hihm-ahn-shu*, (M), (S), cool gazed, moon, another name for Chandra, ★★★

Himmat, *Hihm-muht*, (M), (P), courage, effort, boldness, desire, thought, generosity, blessing, ★★

Hina, *Heen-ah*, (F), (S), perfume, Henna, (P), sword of the finest steel, ★★★

Hir, *Heer*, (M), (S), diamond, necklace, lion, ★★★

Hira, *Heer-ah*, (F), (S), diamond, certain, another name for Lakshmi, ★★★

Hiren, *Heer-aen*, (M), (S), lord of gems, one possessing the qualities of gems, ★★

Hiresh, *Heer-aesh*, (M), (S), lord of gems, one possessing the qualities of gems, ★★

Hit, *Hiht*, (M), (S), well-being, welfare, benefit, friend, friendly, good, auspicious, kind, ★★

Hiya, *Hih-yah*, (F), (S), heart, courage, ★★

Holika, *Hoal-ihk-ah*, (F), (S), auspicious, the festival of Holi, ★★★

Holly, *Hawl-lee*, (F), (O) – English, the holly shrub, name often given to babies born on or near Christmas, ★★★

Hom, *Hoam*, (M), (S), burnt offering, holy sacrifice, ★★★

Honn, *Hoann*, (M), (S), to own, ★★★

Hoor, *Hoor*, (F), (H), (A), fair, beautiful, black eyed, dark haired, celestial nymphs, ★★★

Hosh, *Hoash*, (M), (P), insight, judgement, intelligence, sensibility, consciousness, soul, ★★★

Hresh, *Raesh*, (M), (S), to be glad, to be excited, ★★★

Hridak, *Hrihd-ahk*, (M), (S), of the heart, genuine, lord of the
    heart, ★★

Hridik, *Hrihd-ihk*, (M), (S), of the heart, genuine, lord of the
    heart, ★★

Hrithik, *Hrihth-ihk*, (M), (S), from the heart, derived from the
    Sanskrit word Hriday, ★★

Hrithika, *Hrihth-ihk-ah*, (F), (S), truthful, ★

Huma, *Hum-ah*, (F), (P), auspicious bird, phoenix, ★★★

I

Iccha, *Ih-chch-ah*, (F), (S), ambition, desire, goal, intention, ★★

Ida, *Ih-ddah*, (F), (S), intelligence, perception, the earth, ★★★

Idenya, *Ih-ddaen-yuh*, (M), (S), praiseworthy, ★★★

Idenya, *Ih-ddaen-yah*, (F), (S), praiseworthy, ★★★

Iddham, *Ihd-dhuhm*, (M), (S), brilliant, sunshine, ★★

Idika, *Ih-ddeek-ah*, (F), (S), perception, the earth, another name for Paarvati, ★★★

Idhant, *Ihdh-ahnt*, (M), (S), luminous, one who spreads light, wonderful, ★★

Iha, *Eeh-ah*, (F), (S), desire, labour, exertion, endeavour, ★★★

Iham, *Ee-huhm*, (M), (S), expected, ★★★

Ihin, *Eeh-hihn*, (M), (S), desire, enthusiasm, ★★★

Ihina, *Eeh-hihn-ah*, (F), (S), desire, enthusiasm, ★★★

Ihit, *Ee-hiht*, (F), (S), prize, honour, effort, desire, desired, ★★

Ihita, *Ee-hiht-ah*, (F), (S), prize, effort, desire, desired, ★★

Ijya, *Ihj-yuh*, (M), (S), sacrifice, teacher, divine, ★★★

Iksha, *Eek-shuh*, (M), (S), sight, working of the senses, ★★★

Iksha, *Eek-shah*, (F), (S), sight, working of the senses, ★★★

Ikshan, *Eek-shuhn*, (M), (S), eye, sight, look, care, ★★★

Ikshit, *Eek-shiht*, (M), (S), visible, beheld, ★★★

Ikshita, *Eek-shiht-ah*, (F), (S), visible, beheld, ★★★

Ila, *Eel-ah*, (F), (S), earth, mother, teacher, speech, praise, ★★★

Ilana, *Eel-ahn-ah*, (F), (O) – Hebrew, tree, ★★★

Ilena, *Ihll-eh-nah*, (F), (O) – Greek, bright, shining, ★★★

Ilika, *Ihl-ihk-ah*, (F), (S), earth, transitory, ★★★

Ilil, *Eel-ihl*, (M), (S), very intelligent, ★★★

Ilin, *Eel-ihn*, (M), (S), very intelligent, ★★★

Ilina, *Ihl-ihn-ah*, (F), (S), very intelligent, ★★★

Ilesh, *Ihl-aesh*, (M), (S), king of the earth, ★★★

Ilesha, *Ihl-aesh-ah*, (F), (S), queen of the earth, ★★★

Ilish, *Ihl-eesh*, (M), (S), king of the earth, ★★★

Ilisha, *Ihl-eesh-ah*, (F), (S), queen of the earth, ★★★

Illissa, *Ihl-ee-sah*, (F), (O) – Hebrew, joy, German, noble, ★★★

Ilush, *Ihl-oosh*, (M), (S), a traveller, ★★★

Ilvaka, *Ihl-vuhk-ah*, (F), (S), defending the earth, ★★★

Ilvika, *Ihl-vihk-ah*, (F), (S), defending the earth, ★★★

Ilya, *Ihl-yuh*, (M), (S), heavenly tree, ★★★

Imaan, *Ihm-ahn*, (M), (H), (O) – Urdu, faith, creed, honesty, belief, truth, ★★★

Imaani, *Ihm-ahn-ee*, (F), (H), (O) – Urdu, trustworthy, faithful, honest, truthful, ★★★

In, *Ihn*, (M), (S), strong, sun, ruler, ★★★

Ina, *Ihn-ah*, (F), (S), strong, sun, ruler, ★★★

Inakshi, *Een-ahk-shee*, (F), (S), sharp eyed, ★★★

Inan, *Ihn-uhn*, (M), (S), sun, ruler, royal, ★★★

Inas, *Ihn-uhs*, (M), (S), strong, powerful, brilliant, majestic, another name for Surya, ★★★

Inayat, *Ihn-ah-yuht*, (F), (A), favour, ★★

Indali, *Ihn-duhl-ee*, (F), (S), to ascend, to gain power, ★★

Indira, *Ihn-dihr-ah*, (F), (S), bestows power and prosperity, powerful, another name for Lakshmi, wife of Vishnu, ★★

Indra, *Ihn-druh*, (M), (S), god of the atmosphere and sky, cloud, soul, best, excellent, generous, heroic, ★★

Indrani, *Ihn-drah-nee*, (F), (S), the wife of Indra, ★★

Indu, *Ihn-du*, (F), (S), nectar or Soma, the moon, ★★

Induj, *Ihn-duj*, (M), (S), born of the moon, another name for the planet Mercury, ★★

Induja, *Ihn-duj-ah*, (F), (S), born of the moon, another name for the river Narmada, ★★

Inesh, *Ihn-aesh*, (M), (S), strong, ruler, royal, another name for Vishnu, ★★★

Inika, *Ihn-ihk-ah*, (F), (S), dimunitive for the earth, ★★★

Ipsa, *Eep-sah*, (F), (S), desire, ★★★

Ipsita, *Eep-siht-ah*, (F), (S), desired, ★★★

Ir, *Eer*, (M), (S), wind, influential, to set in motion, ★★★

Ira, *Eer-ah*, (F), (S), the earth, water, wind, refreshment, an apsara or celestial nymph, another name for Saraswati, ★★★

Iraj, *Ihr-ahj*, (M), (S), born of the primal waters, another name for the love god Kaama, ★★★

Iraja, *Eer-uhj-ah*, (F), (S), daughter of the wind and earth, ★★★

Iravaj, *Ihr-ahv-uhj*, (M), (S), born of water, another name for the love god Kaama, ★★

Iravan, *Ihr-ahv-ahn*, (M), (S), filled with water, sea, cloud, ruler, ★★

Iravat, *Ihr-ahv-uht*, (M), (S), cloud, filled with water, ★★

Iresh, *Eer-aesh*, (M), (S), lord of the earth, another name for Vishnu and Ganesh, ★★★

Irika, *Ihr-ihk-ah*, (F), (S), dimunitive for the earth, ★★★

Irish, *Eer-eesh*, (M), (S), lord of the earth, another name for Vishnu and Ganesh, ★★★

Irna, *Ihr-nah*, (F), (A), to fascinate, to celebrate, ★★★

Irhsad, *Ihr-shahd*, (M), (A), command, mandate, ★★

Irya, *Ihr-yuh*, (M), (S), powerful, agile, vigorous, ★★★

Isar, *Ees-uhr*, (M), (S), eminent, another name for Shiva, ★★★

Ish, *Eesh*, (M), (S), divine, master of the universe, ruler, virile, pious, compelling, powerful, fast, (O) – Avestan, wish, ★★★

Isha, *Ihsh-ah*, (F), (S), intellect, power, ★★★

Isha, *Eesh-ah*, (F), (S), plough, another name for Durga, ★★★

Ishan, *Ihsh-uhn*, (M), (S), generous, causing prosperity, ★★★

Ishan, *Eesh-ahn*, (M), (S), ruler, another name for Shiva, Vishnu, Agni and Surya, (P), guide, ★★★

Ishana, *Eesh-ahn-ah*, (F), (S), ruler, another name for Durga, ★★★

Ishani, *Ihsh-ahn-ee*, (F), (S), ruling, owning, another name for Durga, ★★★

Ishanika, *Eesh-ahn-ihk-ah*, (F), (S), of the north-east, ★★★

Ishat, *Eesh-uht*, (M), (S), eminence, superiority, ★★

Ishi, *Eesh-ee*, (F), (S), divine, another name for Durga, ★★★

Ishik, *Ihsh-ihk*, (M), (S), desirable, ★★★

Ishika, *Eesh-ihk-ah*, (M), (S), arrow, paint brush, auspicious pen, ★★★

Ishir, *Ihsh-ihr*, (M), (S), refreshing, powerful, fast, agile, another name for Agni, ★★★

Ishit, *Eesh-iht*, (M), (S), desired, ★★

Ishita, *Eesh-iht-ah*, (F), (S), desired, eminence, superiority, wealth, ★★

Ishmin, *Ihsh-mihn*, (M), (S), fast, spontaneous, ★★★

Ishrit, *Ihsh-riht*, (M), (S), ruler, master of the universe, ★★

Ishtar, *Eesh-tuhr*, (M), (S), desired, dear, ★★

Ishu, *Ihsh-u*, (M), (S), arrow, light, brilliant, ★★★

Ishuk, *Ihsh-uk*, (M), (S), arrow, ★★★

Ishuka, *Ihsh-uk-ah*, (M), (S), arrow, an apsara or celestial nymph, ★★★

Ivana, *Ihv-ahn-ah*, (F), (O) – Hebrew, god is gracious, ★★★

Iya, *Ee-yah*, (F), (S), encompassing, ★★★

J

Jaagrav, *Jahg-ruhv*, (M), (S), alert, awake, watchful, sun, another name for Agni, ★★

Jaagravi, *Jahg-ruhv-ee*, (F), (S), alert, awake, watchful, ★★

Jaagriti, *Jahg-riht-ee*, (F), (S), existence, awakening, ★

Jaahnavi, *Jahn-uhv-ee*, (F), (S), another name for the river Ganges, ★★

Jaamini, *Jahm-ihn-ee*, (F), (S), night, wife of Yama, ★★★

Jaapak, *Jahp-uhk*, (M), (S), meditative, muttering prayers, ★★★

Jag, *Juhg*, (M), (S), universe, the earth, world, ★★★

Jagad, *Juhg-uhd*, (M), (S), universe, world, ★★

Jagan, *Juhg-uhn*, (M), (S), universe, world, ★★★

Jagat, *Juhg-uht*, (M), (S), people, the earth, world, ★★

Jagati, *Juhg-uht-ee*, (F), (S), earth, world, people, belonging to the universe, both heaven and hell, ★★

Jagav, *Juhg-uhv*, (M), (S), born of the world, ★★★

Jagavi, *Juhg-uhv-ee*, (F), (S), born of the world, ★★★

Jai, *Jaeh*, (M), (S), conqueror, victory, the sun, another name for Indra, ★★★

Jaival, *Jae-vuhl*, (M), (S), life giving, ★★★

Jaivat, *Jae-vuht*, (M), (S), victorious, ★★

Jalad, *Juhl-uhd*, (M), (S), cloud, ocean, ★★

Jalaj, *Juhl-uhj*, (M), (S), originating in the water, lotus, the moon, conch shell, ★★★

Jalaja, *Juhl-uhj-ah*, (F), (S), originating in the water, lotus, another name for Lakshmi, ★★★

Jalas, *Juhl-uhs*, (M), (S), water like, joy, soothing, life giving, ★★★

Jaman, *Juhm-uhn*, (M), (S), connoisseur, ★★★

Jamie, *Jaem-ee*, (F), (O) – Hebrew, may god protect, ★★★

Jamie, *Jaem-ee*, (M), (O) – Hebrew, may god protect, ★★★

Janak, *Juhn-uhk*, (M), (S), producing, begetting, father, ★★★

Janaav, *Juhn-ahv*, (M), (S), defender of men, ★★★

Janesh, *Juhn-aesh*, (M), (S), master of men, ★★★

Janhita, *Juhn-iht-ah*, (F), (S), considerate, wanting the welfare of all, ★★

Janish, *Juhn-eesh*, (M), (S), master of men, ★★★

Janisha, *Juhn-eesh-ah*, (M), (S), ruler of humans, ★★★

Janit, *Juhn-iht*, (M), (S), born, ★★

Janita, *Juhn-iht-ah*, (F), (S), born, ★★

Janu, *Juhn-u*, (M), (S), soul, birthplace, ★★★

Januj, *Juhn-uj*, (M), (S), born, son, ★★★

Januja, *Juhn-uj-ah*, (F), (S), born, daughter, ★★★

Janya, *Juhn-yah*, (F), (S), born, lovable, ★★★

Janya, *Juhn-yuh*, (M), (S), born, lovable, father, friend, ★★★

Japan, *Juhp-uhn*, (M), (S), recitation, chanting prayers, ★★★

Jashan, *Juhsh-uhn*, (M), (H), celebration, festival, ★★★

Jasleen, *Juhs-leen*, (M), (S), abode of fame, ★★★

Jasleen, *Juhs-leen*, (F), (S), abode of fame, ★★★

Jasleena, *Juhs-leen-ah*, (F), (S), abode of fame, ★★★

Jasmine, *Jazz-mihn*, (F), (A), (P), jasmine flower, fragrant, ★★★

Jasmit, *Juhs-miht*, (M), (S), celebrated, famous, ★★

Jaspal, *Juhs-pahl*, (M), (S), guarded by fame, ★★★

Jasraj, *Juhs-rahj*, (M), (S), lord of fame, ★★★

Jatan, *Juht-uhn*, (M), (S), nurturing, preserving, ★★

Jatin, *Juht-ihn*, (M), (S), disciplined, ascetic, another name for Shiva, ★★

Javan, *Juhv-uhn*, (M), (S), racer, quick, ★★★

Javin, *Juhv-ihn*, (M), (S), fast, horse, deer, ★★★

Jay, *Jae-y*, (M), (S), the sun, conquest, victorious, another name for Mahavishnu, ★★

Jaya, *Jae-yah*, (F), (S), conquest, victorious, green grass, another name for Paarvati, ★★

Jayan, *Jae-yuhn*, (M), (S), causing victory, ★★

Jayana, *Jae-yuhn-ah*, (F), (S), causing victory, armour, ★★

Jayani, *Jae-yuhn-ee*, (F), (S), auspicious, causing victory, ★★

Jayant, *Jae-yuhnt*, (M), (S), eventual victor, triumphant, the moon, another name for Mahavishnu and Shiva, ★★

Jayanti, *Jae-yuhnt-ee*, (F), (S), eventual victor, triumphant, flag, celebration, another name for Durga, ★★

Jayin, *Jae-yihn*, (M), (S), victor, conqueror, ★★

Jayit, *Jae-yiht*, (F), (S), victorious, ★★

Jayita, *Jae-yiht-ah*, (F), (S), victorious, ★★

Jeet, *Jeet*, (M), (S), mastery, victory, success, ★★

Jeev, *Jeev*, (M), (S), alive, living being, existing, soul, ★★★

Jeevaj, *Jeev-uhj*, (M), (S), born, ★★★

Jeevaa, *Jeev-uhj-ah*, (F), (S), born, ★★★

Jeeval, *Jeev-uhl*, (M), (S), inspiring, lively, causing victory, ★★★

Jeevan, *Jeev-uhn*, (M), (S), life, life giving, son, the sun, water, wind, another name for Shiva, ★★★

Jeevant, *Jeev-uhnt*, (M), (S), medicine, alive, long-lived, ★★

Jeevantika, *Jeev-uhnt-ihk-ah*, (F), (S), giving the blessing of long life, ★★

Jeevika, *Jeev-ihk-ah*, (F), (S), life giving, water, livelihood, ★★★

Jeman, *Jeh-muhn*, (M), (S), victorious, ★★

Jenya, *Jehn-yuh*, (M), (S), noble, true, ★★

Jess, *Jehs*, (F), (P), jasmine, (O) – Hebrew, god is merciful and gracious, ★★★

Jess, *Jehs*, (M), (P), jasmine, (O) – Hebrew, god is merciful and gracious, ★★★

Jessie, *Jehs-ee*, (F), (P), jasmine, (O) – Hebrew, god is merciful and gracious, ★★★

Jessie, *Jehs-ee*, (M), (P), jasmine, (O) – Hebrew, god is merciful and gracious, ★★★

Jharna, *Jhuhrn-ah*, (F), (S), spring, waterfall, fountain, ★★★

Jhata, *Jhuhtt-ah*, (F), (S), daughter, strong, brilliance, ★★★

Jhati, *Jhuhtt-ee*, (F), (S), brilliant, ★★★

Jhillika, *Jhihll-ihk-ah*, (F), (S), light, sunshine, moth, ★★★

Jhilmil, *Jhihl-mihl*, (F), (S), sparkling, twinkling, ★★★

Jhilmit, *Jhihl-miht*, (M), (S), partly visible, ★★

Jigisha, *Jihg-eesh-ah*, (F), (S), ambitious, wanting to win, ★★★

Jihan, *Jih-hahn*, (M), (P), leaping, the world, ★★★

Jin, *Jihn*, (M), (S), victorious, a Buddha, another name for Vishnu, ★★★

Jinesh, *Jihn-aesh*, (M), (S), lord of victors, ★★★

Jiti, *Jiht-ee*, (F), (S), victorious, ★★

Jivaj, *Jeev-uhj*, (M), (S), born, living, ★★★

Jival, *Jeev-uhl*, (M), (S), victorious, lively, ★★★

Josh, *Joash*, (M), (S), approval, zeal, passion, satisfaction, a bud, (P), effervescence, heat, lust, ★★★

Josha, *Joash-ah*, (F), (S), a woman, ★★★

Joshika, *Joash-ihk-ah*, (F), (S), cluster of buds, young, ★★★

Joshit, *Joash-iht*, (M), (S), delighted, ★★

Joshita, *Joash-iht-ah*, (F), (S), delighted, ★★

Jugal, *Jug-uhl*, (M), (S), pair, ★★★

Jugnu, *Jug-nu*, (M), (S), firefly, ornament, ★★★

Juhi, *Joo-hee*, (F), (S), jasmine, light, ★★★

Jushk, *Jushk*, (M), (S), lover, religious, worthy, ★★★

Jusht, *Jush-tt*, (M), (S), amiable, happy, auspicious, worshipped, ★★★

Jushti, *Jush-ttee*, (F), (S), love, service, ★★★

Juvas, *Joo-vuhs*, (M), (S), swiftness, ★★★

Jyot, *Jyoat*, (M), (S), brilliant, ★

Jyota, *Jyoat-ah*, (F), (S), brilliant, ★

Jyoti, *Jyoat-ee*, (F), (S), brilliant, flame, light, dawn, fire, vitality, source of life, energy and intelligence, ★

Jyoti, *Jyoat-ee*, (M), (S), flame, light, brilliant, passionate, scared, ★

Jyotik, *Jyoat-ihk*, (M), (S), flame, brilliant, ★

Jyotika, *Jyoat-ihk-ah*, (F), (S), flame, brilliant, ★

Jyotish, *Jyoat-ihsh*, (M), (S), brilliant, astrology, astronomy, astronomer, the sun, fire, ★

Jyotsna, *Jyoat-snah*, (F), (S), moonlight, lustre, another name for Durga, ★

Jyotsni, *Jyoat-snee*, (F), (S), moonlit night, ★

K

Kaa, *Kah*, (M), (S), creator, another name for Vishnu, ★★★

Kaaberi, *Kah-baer-ee*, (F), (S), water, attractive, a river in
    South India, ★★★

Kaachim, *Kahch-ihm*, (M), (S), where clouds rest, a sacred tree, ★★★

Kaahini, *Kah-hihn-ee*, (F), (S), youthful, spirited, ★★★

Kaai, *Kaiy*, (F), (O) – Greek, pure, the earth, Hawaiian, sea, ★★★

Kaai, *Kaiy*, (M), (O) – Greek, pure, the earth, Hawaiian, sea, ★★★

Kaajal, *Kahj-uhl*, (F), (S), kohl, decoration for women's eyes, ★★★

Kaakali, *Kahk-uhl-ee*, (F), (S), a musical instrument, the melodious
    voice of the cuckoo, ★★★

Kaakalika, *Kahk-uhl-ihk-ah*, (F), (S), softly spoken, melodious, an
    apsara or celestial nymph, ★★

Kaakol, *Kahk-oal*, to drink water, to carry water, ★★★

Kaal, *Kahl*, (M), (S), time, destiny, occasion, black, destruction, death,
    cuckoo, another name for Krishna and Shiva, ★★★

Kaalaka, *Kahl-uhk-ah*, (F), (S), dark, fog, flawed gold, perfumed,
    earth, another name for Durga, ★★★

Kaali, *Kahl-ee*, (F), (S), blackness, night, destroyer, goddess Durga in
    her terrifying form, ★★★

Kaalik, *Kahl-ihk*, (M), (S), darkness, long-lived, ★★★

Kaalika, *Kahl-ihk-ah*, (F), (S), dark, fog, flawed gold, perfumed, earth,
    another name for Durga, ★★★

Kaam, *Kahm*, (M), (S), desire, passion, love, delight, the god of
    love, ★★★

Kaama, *Kahm*, (F), (S), desired, cherished, ★★★

Kaamad, *Kahm-uhd*, (M), (S), generous, another name for the sun, ★★

Kaamada, *Kahm-uhd-ah*, (F), (S), generous, ★★

Kaamaj, *Kahm-uhj*, (M), (S), born of love, ★★★

Kaamana, *Kahm-uhn-ah*, (F), (S), desire, ★★★

Kaamat, *Kahm-uht*, (M), (S), free, unrestrained, ★★

Kaamik, *Kahm-ihk*, (M), (S), desired, ★★★

Kaamika, *Kahm-ihk-ah*, (F), (S), desired, ★★★

Kaamini, *Kahm-ihn-ee*, (F), (S), desirable, beautiful, affectionate, ★★★

Kaamit, *Kahm-iht*, (F), (S), desired, ★★

Kaamita, *Kahm-iht-ah*, (F), (S), desired, ★★

Kaamma, Kahmm-ah, (F), (S), loveble, ★★★

Kaamod, *Kahm-oad*, (M), (S), generous, granting wishes, a musical raag, ★★

Kaamodi, *Kahm-oad-ee*, (F), (S), exciting, ★★

Kaamuk, *Kahm-uk*, (M), (S), passionate, sensual, lover, ★★★

Kaamuk, *Kahm-uk*, (F), (S), desired, sensual, lover, ★★★

Kaamuna, *Kahm-un-ah*, (F), (S), desired, ★★★

Kaamya, *Kahm-yah*, (F), (S), beautiful, lovable, assiduous, successful, ★★★

Kaanan, *Kaa-nuhn*, (M), (S), forest, the mouth of Brahma, ★★★

Kaanan, *Kaa-nuhn*, (F), (S), forest, the mouth of Brahma, ★★★

Kaanchi, *Kahn-chee*, (F), (S), brilliant, a pilgrimage centre in South India, ★★★

Kaanha, *Kahn-hah*, (M), (S), young, another name for Krishna, ★★★

Kaanksha, *Kahnk-shah*, (F), (S), desire, ★★★

Kaankshini, *Kahnk-shihn-ee*, (F), (S), desirous, ★★★

Kaankshita, *Kahnk-shiht-ah*, (F), (S), desired, ★★

Kaant, *Kahnt*, (M), (S), husband, adored, precious, pleasant, spring, the moon, another name for Krishna, ★★

Kaanta, *Kahnt-ah*, (F), (S), adored, fragrant, the earth, ★★

Kaanti, *Kahnt-ee*, (F), (S), beauty, desire, splendour, ornament, another name for Lakshmi, ★★

Kaara, *Kaa-rah*, (F), (O) – Celtic, friend, Italian, dear, Vietnamese, diamond, ★★★

Kaarika, *Kahr-ihk-ah*, (F), (S), philosophical verses, activity, dancer, ★★★

Kaarin, *Kahr-ihn*, (M), (S), to achieve, celebrating, happy, ★★★

Kaaria, *Kahr-ihn-ah*, (F), (S), to achieve, celebrating, happy, ★★★

Kaartik, *Kahr-tihk*, (M), (S), inspiring with courage and joy, ★★

Kaartikeya, *Kahr-tihk-aey-uh*, (M), (S), brave, vigorous, active, inspiring with courage, the planet Mars, ★★

Kaartiki, *Kahr-tihk-ee*, (F), (S), devout, divine, ★★

Kaaru, *Kahru*, (M), (S), poet, ★★★

Kaarunya, *Kahr-un-yah*, (F), (S), kind, compassionate, praiseworthy, ★★★

Kaash, *Kahsh*, (M), (S), appearance, ★★★

Kaashi, *Kahsh-ee*, (F), (S), brilliant, pilgrimage site, the sun, another name for the city of Benaras, ★★★

Kaashik, *Kahsh-ihk*, (M), (S), brilliant, another name for the city of Benaras, ★★★

Kaashin, *Kahsh-ihn*, (M), (S), brilliant, ★★★

Kaashish, *Kahsh-ihsh*, (M), (S), lord of Kashi, another name for Shiva, ★★★

Kaashmir, *Kahsh-meer*, (M), (S), grape, belonging to Kashmir, ★★★

Kaashmira, *Kahsh-meer-ah*, (F), (S), grape, belonging to Kashmir, ★★★

Kaashvi, *Kahsh-vee*, (F), (S), brilliant, beautiful, ★★★

Kaashya, *Kahsh-yuh*, (M), (S), grass, ★★★

Kaashyap, *Kahsh-yuhp*, (M), (S), a famous sage, son of Kashyap, ★★★

Kaaveri, *Kahv-aer-ee*, (F), (S), filled with water, turmeric, ★★

Kaavya, *Kahv-yah*, (F), (S), poem, laden with sentiment, worth,
   learning, foresight, with the qualities of a sage or poet, ★★★

Kaavya, *Kahv-yuh*, (M), (S), poem, laden with sentiment, worth,
   learning, foresight, with the qualities of a sage or poet, ★★★

Kaavyanjali, *Kahv-yahn-juhl-ee*, (F), (S), the offering of poetry, ★★

Kaay, *Kahy*, (M), (S), body, ★★★

Kaaya, *Kah-yah*, (F), (S), body, ★★★

Kabir, *Kuhb-eer*, (M), (A), noble, great, ★★★

Kach, *Kuhch*, (M), (S), hair, splendour, attractiveness, cloud, ★★★

Kachap, *Kuhch-uhp*, (M), (S), leaf, ★★★

Kahan, *Kuh-hahn*, (M), (P), world, universe, ★★★

Kailash, *Kael-ahsh*, (M), (S), a mountain in the Himalayas, Shiva's
   home, temple, ★★

Kaira, *Kah-ee-rah*, (F), (O) – Greek, lady, ★★★

Kairav, *Kaer-uhv*, (M), (S), born of water, lotus, gambler, ★★★

Kairavi, *Kaer-uhv-ee*, (F), (S), moon, moonlight, ★★

Kaishik, *Kaesh-ihk*, (M), (S), fine, hair-like, love, vigour,
   a musical raag, ★★★

Kaitak, *Kaet-uhk*, (M), (S), tree, ★★

Kaitav, *Kaet-uhv*, (M), (S), gambler, deceitful, ★★

Kaivalya, *Kaev-uhl-yuh*, (M), (S), salvation, bliss, ★

Kakshak, *Kuhk-shuhk*, (M), (S), free, forest dweller, ★★★

Kakshap, *Kuhk-shuhk*, (M), (S), tortoise, one who drinks water, ★★★

Kakshi, *Kuhk-shee*, (F), (S), belonging to the jungle,
   fragrant earth, ★★★

Kakud, *Kuhk-ud*, (M), (S), peak, royal sign, ★★

75

Kala, *Kuhl-ah*, (F), (S), an atom, art, talent, initiative, creativity, ★★★

Kalam, *Kuhl-ahm*, (M), (A), speech, philosophy, discussion, compliment, ★★★

Kalap, *Kuhl-ahp*, (M), (S), intelligent, collection, the tail of a peacock, totality, decoration, the moon, ★★★

Kalapak, *Kuhl-ahp-uhk*, (M), (S), skilful, collection, a peacock, decoration, the moon, ★★★

Kalapin, *Kuhl-ahp-ihn*, (M), (S), peacock, cuckoo, ★★★

Kalapini, *Kuhl-ahp-ihn-ee*, (F), (S), night, moon, peacock tail blue, ★★★

Kalash, *Kuhl-ush*, (M), (S), sacred, holy urn, the pinnacle of a temple, ★★★

Kalhan, *Kuhl-huhn*, (M), (S), informative, perceptive, voracious reader, sound, ★★★

Kalhar, *Kuhl-huhr*, (M), (S), water lily, lotus, ★★★

Kali, *Kuhl-ee*, (F), (S), bud, ★★★

Kalika, *Kuhl-ihk-ah*, (F), (S), bud, fragrant, ★★★

Kalil, *Kuhl-ihl*, (M), (S), profound, difficult to attain, ★★★

Kalind, *Kuhl-ihnd*, (M), (S), bestowing arts and skills, the sun, ★★★

Kaling, *Kuhl-ihng*, (M), (S), artistic, ★★★

Kalini, *Kuhl-ihn-ee*, (F), (S), plant, full of blossoms and bloom, another name for the river Yamuna, ★★★

Kalit, *Kuhl-iht*, (M), (S), understood, ★★

Kalita, *Kuhl-iht-ah*, (F), (S), understood, ★★

Kalp, *Kuhlp*, (M), (S), appropriate, competent, rule, healthy, perfect, will, generous, a day in the life of Brahma, another name for Shiva, ★★★

Kalpak, *Kuhl-puhk*, (M), (S), getting to a benchmark, ceremony, ★★★

Kalpana, *Kuhl-puhn-ah*, (F), (S), imagination, creating, invention, embellishment, ★★★

Kalpesh, *Kuhl-paesh*, (M), (S), lord of perfection, ★★★

Kalpit, *Kuhl-piht*, (M), (S), imagined, appropriate, exact, invented, ★★

Kalpita, *Kuhl-piht-ah*, (F), (S), imagined, invented, ★★

Kalya, *Kuhl-yah*, (F), (S), morning, praise, clever, auspicious, healthy, ★★★

Kalyan, *Kuhl-yahn*, (M), (S), welfare, worth, fortune, noble, auspicious, handsome, pleasant, wealthy, joyful, ★★★

Kalyani, *Kuhl-yahn-ee*, (F), (S), auspicious, excellent, fortune, welfare, a sacred cow, another name for Paarvati, ★★★

Kalyanin, *Kuhl-yahn-ihn*, (M), (S), happy, lucky, propitious, wealthy, worthy, eminent, ★★★

Kama, *Kuhm-ah*, (F), (S), beauty, briliance, ★★★

Kamal, *Kuhm-ahl*, (M), (A), perfection, miracle, art, ★★★

Kamal, *Kuhm-uhl*, (M), (S), lotus, water, rose-coloured, another name for Brahma, (A), perfect, complete, ★★★

Kamala, *Kuhm-uhl-ah*, (F), (S), born of a lotus, spring, passionate, beautiful, eminent, prosperity, another name for Lakshmi, ★★★

Kamalika, *Kuhm-uhl-ihk-ah*, (F), (S), lotus, ★★★

Kamalini, *Kuhm-uhl-ihn-ee*, (F), (S), a pondful of lotuses, beautiful, auspicious, ★★★

Kamboj, *Kuhm-boaj*, (M), (S), shell, elephant, ★★

Kamran, *Kahm-rahn*, (M), (P), successful, lucky, happy, ★★★

Kanak, *Kuhn-uhk*, (M), (S), gold, sandalwood, ★★★

Kanaka, *Kuhn-uhk-ah*, (F), (S), another name for Sita, ★★★

Kanal, *Kuhn-uhl*, (M), (S), brilliant, ★★★

Kanav, *Kuhn-uhv*, (M), (S), wise, beautiful, a sage, ★★★

Kanch, *Kuhnch*, (M), (S), brilliant, glass, ★★★

Kanchan, *Kuhnch-uhn*, (M), (S), gold, wealth, a Buddha, ★★★

Kanchan, *Kuhnch-uhn*, (F), (S), gold, wealth, ★★★

Kanchana, *Kuhnch-uhn-ah*, (F), (S), gold, wealth, ★★★

Kaneen, *Kuhn-een*, (M), (S), young, ★★★

Kanik, *Kuhn-ihk*, (M), (S), small, a grain, an atom, ★★★

Kanika, *Kuhn-ihk-ah*, (F), (S), small, girl, an atom, ★★★

Kanishk, *Kuhn-ihshk*, (M), (S), small, a king who followed
    Buddhism, ★★★

Kanita, *Kuhn-iht-ah*, (F), (S), the iris, ★★

Kanj, *Kuhnj*, (M), (S), born of water, born of the head, lotus, another
    name for Brahma, ★★★

Kanjak, *Kuhnj-uhk*, (M), (S), born of water, born of the earth, ★★★

Kanjam, *Kuhn-juhm*, (M), (S), lotus, nectar, ★★★

Kanjan, *Kuhnj-uhn*, (M), (S), born of water, another name for the
    love god Kaama, ★★★

Kanjira, *Kuhn-jihr-ah*, (F), (S), tambourine, ★★★

Kank, *Kuhnk*, (M), (S), fragrance of the lotus, heron, ★★★

Kanka, *Kuhnk-ah*, (F), (S), fragrance of the lotus, ★★★

Kankana, *Kuhnk-uhn-ah*, (F), (S), bangle, ★★★

Kanv, *Kuhnv*, (M), (S), admired, skilful, intelligent, ★★★

Kanvak, *Kuhnv-uhk*, (M), (S), born of a skilful person, ★★

Kanval, *Kuhnv-uhl*, (M), (S), lotus, ★★

Kanvar, *Kuhnv-uhr*, (M), (S), young prince, ★★

Kapil, *Kuhp-ihl*, (M), (S), the sun, fire, a famous sage, an
    incarnation of Vishnu, another name for Vishnu, Shiva and
    Surya, ★★★

Kapila, *Kuhp-ihl-ah*, (F), (S), fragrance, a celestial cow, ★★★

Kapish, *Kuhp-ihsh*, (M), (S), Hanuman, lord of the monkeys, golden, incense, another name for Shiva and the sun, ★★★

Karam, *Kuhr-uhm*, (M), (S), destiny, code, duty, action, ★★★

Karan, *Kuhr-uhn*, (M), (S), talented, intelligent, ear, document, another name for Brahman or the Supreme Spirit, ★★★

Kareena, *Kuhr-een-ah*, (F), (H), manner, mode, order, (O) – Greek, pure, Scandinavian, beloved, variant of Katherine, ★★★

Karim, *Kuhr-eem*, (M), (A), generous, noble, precious, ★★★

Karima, *Kuhr-eem-ah*, (F), (A), generous, kind, ★★★

Karishma, *Kuhr-ishm-ah*, (F), (S), miracle, magic, (P), unusual, ★★★

Karma, *Kuhr-muh*, (M), (S), destiny, code, duty, action, ★★★

Karmash, *Kuhr-muhsh*, (M), (S), dutiful, ★★

Karnak, *Kuhr-nuhk*, (M), (S), of the ear, attentive, ★★★

Karshin, *Kuhr-shihn*, (M), (S), attractive, another name for the love god Kaama, ★★

Karnika, *Kuhr-nihk-ah*, (F), (S), lotus, heart of a lotus, earring, an apsara or celestial nymph, ★★★

Kartaar, *Kuhr-tahr*, (M), (S), master of all creation, ★★

Karun, *Kuhr-un*, (M), (S), kind, merciful, gentle, another name for Brahman or the Supreme Spirit, ★★★

Karuna, *Kuhr-un-ah*, (F), (S), compassion, gentleness, mercy, ★★★

Karush, *Kuhr-oosh*, (M), (S), dry, hard, ★★★

Kashmira, *Kuhsh-meer-ah*, (F), (S), belonging to Kashmir, another name for Paarvati, ★★★

Kastur, *Kuhs-toor*, (M), (S), musk, ★★

Kasturi, *Kuhs-toor-ee*, (F), (S), smelling of musk, ★★

Kashyap, *Kuhsh-yuhp*, (M), (S), one who drinks water, lily, a sage, ★★★

Kashyapi, *Kuhsh-yuhp-ee*, (F), (S), the earth, belonging to
Kashyap, ★★★

Katam, *Kuht-uhm*, (M), (S), handsome, best, ★★

Kathak, *Kuhth-uhk*, (F), (S), narrator, heroine, ★★

Kathak, *Kuhth-uhk*, (M), (S), narrator, hero, ★★

Kathit, *Kuhth-iht*, (M), (S), universally liked, praised, much talked
about, well-recited, ★★

Katrina, *Kuhtt-reen-ah*, (F), (O) – Greek, pure, ★★★

Kaush, *Kaw-sh*, (M), (S), silken, talent, ★★★

Kaushal, *Kosh-uhl*, (M), (S), welfare, wealth, skill, happiness, ★★

Kaushala, *Kosh-uhl-ah*, (F), (S), happiness, skill, a wife of Krishna, ★★

Kaushalya, *Kosh-uhl-yah*, (F), (S), talent, welfare, intelligence, mother
of Raam, ★★

Kaushik, *Kosh-ihk*, (M), (S), love, with knowledge of hidden treasure,
another name for Indra and Shiva, ★★★

Kaushika, *Kosh-ihk-ah*, (F), (S), silk, cup, ★★★

Kaushiki, *Kosh-ihk-ee*, (F), (S), silken, hidden, another name for
Durga, ★★★

Kautilya, *Kott-ihl-yuh*, (M), (S), strategic, shrewd, wily, celebrated
writer of the Arthashastra, ★

Kavach, *Kuhv-uhch*, (M), (S), armour, ★★★

Kavachin, *Kuhv-uhch-ihn*, (M), (S), armoured, another name for
Shiva, ★★★

Kavan, *Kuhv-uhn*, (M), (S), water, ★★★

Kavash, *Kuhv-uhsh*, (M), (S), shield, ★★★

Kavi, *Kuhv-ee*, (M), (S), knowledgeable, poet, learned, talented, a
physician, a singer, the sun, another name for Brahma, ★★★

Kavika, *Kuhv-ihk-ah*, (F), (S), poetess, ★★★

Kavin, *Kuhv-ihn*, (M), (S), another name for Ganesh, (O) – Irish, handsome, ★★★

Kavish, *Kuhv-ihsh*, (M), (S), master poet, best physician, a sage, ★★★

Kavita, *Kuhv-iht-ah*, (F), (S), poem, ★★

Kay, *Kaey*, (F), (O) – Greek, pure, ★★★

Kay, *Kaey*, (M), (O) – Greek, pure, ★★★

Kayan, *Kuh-yuhn*, (M), (P), king, name of a royal dynasty in Persia, ★★

Kedar, *Kaed-ahr*, (M), (S), meadow, the peak of the Himalayas, a musical raag, another name for Shiva, ★★

Keenan, *Keen-uhn*, (M), (O) – Celtic, little ancient one, ★★★

Keertan, *Keer-tuhn*, (M), (S), praise, praiser, ★★

Keertenya, *Keer-taen-yuh*, (M), (S), praiseworthy, ★

Keerti, *Keer-tee*, (F), (S), fame, reputation, happiness, ★★

Keertiman, *Keer-tihm-ahn*, (M), (S), famous, ★★

Keertimay, *Keer-tihm-uhy*, (M), (S), famous, ★★

Keertit, *Keer-tiht*, (M), (S), famous, ★

Keira, *Kee-rah*, (F), (O) – Celtic, dark haired, dusky, Greek, noble lady, ★★★

Keiron, *Keer-uhn*, (M), (O) – Celtic, dark haired, dusky, ★★★

Kelaka, *Kael-uhk-ah*, (F), (S), playful, artistic, ★★★

Kelik, *Kael-ihk*, (M), (S), playful, ★★★

Kesar, *Kaes-uhr*, (M), (S), saffron, mane of a horse or lion, eyebrow, ★★★

Keshat, *Kaesh-uht*, (M), (S), blessed, virile, an arrow of Kaama, another name for Vishnu, ★★

Keshav, *Kaesh-uhv*, (M), (S), long haired, another name for Vishnu and Krishna, ★★★

Keshik, *Kaesh-ihk*, (M), (S), long haired, ★★★

Keshika, *Kaesh-ihk-ah*, (F), (S), long haired, ★★★

Keshin, *Kaesh-ihn*, (M), (S), long haired, lion, ★★★

Keshini, *Kaesh-ihn-ee*, (F), (S), long haired, with beautiful hair, an apsara or celestial nymph, another name for Durga, ★★★

Ketak, *Kaet-uhk*, (M), (S), flag, gold ornament for the hair, a flower, ★★

Ketaki, *Kaet-uhk-ee*, (F), (S), golden, a flower, ★★

Ketan, *Kaet-uhn*, (M), (S), abode, flag, signal, invitation, ★★

Ketana, *Kaet-uhn-ah*, (F), (S), residence, ★★

Ketit, *Kaet-iht*, (M), (S), invited, called, ★★

Ketu, *Kaet-u*, (M), (S), brilliance, intellect, leader, shape, comet, flag, a planet, flame, another name for Shiva, ★★

Keva, *Kaev-ah*, (F), (O) – Celtic, fair, beautiful, gentle, ★★★

Keval, *Kaev-uhl*, (M), (S), sole, one, complete, perfect, unblemished, ★★★

Kevali, *Kaev-uhl-ee*, (F), (S), one, she who has attained the absolute, ★★★

Kevalin, *Kaev-uhl-ihn*, (M), (S), seeking of the absolute, ★★★

Kevika, *Kaev-ihk-ah*, (F), (S), flower, ★★★

Key, *Kaey*, (M), (S), speed, ★★★

Keya, *Kae-yah*, (F), (S), speed, a monsoon flower, ★★★

Keyan, *Keey-awn*, (M), (P), royal, (O) – Gaelic, Irish, ancient, ★★★

Keyur, *Kaey-oor*, (M), (S), armlet, ★★★

Keyura, *Kaey-oor-ah*, (F), (S), armlet, ★★★

Keyuri, *Kaey-oor-ee*, (F), (S), armlet, ★★★

Keyurin, *Kaey-oor-ihn*, (M), (S), with an armlet, ★★★

Khadir, *Khuhd-ihr*, (M), (S), heavenly, the Acacia tree, the moon, another name for Indra, ★

Khajit, *Khuhj-iht*, (M), (S), conquering heaven, a Buddha, ★★

Khanak, *Khuhn-uhk*, (M), (S), miner, digger, mouse, ★★

Khasha, *Khush-ah*, (F), (S), perfume, ★★

Khasam, *Khuhs-uhm*, (M), (S), in the air, a Buddha, ★★

Khushboo, *Khush-boo*, (F), (P), fragrance, ★★

Khushal, *Khush-ahl*, (M), (P), happy, ★★

Khusheel, *Khuhsh-eel*, (M), (H), happy, pleasant, ★★★

Khushi, *Khush-ee*, (F), (H), (P), delight, happiness, ★★

Kian, *Kee-ahn*, (M), (P), royal, (O) – Gaelic, ancient, ★★★

Kiara, *Kee-ahr-ah*, (F), (O) – Gaelic, dark haired, dusky, ★★★

Kieran, *Keer-uhn*, (M), (O) – Celtic, dark haired, dusky, ★★★

Kimaya, *Keem-yah*, (F), (S), divine, ★★★

Kiran, *Kihr-uhn*, (F), (S), ray of light, heat, ★★★

Kiran, *Kihr-uhn*, (M), (S), ray of light, heat, ★★★

Kirik, *Kihr-ihk*, (M), (S), sparkling, brilliant, ★★★

Kirin, *Kihr-ihn*, (M), (S), poet, writer, orator, ★★★

Kirit, *Kihr-iht*, (M), (S), crown, ★★

Kirmi, *Kihr-mee*, (F), (S), golden image, ★★★

Kirtan, *Keer-tuhn*, (M), (S), praise, ★★

Kirti, *Keer-tee*, (F), (S), fame, reputation, happiness, ★★

Kirtin, *Keer-tihn*, (M), (S), praise, ★★

Kirtit, *Keer-tiht*, (M), (S), famous, praised, ★★

Kishor, *Kihsh-oar*, (M), (S), youth, youthful, the sun, another name for Krishna, ★★★

Kishori, *Kihsh-oar-ee*, (F), (S), young, maiden, ★★★

Kismet, *Kihs-meht*, (F), (H), (A), (O) – Turkish, destiny, fate, ★★

Kitav, *Kiht-uhv*, (M), (S), gambler, rogue, ★★

Kiva, *Keev-ah*, (F), (O) – Hebrew, shelter, ★★★

Kiya, *Kih-yah*, (F), (S), a bird's cooing, melodious, (O) – Greek, pure, Egyptian, beloved, good natured, happy, ★★★

Koel, *Koa-yuhl*, (F), (S), the cuckoo bird, ★★

Kokil, *Koak-ihl*, (M), (S), the cuckoo bird, ★★★

Kokila, *Koak-ihl-ah*, (F), (S), the cuckoo bird, ★★★

Komal, *Koam-uhl*, (F), (S), gentle, soft, sweet, beautiful, ★★★

Komal, *Koam-uhl*, (M), (S), gentle, soft, sweet, handsome, ★★★

Komala, *Koam-uhl-ah*, (F), (S), gentle, soft, sweet, beautiful, ★★★

Koshin, *Koash-ihn*, (M), (S), bud, ★★★

Kotir, *Koat-ihr*, (M), (S), horned, another name for Indra, ★★

Kovid, *Koav-ihd*, (M), (S), erudite, skilled, cultured, experienced, ★★

Koyal, *Koa-yuhl*, (F), (S), the cuckoo bird, ★★★

Kram, *Kruhm*, (M), (S), order, method, custom, ★★★

Kraman, *Kruhm-uhn*, (M), (S), foot, horse, ★★★

Krip, *Krihp*, (M), (S), generosity, grace, gentleness, compassion, mercy, lustre, attractiveness, ★★★

Kripa, *Krihp-ah*, (F), (S), compassion, grace, gentleness, mercy, ★★★

Kripal, *Krihp-ahl*, (M), (S), kind, generous, ★★★

Kripan, *Krihp-ahn*, (M), (S), sword, ★★★

Kripi, *Krihp-ee*, (F), (S), beautiful, ★★★

Krish, *Krihsh*, (M), (S), thin, divine sage, ★★★

Krisha, *Krihsh-ah*, (F), (S), thin, ★★★

Krishak, *Krihsh-uhk*, (M), (S), farmer, a sage, ★★★

Krishan, *Krihsh-uhn*, (M), (S), pearl, gold, shape, oyster, antelope, another name for Krishna, ★★★

Krishang, *Krihsh-uhng*, (M), (S), thin, another name for Shiva, ★★★

Krishanga, *Krihsh-uhng-ah*, (F), (S), slender, an apsara or celestial nymph, ★★★

Krishangi, *Krihsh-uhng-ee*, (F), (S), slender, an apsara or celestial nymph, ★★★

Krishav, *Krihsh-uhv*, (M), (S), uniting the names of the gods Krishna and Shiva, ★★★

Krishi, *Krihsh-ee*, (F), (S), cultivation, farming, the earth, ★★★

Krishiv, *Krihsh-ihv*, (M), (S), uniting the names of the gods Krishna and Shiva, ★★★

Krishna, *Krihsh-nah*, (F), (S), dusky, blue, black, night, the pupil of the eye, perfume, a river in South India, another name for Durga, ★★★

Krishna, *Krihsh-nuh*, (M), (S), dusky, blue, black, the dark half of the lunar month, an incarnation of Vishnu, ★★★

Krishnan, *Krihsh-nuhn*, (M), (S), darkness, ★★★

Krishni, *Krihsh-nee*, (F), (S), dark, night, ★★★

Krishnik, *Krihsh-nihk*, (M), (S), linked to Krishna, linked to darkness, ★★★

Krishti, *Krihsh-ttee*, (F), (S), harvest, attractive, ploughing, ★★

Krit, *Kriht*, (M), (S), accomplished, appropriate, work, sacrifice, golden age, ★★

Kritak, *Kriht-uhk*, (M), (S), produced, adopted, made, ★★

Kriteyu, *Kriht-ae-yu*, (M), (S), lord of his own time, immortal, ★

Kriti, *Kriht-ee*, (F), (S), achievement, creation, magic, action, work, ★★

Kritin, *Kriht-ihn*, (M), (S), active, talented, accomplished, proficient, intelligent, pure, devout, happy, fortunate, worthy, ★★

Krittika, *Kriht-ihk-ah*, (F), (S), a constellation, ★★

Kritvi, *Kriht-vee*, (F), (S), accomplished, ★★

Kritya, *Kriht-yah*, (F), (S), action, accomplishment, appropriate, magic, performance, ★★

Kritya, *Kriht-yuh*, (M), (S), action, accomplishment, appropriate, magic, performance, ★★

Krityak, *Kriht-yuhk*, (M), (S), accomplished, ★★

Krityaka, *Kriht-yuhk-ah*, (F), (S), accomplished, ★★

Krivi, *Krihv-ee*, (M), (S), cloud, ★★★

Krivi, *Krihv-ee*, (F), (S), cloud, ★★★

Kriya, *Krih-yuh*, (M), (S), literary composition, knowledge, activity, ability, achievement, worship, Aries, ★★★

Kriya, *Krih-yah*, (F), (S), performance, activity, labour, ceremony, sacrifice, ★★★

Krupal, *Krup-ahl*, (M), (S), kind, generous, ★★★

Krushak, *Krush-uhk*, (M), (S), farmer, a sage, ★★★

Kshaa, *Shah*, (F), (S), the earth, patient, soothing, healing, ★★★

Kshaanti, *Shahn-tee*, (F), (S), patience, peace, indulgence, ★★

Kshaantu, *Shahn-tu*, (M), (S), patient, peaceful, enduring, ★★

Ksham, *Shuhm*, (M), (S), earthly, patient, compassionate, appropriate, quiet, forgiving, ★★★

Kshama, *Shuhm-ah*, (F), (S), earthly, patience, forgiveness, compassion, indulgence, the number one, another name for Durga and the earth, ★★★

Kshamak, *Shuhm-uhk*, (M), (S), kind, compassionate, ★★★

Kshaman, *Shuhm-uhn*, (M), (S), earth, soil, ★★★

Kshamya, *Shuhm-yah*, (F), (S), earthly, ★★★

Kshanik, *Shuhn-ihk*, (M), (S), ephemeral, ★★★

Kshanika, *Shuhn-ihk-ah*, (F), (S), ephemeral, ★★★

Kshapan, *Shuhp-uhn*, (M), (S), disciplined, religious, fasting, ★★★

Kshaunish, *Shaw-nihsh*, (M), (S), ruler, ★★

Kshay, *Sheh-y*, (M), (S), home, ★★★

Kshayan, *Shuh-yuhn*, (M), (S), home, a place with calm water, ★★★

Kshayat, *Shuh-yuht*, (M), (S), to rule, ★★

Kshem, *Shaem*, (M), (S), happiness, safety, peace, salvation, ★★★

Kshema, *Shaem-ah*, (F), (S), happiness, safety, peace, salvation,, an apsara or celestial nymph, another name for Durga, ★★★

Kshemak, *Shaem-uhk*, (M), (S), protector, fragrance, ★★★

Kshemya, *Shaem-yah*, (F), (S), goddess of welfare, another name for Durga, ★★★

Kshemya, *Shaem-yuh*, (M), (S), one who brings peace, healthy, wealthy, auspicious, another name for Shiva, ★★★

Kshipra, *Shihp-rah*, (F), (S), fast, stream,★★★

Kshipra, *Shihp-ruh*, (M), (S), fast,★★★

Kshiraj, *Sheer-uhj*, (M), (S), produced of milk, nectar, pearl, the moon, ★★★

Kshirin, *Sheer-een*, (F), (S), milky, ★★★

Kshiti, *Shiht-ee*, (F), (S), home, the earth, soil, races of men, ★★

Kshitij, *Shiht-ihj*, (M), (S), son of the earth, tree, horizon, Mars, ★★

Kshitija, *Shiht-ihj-ah*, (F), (S), daughter of the earth, another name for Sita, ★★

Kshitish, *Shiht-eesh*, (M), (S), master of the earth, ★★

Kshona, *Shoan-ah*, (F), (S), firm, immovable, the earth, ★★★

Kshoni, *Shoan-ee*, (F), (S), firm, immovable, the earth, ★★★

Kuber, *Kub-aer*, (M), (S), slow, god of riches, ★★★

Kuj, *Kuj*, (M), (S), son of the earth, tree, Mars, ★★★

Kuja, *Kuj-ah*, (F), (S), daughter of the earth, horizon, another name for Durga and Sita, ★★★

Kulaj, *Kul-uhj*, (M), (S), noble, from a good family, ★★★

Kulamba, *Kul-uhmb-ah*, (F), (S), family deity, ★★★

Kulik, *Kul-ihk*, (M), (S), from a good family, ★★★

Kulika, *Kul-ihk-ah*, (F), (S), from a good family, ★★★

Kulin, *Kul-ihn*, (M), (S), from a good family, ★★★

Kulish, *Kul-ihsh*, (M), (S), dazzling, diamond, thunderbolt, ★★★

Kulya, *Kul-yah*, (F), (S), worthy, from a good family, ★★★

Kulya, *Kul-yuh*, (M), (S), from a good family, worthy, ★★★

Kumar, *Kum-ahr*, (M), (S), boy, young, prince, ★★★

Kumari, *Kum-ahr-ee*, (F), (S), daughter, young girl, Jasmine, gold, another name for Durga and Sita, ★★★

Kumarika, *Kum-ahr-ihk-ah*, (F), (S), young girl, Jasmine, another name for Durga and Sita, ★★★

Kumaril, *Kum-ahr-ihl*, (M), (S), young, clever, ★★★

Kumud, *Kum-ud*, (M), (S), joy of the earth, water lily, lotus, another name for Vishnu, ★

Kumuda, *Kum-ud-ah*, (F), (S), joy of the earth, water lily, lotus, ★

Kunal, *Kun-ahl*, (M), (S), lotus, a bird, ★★★

Kunalika, *Kun-ahl-ihk-ah*, (F), (S), the cuckoo bird, ★★★

Kundan, *Kun-duhn*, (F), (S), pure, brilliant, gold, jasmine, ★★

Kundan, *Kun-duhn*, (M), (S), pure, brilliant, gold, jasmine, ★★

Kundanika, *Kun-duhn-ihk-ah*, (F), (S), Jasmine, ★★

Kunj, *Kunj*, (M), (S), living in greenery, ★★★

Kunja, *Kunj-ah*, (F), (S), living in greenery, ★★★

Kunjal, *Kun-juhl*, (M), (S), living in greenery, the cuckoo bird, ★★★

Kunjan, *Kun-juhn*, (F), (S), living in greenery, ★★★

Kunjar, *Kun-juhr*, (M), (S), living in greenery, an elephant, the
number 8, ★★★

Kunjika, *Kun-jihk-ah*, (F), (S), of the forest, ★★★

Kunjit, *Kun-jiht*, (M), (S), hidden in the forest, ★★

Kunsh, *Kunsh*, (M), (S), shining, articulate, ★★★

Kunshi, *Kunsh-ee*, (F), (S), shining, ★★★

Kupat, *Kup-uht*, (M), (S), excellent, ★★

Kush, *Kush*, (M), (S), scared grass, a son of the god Raam, ★★★

Kushad, *Kush-uhd*, (M), (S), cloud, ★★

Kushal, *Kush-uhl*, (M), (S), proficient, expert, good, happy, wise,
wealthy, healthy, auspicious, pious, another name for Shiva, ★★★

Kushalin, *Kush-uhl-ihn*, (M), (S), healthy, wise, successful,
auspicious, ★★★

Kushan, *Kush-ahn*, (M), (S), king, the Kushan dynasty that ruled
parts of India, ★★★

Kushanu, *Kush-ahn-u*, (M), (S), fire, ★★★

Kushin, *Kush-ihn*, (M), (S), another name for the celebrated sage
Vaalmiki, ★★★

Kusum, *Kus-um*, (M), (S), flower, blossom, fire, ★★★

Kusuma, *Kus-um-ah*, (F), (S), flower like, ★★★

Kuval, *Kuv-uhl*, (M), (S), informative, clever, water lily,
pearl, water, ★★★

Kuvam, *Kuv-uhm*, (M), (S), producer of the earth, the sun, ★★★

Kuvar, *Kuv-uhr*, (M), (S), fragrant, ★★★

L

Laakini, *Lahk-ihn-ee*, (F), (S), divine, a goddess who gives and takes, ★★★

Laal, *Lahl*, (M), (S), red, heart, child, beloved, ruby, ★★★

Laalima, *Lahl-ihm-ah*, (F), (S), reddish glow, supreme, beautiful, charming, symbol, ★★★

Laana, *Lahn-ah*, (F), (O) – Celtic, peaceful, little rock, Latin, wool, Greek, bright, shining, Hawaiian, buoyant, ★★★

Laara, *Lahr-ah*, (F), (O) – Latin, laurel, bright, famous, protection, Greek, Russian, lovely, ★★★

Laasak, *Lahs-uhk*, (M), (S), dancer, body, playful, peacock, another name for Shiva, ★★★

Laayak, *Lah-yuhk*, (M), (H), fit, clever, capable, ★★★

Laboni, *Luhb-oan-ee*, (F), (S), graceful, beautiful, ★★★

Labonya, *Lub-oan-yah*, (F), (S), brilliant, beautiful, ★★★

Lagan, *Luhg-uhn*, (M), (S), the rising of the sun or planets, (H), attachment, love, devotion, ★★★

Lahar, *Leh-hehr*, (F), (H) wave, surf, ripple, whim, ★★★

Lahar, *Leh-hehr*, (M), (H) wave, surf, ripple, whim, ★★★

Lahari, *Leh-hehr-ee*, (F), (S), wave, ★★

Laila, *Laey-lah*, (F), (A), night, sweetheart, ★★★

Lajja, *Luhjj-ah*, (F), (S), shyness, modesty, ★★★

Lajjak, *Luhjj-uhk*, (M), (S), modesty, ★★★

Lajjaka, *Luhjj-uhk-ah*, (F), (S), modesty, ★★★

Lajjan, *Luhjj-uhn*, (M), (S), modesty, ★★★

Lajjana, *Luhjj-uhn-ah*, (F), (S), modesty, ★★★

Lajjit, *Luhjj-iht*, (M), (S), shy, modest, blushing, ★★

Lajjita, *Luhjj-iht-ah*, (F), (S), shy, modest, blushing, ★★

Lakhan, *Luhkh-uhn*, (M), (S), successful, achiever, distinguished, with auspicious marks, ★★

Lak, *Luhk*, (M), (S), successful, achiever, distinguished, forehead, with auspicious marks, ★★★

Laksh, *Luhksh*, (M), (S), goal, sign, 100,000, ★★★

Laksha, *Luhksh-ah*, (F), (S), 100,000, rose, a decorative red dye used by women of ancient India, ★★★

Lakshak, *Luhksh-uhk*, (M), (S), expressing indirectly, ray of beauty, ★★★

Lakshan, *Luhksh-uhn*, (M), (S), propitious, distinguished, mark, the half-brother of god Raam, ★★★

Lakshana, *Luhksh-uhn-ah*, (F), (S), goal, vision, metaphor, an apsara or celestial nymph, ★★★

Lakshanya, *Luhksh-uhn-yuh*, (M), (S), successful, distinguished, achiever, objective, ★★★

Lakshin, *Luhksh-ihn*, (M), (S), propitious, distinguished, ★★★

Lakshit, *Luhksh-iht*, (M), (S), regarded, distinguished, ★★

Lakshita, *Luhksh-iht-ah*, (F), (S), regarded, distinguished, ★★

Lakshman, *Luhksh-muhn*, (M), (S), successful, distinguished, loyal, fortunate, half-brother of god Raam, ★★★

Lakshmi, *Luhksh-mee*, (F), (S), fortune, charm, beauty, brilliance, pearl, turmeric, the goddess of fortune, prosperity and success and the consort of Mahavishnu, ★★★

Lakshya *Luhk-shyah*, (F), (S), target, aim, meaning, ★★★

Lakshya *Luhk-shyuh*, (M), (S), target, aim, meaning, ★★★

Lalit, *Luhl-iht*, (F), (S), beautiful, desirable, voluptuous, gentle, graceful, sporting, a musical raag, ★★

Lalit, *Luhl-iht*, (M), (S), attractive, desirable, gentle, graceful, charming, sporting, a musical raag, ★★

Lalita, *Luhl-iht-ah*, (F), (S), woman, beautiful, desirable, graceful, musk, a musical raag, another name for Durga, ★★

Lashit, *Luhsh-iht*, (M), (S), desired, ★★

Lashita, *Luhsh-iht-ah*, (F), (S), desired, ★★

Lata, *Luht-ah*, (F), (S), vine, slender, an apsara or celestial nymph, ★★

Latika, *Luht-ihk-ah*, (F), (S), a small vine, the vermillion dot applied by women on the forehead, a pearl necklace, ★★

Larissa, *Luhr-ihs-ah*, (F), (O) – Greek, lovely, cheerfulness, ★★★

Lav, *Luhv*, (M), (S), small, bit, a moment of time, harvesting, the son of god Raam, ★★★

Lavaleen, *Luhv-uhl-een*, (F), (S), devoted, absorbed, ★★★

Lavali, *Luhv-uhl-ee*, (F), (S), vine, ★★★

Lavalika, *Luhv-uhl-eek-ah*, (F), (S), a small vine, ★★★

Lavam, *Luhv-uhm*, (M), (S), small, clove, ★★★

Lavan, *Luhv-uhn*, (M), (S), handsome, salt, ★★★

Lavana, *Luhv-uhn-ah*, (F), (S), brilliant, beauty, ★★★

Lavanya, *Luhv-uhn-yah*, (F), (S), brilliant, beautiful, ★★★

Lavanya, *Luhv-uhn-yuh*, (M), (S), brilliance, attractiveness, ★★★

Lay, *Laey*, (M), (S), concentration, peace, another name for Brahman or the Supreme Spirit, ★★★

Layla, *Laey-lah*, (F), (A), night, sweetheart, ★★★

Leela, *Leel-ah*, (F), (S), play, joy, comfort, beauty, grace, ★★★

Leena, *Leen-ah*, (F), (S), devoted, united, ★★★

Leher, *Leh-hehr*, (F), (H), wave, wave, ★★★

Leher, *Leh-hehr*, (M), (H), wave, wave, ★★★

Leheri, *Leh-hehr-ee*, (F), (S), wave, ★★

Leilani, *Lehy-lahn-ee*, (F), (O) – Hawaiian, heavenly flower, ★★★

Lekh, *Laekh*, (M), (S), document, signature, deity, ★★

Lekha, *Laekh-ah*, (F), (S), line, record, lightening, the crescent
    moon, mark, horizon, ★★

Leo, *Lee-oah*, (M), (O) – Latin, lion, brave, great, ★★★

Lesh, *Laesh*, (M), (S), small, bit, a small song, ★★★

Lewis, *Lu-wihs*, (M), (O) – German, fame, brave, fighter, ★★★

Liam, *Lee-uhm*, (M), (O) – German, will, desire, protection, ★★★

Libni, *Lihb-nee*, (F), (S), a manuscript of the gods, ★★★

Likhit, *Lihkh-iht*, (M), (S), drawn, written, ★★

Lily, *Lih-lee*, (F), (O) – English, the Lily flower, ★★★

Lipi, *Lihp-ee*, (F), (S), alphabet, manuscript, script, writing, ★★★

Lipika, *Lihp-ihk-ah*, (F), (S), alphabet, manuscript, script,
    writing, writer, ★★★

Lipshit, *Lihp-shiht*, (M), (S), desired, ★★

Lochan, *Loach-uhn*, (M), (S), eye, sight, ★★★

Lochan, *Loach-uhn*, (F), (S), eye, sight, ★★★

Lochana, *Loach-uhn-ah*, (F), (S), eye, illuminating, ★★★

Logan, *Loag-uhn*, (M), (O) – Celtic, little hollow, ★★★

Lohit, *Loa-hiht*, (M), (S), red, saffron, copper, battle,
    sandalwood, Mars, ★★

Lohita, *Loa-hiht-ah*, (F), (S), red, saffron, ruby, copper, ★★

Lok, *Loak*, (M), (S), heaven, earth, humanity, humankind, ★★★

Lokavya, *Loak-uhv-yah*, (F), (S), virtuous, deserving of
    heaven, ★★★

Lokavya, *Loak-uhv-yuh*, (M), (S), virtuous, deserving of heaven, ★★★

Lokesh, *Loak-aesh*, (M), (S), king, lord of the world, another name
    for Brahma, ★★★

Lokin, *Loak-ihn*, (M), (S), winning the next world, having dominion over a world, ★★★

Lola, *Loal-ah*, (F), (S), beautiful, varying, lightning, another name for Lakshmi, (O) – Latin, laurel, Spanish, sorrow, German, free, ★★★

Lolita, *Loal-iht-ah*, (F), (S), agitated, varying, ★★

Lolita, *Loal-eett-ah*, (F), (O) – Latin, laurel, Spanish, sorrow, German, free, ★★★

Lomash, *Loam-uhsh*, (M), (S), a sage, one covered with hair, ★★

Lop, *Loap*, (M), (S), disappearing, imperceptible, ★★★

Lopa, *Loap-ah*, (F), (S), disappearing, imperceptible, ★★★

Lotika, *Loat-ihk-ah*, (F), (S), herb, light reddish-brown, ★★

Lubna, *Lub-nah*, (F), (A), a tree with a milk sweeter than honey, ★★★

Lumbika, *Lumb-ihk-ah*, (F), (S), musical instrument, ★★★

Lumbini, *Lumb-ihn-ee*, (F), (S), the grove where Buddha was born, ★★★

Lush, *Lush*, (M), (S), saffron, desire, appetite, ★★★

Luv, *Luv*, (M), (S), small, bit, a moment of time, harvesting, the son of god Raam, ★★★

M

Maadhav, *Mahdh-uhv*, (M), (S), of spring, relating to wine, another
  name for Krishna, Shiva and Indra, ★★

Maadhava, *Mahdh-uhv-ah*, (F), (S), of spring, intoxicating, exciting,
  an apsara or celestial nymph, ★★

Maadhavi, *Mahdh-uhv-ee*, (F), (S), a vine, honey–sugar drink
  intoxicating, another name for Durga, ★★

Maadhavik, *Mahdh-uhv-ihk*, (M), (S), one who collects honey,
  a creeper, ★★

Maadhuri, *Mah-dhur-ee*, (F), (S), beauty, charm, wine, sweetness, ★★

Maagh, *Mahgh*, (M), (S), rewarding, the month of January /
  February, a great poet, ★★

Maaghi, *Mahgh-ee*, (F), (S), rewarding, the day of the full moon in
  the month of January / February, ★★

Maaghoni, *Mahgh-oan-ee*, (F), (S), generosity, the east, ★★

Maaghya, *Mahgh-yah*, (F), (S), born in the month of Maagh, i.e.,
  January / February, Jasmine, ★★

Maaha, *Mah-hah*, (F), (S), wonderful, substantial, cow, ★★★

Maahin, *Mah-hihn*, (M), (S), delightful, happy, great, ★★★

Maahir, *Mah-hihr*, (M), (A), expert, wise, ★★★

Maaia, *Mah-yah*, (F), (S), illusion, magic, wonder, wealth, art,
  wisdom, kindness, the limiting illusory world that we perceive,
  another name for Lakshmi, (P), generous, money, (O) – Hebrew,
  spring, brook, ★★★

Maaki, *Mah-kee*, (F), (S), both heaven and earth, ★★★

Maala, *Mahl-ah*, (F), (S), garland, rosary, line, ★★★

Maalank, *Mahl-ahnk*, (M), (S), garlanded, ruler, ★★

Maalati, *Mahl-uht-ee*, (F), (S), jasmine, a bud, young girl, moonlight, ★★

Maalav, *Mahl-uhv*, (M), (S), horse keeper, a musical raag, ★★★

Maalavi, *Mahl-uhv-ee*, (F), (S), princess, a musical raag, ★★★

Maalavika, *Mahl-uhv-ihk-ah*, (F), (S), princess, ★★★

Maalia, *Mahl-ee-ah*, (F), (O), Hawaiian, calm and peaceful, Hebrew, derived from Mary, ★★★

Maalik, *Mahl-ihk*, (M), (S), gardener, (H), owner, master, husband, ★★★

Maalika, *Mahl-ihk-ah*, (F), (S), daughter, jasmine, garland, intoxicating drink, ★★★

Maalin, *Mahl-ihn*, (M), (S), wearing a garland, crowned, gardener, ★★★

Maalini, *Mahl-ihn-ee*, (F), (S), wearing a garland, fragrant, jasmine, gardener, another name for Durga and the Ganges, ★★★

Maalya, *Mahl-yah*, (F), (S), wealth, garland, mass of flowers, ★★★

Maalya, *Mahl-yuh*, (M), (S), wealth, garland, mass of flowers, ★★★

Maan, *Mahn*, (M), (S), opinion, respect, devotion, home, pride, respect, ★★★

Maanada, *Mahn-uhd-ah*, (F), (S), respectful, ★★

Maanas, *Mahn-uhs*, (M), (S), produced from the mind, mind, soul, intellect, spiritual thought, heart, another name for Vishnu, (O), Latin, Manus is translated as hand, ★★★

Maanasi, *Mahn-uhs-ee*, (F), (S), intellectual or spiritual endeavour, another name for Saraswati, ★★★

Maanasik, *Mahn-uhs-ihk*, (M), (S), intellectual, fanciful, psychic, ★★★

Maanav, *Mahn-uhv*, (M), (S), youth, relating to Manu, humankind, human being, pearl, treasure, ★★★

Maanavi, *Mahn-ahv-ee*, (F), (S), wife of Manu, born of man, ★★★

Maanavika, *Mahn-uhv-ihk-ah*, (F), (S), young girl, ★★★

Maandav, *Mahn-duhv*, (M), (S), fit, competent, administrator, ★★

Maandavi, *Mahn-duhv-ee*, (F), (S), fit, competent, administrator, ★★

Maandavik, *Mahn-duhv-ihk*, (M), (S), administrator, belonging
   to people, ★

Maandavika, *Mahn-duhv-ihk-ah*, (F), (S), administrator,
   belonging to people, ★

Maandhan, *Mahn-dhuhn*, (M), (S), honourable, ★★

Maandhar, *Mahn-dhuhr*, (M), (S), honourable, ★★

Maandhari, *Mahn-dhahr-ee*, (F), (S), honourable, ★★

Maanik, *Mahn-ihk*, (M), (S), ruby, valued, honoured, ★★★

Maanika, *Mahn-ihk-ah*, (F), (S), ruby, of jewels, ★★★

Maanikya, *Mahn-ihk-yuh*, (M), (S), ruby, ★★★

Maanini, *Mahn-ihn-ee*, (F), (S), determined, proud, angry, self-
   respecting, an apsara or celestial nymph, ★★★

Maansar, *Mahn-suhr*, (M), (O) – Pahlavi, holy words, ★★★

Maansi, *Mahn-see*, (F), (S), intellectual or spiritual endeavour,
   another name for Saraswati, ★★★

Maansik, *Mahn-sihk*, (M), (S), intellectual, fanciful, psychic, ★★★

Maanushi, *Mahn-ush-ee*, (F), (S), woman, kind, ★★★

Maanya, *Mahn-yah*, (F), (S), respected, honourable, ★★★

Maargin, *Mahr-gihn*, (M), (S), pioneer, ★★★

Maargit, *Mahr-giht*, (M), (S), desired, needed, ★★★

Maarish, *Mahr-ihsh*, (M), (S), worthy, respectable, ★★★

Maarisha, *Mahr-ihsh-ah*, (F), (S), worthy, respectable, ★★★

Maariya, *Mahr-ee-yah*, (F), (S), one who belongs to the love
   god Kaama, ★★★

Maarmik, *Mahr-mihk*, (M), (S), intelligent, influential, insightful, ★★★

Maarshak, *Mahr-shuhk*, (M), (S), worthy, respectable, ★★★

Maarut, *Mahr-ut*, (M), (S), air, belonging to the wind, god of the wind, another name for Vishnu, ★★

Maathar, *Mah-thuhr*, (M), (S), voyager, ★★

Maathur, *Mah-thur*, (M), (S), from or relating to Mathura, ★★

Maaya, *Mah-yah*, (F), (S), illusion, magic, wonder, wealth, art, wisdom, kindness, the limiting illusory world that we perceive, another name for Lakshmi, (P), generous, money, (O) – Hebrew, spring, brook, ★★★

Maayan, *Mah-yuhn*, (M), (S), indifferent to wealth, ★★★

Maayin, *Mah-yihn*, (M), (S), illusionary, wily, magician, enchanting, another name for Brahma, Shiva, Agni and the love god Kaama, ★★★

Madan, *Muhd-uhn*, (M), (S), passion, love, spring, another name for the love god Kaama, ★★

Madhu, *Muh-dhu*, (F), (S), sweet, honey, nectar, charming, ★★

Madhu, *Muh-dhu*, (M), (S), sweet, honey, nectar, charming, ★★

Madhuj, *Muh-dhuj*, (M), (S), sweet, sugar, ★★

Madhuja, *Muh-dhuj-ah*, (F), (S), sweet, honeycomb, the earth, ★★

Madhuk, *Muh-dhuk*, (M), (S), a bird, honey coloured, sweet, melodious, ★★

Madhukar, *Muh-dhuk-uhr*, (M), (S), bee, lover, the Mango tree, ★★

Madhul, *Muh-dhul*, (M), (S), sweet, intoxicating, a drink, ★★

Madhulika, *Muh-dhul-ihk-ah*, (F), (S), honey, sweetness, bee, ★★

Madhup, *Muhdh-up*, (M), (S), bee, ★★

Madhur, *Muh-dhur*, (M), (S), sweet, amiable, melodious, ★★

Madhur, *Muh-dhur*, (F), (S), sweet, amiable, melodious, ★★

Madin, *Muhd-ihn*, (M), (S), intoxicating, pleasing, handsome, ★★

Madir, *Muhd-ihr*, (M), (S), nectar, intoxicating, wine, ★★

Madira, *Muhd-ihr-ah*, (F), (S), nectar, intoxicating, wine, another name for Durga, ★★

Madur, *Muhd-ur*, (M), (S), a bird, ★★

Madvan, *Muhd-vuhn*, (M), (S), intoxicating, delightful, drunk with joy, another name for Shiva, ★★

Magan, *Muhg-uhn*, (M), (S), absorbed, immersed, ★★★

Mahaj, *Muh-huhj*, (M), (S), from a noble family, ★★★

Mahak, *Muh-huhk*, (M), (S), eminent, a great person, a tortoise, another name for Vishnu, (H), fragrance, ★★★

Mahalika, *Muh-huhl-ihk-ah*, (F), (S), woman, attendant, ★★★

Mahan, *Muh-hahn*, (M), (S), great, powerful, eminent, ★★★

Mahash, *Muh-huhsh*, (M), (S), serious, unsmiling, ★★★

Mahelika, *Muh-hael-ihk-ah*, (F), (S), woman, ★★★

Mahesh, *Muh-haesh*, (M), (S), great, divine, an incarnation of Shiva, a Buddhist deity, ★★

Maheshani, *Muh-haesh-uhn-ee*, (F), (S), great, consort of Mahesh, another name for Paarvati, ★★

Mahi, *Muh-hee*, (F), (S), earth, the union of heaven and earth, the number one, ★★★

Mahika, *Muh-hihk-ah*, (F), (S), dew, mist, frost, ★★★

Mahima, *Muh-hihm-ah*, (F), (S), greatness, splendour, majesty, dignity, power, ★★★

Mahiman, *Muh-hihm-uhn*, (M), (S), greatness, dignity, power, ★★★

Mahir, *Muh-hihr*, (M), (S), expert, proficient, the sun, another name for Indra, ★★★

Mahish, *Muh-hihsh*, (M), (S), mighty, great, buffalo, lord of the earth, the sun, ★★★

Mahit, *Muh-hiht*, (M), (S), respected, excellent, revered, ★★

Mahita, *Muh-hiht-ah*, (F), (S), river, respected, excellent, revered, ★★

Mahiya, *Muh-hee-yah*, (F), (S), happiness, exultation, ★★★

Mahok, *Muh-hoak*, (M), (S), eminent, another name for Vishnu, ★★★

Maholka, *Muh-hoalk-ah*, (F), (S), fiery, portent, meteor, ★★★

Mahtab, *Maeh-tahb*, (M), (P), moonlight, adored, ★★

Mahuli, *Muh-hul-ee*, (F), (S), melodious, a musical raag, ★★★

Maina, *Maen-ah*, (F), (S), intelligence, a bird, ★★★

Mainak, *Maen-ahk*, (M), (S), a mountain near Kailash, ★★★

Maira, *Meh-rah*, (F), (O) – Latin, marvellous, myrrh, Hebrew, bitterness, ★★★

Mairav, *Maer-uhv*, (M), (S), relating to Mount Meru, ★★

Maithili, *Maith-ihl-ee*, (F), (S), another name for Sita, ★

Maitra, *Maet-ruh*, (M), (S), friendly, kind, ★★

Maitreya, *Maet-reh-yuh*, (M), (S), friendly, kind, ★

Maitreyi, *Maet-reh-yee*, (F), (S), friendly, ★

Maitri, *Maet-ree*, (F), (S), friendship, kindness, goodwill, ★

Makshi, *Muhk-shee*, (F), (S), bee, ★★★

Makshika, *Muhk-shee-kah*, (F), (S), bee, honey, ★★★

Makul, *Muhk-ul*, (M), (S), a bud, ★★★

Makur, *Muhk-ur*, (M), (S), a bud, reflection, mirror, jasmine, ★★★

Malada, *Muhl-uhd-ah*, (F), (S), auspicious, lucky, ★★

Malaika, *Muhl-ai-kah*, (F), (S), amorous, affectionate, ★★

Malaka, *Muhl-ah-kah*, (F), (S), amorous, affectionate, ★★

Malay, *Muhl-uhy*, (M), (S), fragrant, sandalwood, a mountain range in South India famous for its spices, ★★★

Malaya, *Muhl-uhy-ah*, (M), (S), fragrant, sandalwood, ★★★

Malhar, *Muhl-hahr*, (M), (S), inspiring rain, a musical raag of the monsoon season, ★★★

Maliha, *Muhl-ee-hah*, (F), (A), beautiful, pleasant, clever, quick-witted, ★★★

Malik, *Muhl-ihk*, (M), (A), master, ★★★

Mallika, *Muhll-ihk-ah*, (F), (S), Jasmine, garland, queen, daughter, (A), queen, ★★★

Mamata, *Muhm-uht-ah*, (F), (S), maternal love, deep, attachment★★

Manahar, *Muhn-uh-huhr*, (M), (S), attractive, pleasant, ★★★

Manaj, *Muhn-uhj*, (M), (S), created in the mind, imagined another name for the love god Kaama, ★★★

Manajit, *Muhn-uhj-iht*, (M), (S), one who has conquered thought, ★★

Manajna, *Muhn-uhj-nah*, (F), (S), princess, beautiful, pleasant, ★★★

Manak, *Muhn-ahk*, (M), (S), related to the mind, affectionate, ★★★

Manaka, *Muhn-ahk-ah*, (F), (S), related to the mind, affectionate, ★★★

Manal, *Muhn-uhl*, (M), (S), a bird, ★★★

Manali, *Muhn-uhl-ee*, (F), (S), a bird, ★★★

Manan, *Muhn-uhn*, (M), (S), reflection, thoughtful, intelligence, understanding, ★★★

Manank, *Muhn-ahnk*, (M), (S), affectionate, kind, ★★★

Mananya, *Muhn-uhn-yuh*, (M), (S), praiseworthy, ★★★

Manap, *Muhn-ahp*, (M), (S), attractive, ★★★

Manas, *Muhn-uhs*, (M), (S), mind, intelligence, insight, desire, (A), cheerfulness, ★★★

Manasa, *Muhn-uhs-ah*, (F), (S), born in the mind, intellect, mind, heart, ★★★

Manasi, *Muhn-uhs-ee*, (F), (S), sensible, intelligent, ★★★

Manasij, *Muhn-uhs-ihj*, (M), (S), passion, love, the moon, another
name for the love god Kaama, ★★★

Manasvi, *Muhn-uhs-vee*, (F), (S), self-respecting, self-controlled,
intelligence, wise, sensible, ★★★

Manasvin, *Muhn-uhs-vihn*, (M), (S), self-respecting, self-controlled,
intelligence, wise, sensible, ★★★

Manasvini, *Muhn-uhs-vihn-ee*, (F), (S), self-respecting,
self-controlled, intelligence, wise, sensible, virtuous,
another name for Durga, ★★

Manasyu, *Muhn-uhs-yu*, (M), (S), desirous, ★★

Mandakini, *Muhn-dahk-ihn-ee*, (F), (S), the Milky Way, a tributary of
the river Ganges, ★

Mandan, *Muhn-duhn*, (M), (S), loving, decoration, ★★

Mandana, *Muhn-duhn-ah*, (F), (S), cheerful, ★★

Mandar, *Muhn-dahr*, (M), (S), heavenly, large, firm, slow, ★★

Mandar, *Muhn-duhr*, (M), (S), heavenly, large, firm, slow, ★★

Mandara, *Muhn-duhr-ah*, (F), (S), heavenly, large, firm, slow, ★★

Mandarika, *Muhn-dahr-ihk-ah*, (F), (S), the Coral tree, ★★

Mandin, *Muhn-dihn*, (M), (S), delighting, nectar, ★★

Mandira, *Muhn-dihr-ah*, (F), (S), sacred, temple, sea, melodious, the
melodious sound produced by cymbals, ★★

Mandit, *Muhn-diht*, (M), (S), decorated, ★★

Mandita, *Muhn-diht-ah*, (F), (S), decorated, ★★

Mangal, *Muhn-guhl*, (M), (S), welfare, joy, auspiciousness, another
name for Agni and Mars, ★★★

Mangala, *Muhn-guhl-ah*, (F), (S), auspicious, sacred grass, jasmine,
another name for Uma and Durga, ★★★

Mangali, *Muhn-guhl-ee*, (F), (S), auspicious, fragrant, ★★★

Manhan, *Muhn-huhn*, (M), (S), gift, ★★★

Mani, *Muhn-ee*, (M), (S), jewel, magnet, ★★★

Manich, *Muhn-eech*, (M), (S), pearl, flower, hand, ★★★

Manik, *Muhn-ihk*, (M), (S), ruby, ★★★

Manika, *Muhn-ihk-ah*, (F), (S), ruby, ★★★

Maninga, *Muhn-ihng-ah*, (F), (S), treasure, a river, ★★★

Manish, *Muhn-eesh*, (M), (S), lord of the mind, deep thinker, ★★★

Manish, *Muhn-ihsh*, (M), (P), joyful temperament, mind, soul, heart, pride, ★★★

Manisha, *Muhn-eesh-ah*, (F), (S), thought, intellect, wisdom, thoughtfulness, hymn, wish, ★★★

Manishi, *Muhn-ihsh-ee*, (F), (S), desired, ★★★

Manishika, *Muhn-eesh-ihk-ah*, (F), (S), consideration, intelligence, ★★★

Manishin, *Muhn-eesh-ihn*, (M), (S), considerate, intelligent, wise, pious, ★★★

Manishit, *Muhn-eesh-iht*, (M), (S), desired, ★★

Manishita, *Muhn-eesh-iht-ah*, (F), (S), desired, ★★

Manishka, *Muhn-ihsh-kah*, (F), (S), wisdom, intellect, ★★★

Manit, *Muhn-iht*, (M), (S), highly regarded, celebrated, understood, ★★

Manjav, *Muhn-juhv*, (M), (S), swift, ★★★

Manjira, *Muhn-jihr-ah*, (F), (S), anklet, ★★★

Manju, *Muhn-ju*, (F), (S), beautiful, pleasant, ★★★

Manjula, *Muhn-ju-lah*, (F), (S), beautiful, likeable, a spring, ★★★

Manjulika, *Muhn-jul-ihk-ah*, (F), (S), beautiful, likeable, ★★

Mankan, *Muhn-kuhn*, (M), (S), of the mind, ★★★

Manksh, *Muhnksh*, (M), (S), desire, ★★★

Mankur, *Muhn-kur*, (M), (S), reflecting the mind, a mirror, ★★★

Mannan, *Muhn-nahn*, (M), (A), liberal, generous, another name for god, ★★★

Mannat, *Muhn-nuht*, (M), (S), devoted, a promise to god, ★★

Manohar, *Muhn-oa-huhr*, (M), (S), loveble, another name for Krishna, ★★

Manohara, *Muhn-oa-huhr-ah*, (F), (S), loveble, an apsara or celestial nymph, ★★

Manohari, *Muhn-oa-huhr-ee*, (F), (S), loveble, Jasmine, an apsara or celestial nymph, ★★

Manoj, *Muhn-oaj*, (M), (S), love, originating in the mind, another name for the love god Kaama, ★★★

Manojna, *Muhn-oaj-nah*, (F), (S), princess, beautiful, pleasant, ★★★

Manorama, *Muhn-oar-uhm-ah*, (F), (S), beautiful, pleasant, ★★★

Manorit, *Muhn-oar-iht*, (M), (S), desire, of the mind, ★★

Manorita, *Muhn-oar-iht-ah*, (F), (S), desire, of the mind, ★★

Manot, *Muhn-oat*, (M), (S), originating in the mind, ★★

Manoti, *Muhn-oat-ee*, (F), (S), originating in the mind, promise to god, ★★

Mant, *Muhnt*, (M), (S), thought, devotion, ★★

Mantik, *Muhnt-ihk*, (M), (S), thoughtful, devoted, ★★

Mantika, *Muhnt-ihk-ah*, (F), (S), thoughtful, devoted, ★★

Mantra, *Muhnt-ruh*, (M), (S),Vedic hymn, prayer, another name for Vishnu and Shiva, ★★

Mantrana, *Muhnt-ruhn-ah*, (F), (S), advice, thought, ★★

Mantrin, *Muhnt-rihn*, (M), (S), wise, articulate, adviser, with knowledge of the sacred texts, ★★

Manu, *Muhn-oo*, (F), (S), wise, attractive, an apsara or celestial nymph, ★★★

Manu, *Muhn-u*, (M), (S), wise, intelligent, man, humankind, thought, prayer, (P), paradise, ★★★

Manuj, *Muhn-uj*, (M), (S), born of Manu, man, ★★★

Manuja, *Muhn-uj-ah*, (F), (S), born of Manu, woman, ★★★

Maral, *Muhr-ahl*, (M), (S), soft, gentle, ★★★

Maralika, *Muhr-ahl-ihk-ah*, (F), (S), small swan, ★★★

Marina, *Muhr-een-ah*, (F), (O) – Latin, of the sea, ★★★

Marisa, *Muhr-ihs-ah*, (F), (O) – Latin, of the sea, Hebrew, bitterness, ★★★

Marsh, *Muhrsh*, (M), (S), patience, deliberation, ★★★

Marshan, *Muhrsh-uhn*, (M), (S), patient, ★★★

Marut, *Muhr-ut*, (M), (S), brilliant, air, wind, breeze, the storm god, ★★

Marya, *Muhr-yah*, (F), (S), boundary, ★★★

Maryada, *Muhr-yah-dah*, (F), (S), boundary, rule, decorum, ★★

Masar, *Muhs-ahr*, (M), (S), jewel, sapphire, emerald, ★★★

Masma, *Muhs-mah*, (F), (S), fair, ★★★

Mastak, *Muhs-tuhk*, (M), (S), forehead, pinnacle, another name for Shiva, ★★

Mat, *Muht*, (M), (S), thought, opinion, honoured, wanted, ★★

Mati, *Muht-ee*, (F), (S), thought, prayer, mind, decision, respect, will, opinion, intelligence, memory, ★★

Matil, *Muht-ihl*, (M), (S), intelligent, ★★

Maulik, *Mohl-ihk*, (M), (S), precious, dear, (H), ultimate, original, essential, ★★

Maushmi, *Moh-sh-mee*, (F), (S), monsoon wind, ★★

May, *Muhy*, (M), (S), illusion, architect, ★★★

Mayank, *Muhy-uhnk*, (M), (S), distinguished, the moon, ★★★

Mayas, *Muhy-uhs*, (M), (S), pleasure, joy, ★★★

Mayur, *Muh-yoor*, (M), (S), peacock, ★★★

Mayuri, *Muh-yoor-ee*, (F), (S), peahen, ★★★

Medha, *Maedh-ah*, (F), (S), wisdom, capacity for learning,
    intelligence, a form of Saraswati, ★★

Medhani, *Maedh-uhn-ee*, (F), (S), intellect, the consort of Brahma, ★★

Medhas, *Maedh-uhs*, (M), (S), sacrifice, sacrificed, ★★

Medhavin, *Maedh-ahv-ihn*, (M), (S), wise, erudite, intelligent, with a
    good memory, ★

Medhir, *Maedh-ihr*, (M), (S), wise, ★★

Medini, *Maed-ihn-ee*, (F), (S), fertile, land, the earth goddess, ★★

Megh, *Maegh*, (M), (S), cloud, a musical raag, (P), cloud, mist, ★★

Megha, *Maegh-ah*, (F), (S), cloud, a musical raag, ★★

Meghaj, *Maegh-uhj*, (M), (S), water, ★★

Meghaja, *Maegh-uhj-ah*, (F), (S), water, ★★

Meghana, *Maegh-uhn-ah*, (F), (S), thunder, ★★

Mehal, *Meh-huhl*, (M), (S), rain, ★★

Mehek, *Meh-hehk*, (F), (H), fragrance, scent, ★★★

Mehek, *Meh-hehk*, (M), (H), fragrance, scent, ★★★

Meher, *Meh-hehr*, (F), (O) – Pahlavi, alternative name for
    Mithra, the Zoroastrian god associated with the sun
    and friendship, kind, ★★

Mehul, *Meh-hul*, (M), (S), rain, ★★★

Men, *Maen*, (M), (S), knowledgeable, ★★★

Mena, *Maen-ah*, (F), (S), intelligence, speech, an apsara or celestial nymph, ★★★

Menaka, *Maen-uhk-ah*, (F), (S), daughter, originating in the mind, relating to the mountains, an apsara or celestial nymph, ★★★

Menit, *Maen-iht*, (M), (S), wise, ★★★

Menita, *Maen-iht-ah*, (F), (S), wise, ★★★

Meru, *Maer-u*, (M), (S), peak, principle, golden, a divine mountain said to be made of gold, ★★★

Meruk, *Maer-uk*, (M), (S), incense, ★★★

Mev, *Maev*, (M), (S), to worship, admire, ★★★

Mia, *Mee-ah*, (F), (O) – Italian, Latin, mine, desired, Hebrew, bitterness, one who is like god, ★★★

Mihika, *Mih-ihk-ah*, (F), (S), mist of innocence, ignorance, fog, snow, ★★★

Mihin, *Mih-heen*, (M), (P), best, subtle, ★★★

Mihir, *Mih-hihr*, (M), (S), light and rain, the sun, the moon, cloud, air, a sage, (O) – Pahlavi, light, ★★★

Mikul, *Mihk-ul*, (M), (S), bud, first bloom, ★★★

Milan, *Mihl-uhn*, (M), (S), together, meeting, ★★★

Miland, *Mihl-uhnd*, (M), (S), bee, to seek a meeting, ★★

Milap, *Mihl-ahp*, (M), (S), embrace, ★★★

Mili, *Mihl-ee*, (F), (S), union, ★★★

Milika, *Mihl-ihk-ah*, (F), (S), desiring union, ★★★

Milind, *Mihl-ihnd*, (M), (S), bee, to seek a meeting, ★★

Milit, *Mihl-iht*, (M), (S), friendship, encounter, ★★

Mina, *Meen-ah*, (F), (S), gem, glass, fish, Pisces, (P), glass, blue, heaven, (A), harbour, ★★★

Minakshi, *Meen-ahk-shee*, (F), (S), fish eyed, an incarnation of
Paarvati, ★★★

Minali, *Meen-ahl-ee*, (F), (S), fisherwoman, ★★★

Minnat, *Mihn-nuht*, (F), (A), favour, gift, ★★

Mir, *Meer*, (M), (P), chief, ruler, ★★★

Mira, *Meer-ah*, (F), (S), ocean, boundary, poetess and devotee of
Krishna, ★★★

Mirat, *Mihr-uht*, (M), (S), mirror, reflective, ★★

Mishi, *Mihsh-ee*, (F), (S), sugarcane, ★★★

Mishrak, *Mihsh-ruhk*, (M), (S), varied, Indra's garden of paradise, ★★★

Mit, *Meet*, (F), (S), friend, ★★

Mita, *Meet-ah*, (F), (S), friend, ★★

Mitali, *Miht-ahl-ee*, (F), (S), friendship, ★★

Miti, *Meet-ee*, (F), (S), friend, ★★

Mitul, *Miht-ul*, (M), (S), balanced, moderate, ★★

Miya, *Mee-yah*, (F), (O) – Latin, great, big, Japanese, temple, ★★★

Mod, *Moad*, (M), (S), happiness, fragrance, ★★

Modak, *Moad-uhk*, (M), (S), delightful, ★★

Modaki, *Moad-uhk-ee*, (F), (S), delightful, ★★

Modini, *Moad-ihn-ee*, (F), (S), happy, cheerful, ★★

Moh, *Moa-h*, (M), (S), worldly attachment, infatuation, ★★★

Mohak, *Moa-huhk*, (M), (S), infatuating, handsome, ★★★

Mohal, *Moa-huhl*, (M), (S), attractive, ★★★

Mohan, *Moa-huhn*, (M), (S), infatuating, handsome, charming,
another name for Shiva and Krishna, ★★★

Mohana, *Moa-huhn-ah*, (F), (S), charming, infatuating,
beautiful, ★★★

Mohani, *Moa-huhn-ee*, (F), (S), charming, infatuating, beautiful, an apsara or celestial nymph, ★★★

Mohin, *Moa-hihn*, (M), (S), bewildering, fascinating, ★★★

Mohini, *Moa-hihn-ee*, (F), (S), fascinating, jasmine, an apsara or celestial nymph, ★★★

Mohit, *Moa-hiht*, (M), (S), infatuated, bewildered, ★★

Mohita, *Moa-hiht-ah*, (F), (S), infatuated, bewildered, ★★

Mohona, *Moa-hoan-ah*, (F), (S), attractive, ★★★

Moksh, *Moak-sh*, (M), (S), salvation, another name for Mount Meru, ★★★

Mokshin, *Moak-shihn*, (M), (S), free from attachment, seeking salvation, liberated, ★★★

Mokshit, *Moak-shiht*, (M), (S), liberated, ★★★

Mokshita, *Moak-shiht-ah*, (F), (S), liberated, ★★★

Mona, *Moan-ah*, (F), (S), solitary, ★★★

Monika, *Moan-ihk-ah*, (F), (S), solitary, ★★★

Monish, *Moa-neesh*, (M), (S), attractive, another name for Krishna, ★★★

Monisha, *Moa-neesh-ah*, (F), (S), beautiful, solitary, ★★★

Mriduk, *Mrihd-uhk*, (M), (S), gentle, soft, ★★

Mriduka, *Mrihd-uhk-ah*, (F), (S), gentle, soft, an apsara or celestial nymph, ★★

Mridul, *Mrihd-ul*, (M), (S), water, soft, gentle, ★★

Mridula, *Mrihd-ul-ah*, (F), (S), gentle, sweet, soft, ★★

Mridur, *Mrihd-ulr* (M), (S), born of water, ★★

Mridvika, *Mrihd-ihk-ah*, (F), (S), gentleness, a vine, ★★

Mrigad, *Mrihg-uhd*, (M), (S), tiger, ★★

Mrigaj, *Mrihg-uhj*, (M), (S), born of the moon, ★★

Mrigank, *Mrihg-ahnk*, (M), (S), distinguished, the moon, wind, ★

Mrinal, *Mrihn-ahl*, (F), (S), delicate, the root of a lotus, ★★★

Mrinal, *Mrihn-ahl*, (M), (S), delicate, the root of a lotus, ★★★

Mrinali, *Mrihn-ahl-ee*, (F), (S), lotus stalk, ★★★

Mrinalika, *Mrihn-ahl-ihk-ah*, (F), (S), lotus root, ★★★

Mrinalini, *Mrihn-ahl-ihn-ee*, (F), (S), fragrant, soft, holy, many lotuses, ★★

Mrinmay, *Mrihn-muhy*, (M), (S), earthly, ★★

Mrinmayi, *Mrihn-muhy-ee*, (F), (S), earthly, ★★

Mudit, *Mud-iht*, (M), (S), happy, satisfied, ★★

Mudita, *Mud-iht-ah*, (F), (S), happy, satisfied, ★★

Muhir, *Mu-hihr*, (M), (S), passionate, dazzling, another name for the love god Kaama, ★★★

Mukesh, *Muk-aesh*, (M), (S), to liberate, another name for Shiva, ★★★

Mukt, *Mukt*, (M), (S), liberated, pearl, ★★

Mukta, *Mukt-ah*, (F), (S), liberated, pearl, ★★

Mukti, *Mukt-ee*, (F), (S), freedom, final release, ★★

Mukul, *Muk-ul*, (M), (S), bud, first bloom, ★★★

Mukund, *Muk-und*, (M), (S), gem, liberater, another name for Vishnu and Krishna, ★★

Mukunda, *Muk-und-ah*, (F), (S), gem, liberater, ★★

Mumtaz, *Mum-tahz*, (F), (A), distinguished, precious, special, ★★

Munish, *Mun-eesh*, (M), (S), chief of the sages, a Buddha, ★★★

Murad, *Mur-ahd*, (M), (A), desire, will, ★★

Muskan, *Mus-kahn*, (F), (H), smile, ★★★

N

Naabhak, *Nahbh-uhk*, (M), (S), belonging to the sky, ★★

Naabhas, *Nahbh-uhs*, (M), (S), sky, ocean, heavenly, ★★

Naarang, *Nahr-uhng*, (M), (S), orange, human, a twin, (P),
orange, ★★★

Naarayan, *Nahr-ah-yuhn*, (M), (S), son of the original man, an
incarnation of Vishnu, ★★

Naarayani, *Nahr-ah-yuhn-ee*, (F), (S), belonging to Naarayan,
Vishnu or Krishna, another name for Durga, Lakshmi and
the river Ganges, ★★

Naasik, *Nahs-ihk*, (M), (A), pious, ★★★

Naathan, *Nahth-uhn*, (M), (S), desire, protector, lord, another name
for Krishna, ★★

Naatika, *Nahtt-ihk-ah*, (F), (S), a play, with dancers / actors,
a musical raagini, ★★

Naayab, *Nah-yahb*, (M), (P), unattainable, precious, ★★★

Naaz, *Nahz*, (F), (P), coquetry, pride, elegance, young,
gentle, ★★★

Nabh, *Nuhbh*, (M), (S), the sky, ★★

Nabha, *Nuhbh-ah*, (F), (S), the sky, ★★

Nabhanya, *Nuhbh-uhn-yah*, (F), (S), ethereal, celestial, ★★★

Nabhanyu, *Nuhbh-uhn-yu*, (M), (S), ethereal, celestial, ★★★

Nabhas, *Nuhbh-uhs*, (M), (S), sun, sky, monsoon, atmosphere, cloud,
another name for Shiva, ★★

Nadish, *Nuhd-ihsh*, (M), (S), ocean, lord of water, ★★

Naghma, *Nuhgh-mah*, (F), (A), melody, melodious, ★★★

Naiba, *Naeb-ah*, (F), (O) – Pahlavi, beautiful, ★★★

Naima, *Naem-ah*, (F), (S), belonging to one, striving for the absolute, ★★★

Naimish, *Naem-ihsh*, (M), (S), transient, ★★★

Naimisha, *Naem-ihsh-ah*, (F), (S), transient, ★★★

Naina, *Naen-ah*, (F), (S), eyes, ★★★

Nairit, *Naer-iht*, (M), (S), direction, south-west, ★★

Naissa, *Naeh-ssah*, (F), (O) – French, rebirth, ★★★

Naisha, *Naesh-ah*, (F), (S), pertaining to Nishadha, special, ★★★

Naishadh, *Naesh-ahdh*, (M), (S), pertaining to Nishadha, an epic poem, ★

Naishadha, *Naesh-ahdh-ah*, (F), (S), pertaining to Nishadha, an epic poem, ★

Naksh, *Nuhksh*, (M), (S), to achieve, ★★★

Nakul, *Nuhk-ul*, (M), (S), son, a musical instrument, the fourth Pandava prince from the Mahabharata, mongoose, another name for Shiva, ★★★

Nalin, *Nuhl-ihn*, (M), (S), lotus, water lily, crane, water, ★★★

Nalini, *Nuhl-ihn-ee*, (F), (S), lotus, pond of lotuses, flower, the stalk of the water lily, beautiful, fragrant, auspicious, a tributary of the Ganges, ★★★

Naman, *Nuhm-uhn*, (M), (S), bowing, to pay homage, ★★★

Namat, *Nuhm-uht*, (M), (S), bowing, to pay homage, ★★

Namish, *Nuhm-ihsh*, (M), (S), celebrated, famous, another name for Vishnu, ★★★

Namit, *Nuhm-iht*, (M), (S), bowing, worshipper, ★★

Namita, *Nuhm-iht-ah*, (F), (S), bowing, worshipper, ★★

Namrata, *Nuhm-ruht-ah*, (F), (S), humble, submissive, ★★

Namya, *Nuhm-yah*, (F), (S), venerable, night, ★★★

Namya, *Nuhm-yuh*, (M), (S), venerable, ***

Nand, *Nuhnd*, (M), (S), joy, son, prosperous, a flute, number 9, another name for Vishnu, **

Nanda, *Nuhn-dah*, (F), (S), happiness, wealth, an apsara or celestial nymph, another name for Durga, **

Nandak, *Nuhn-duhk*, (M), (S), celebrating, delightful, Krishna's sword, **

Nandan, *Nuhn-duhn*, (M), (S), son, celebrating, heartening, temple, another name for Shiva and Vishnu, **

Nandana, *Nuhn-duhn-ah*, (F), (S), daughter, celebrating, heartening, Indra's paradise, another name for Durga, **

Nandi, *Nuhn-dee*, (F), (S), happiness, prosoerity, Shiva's bull, another name for Durga, **

Nandik, *Nuhn-dihk*, (M), (S), Shiva's bull, prosperous, happy, pleasing, **

Nandika, *Nuhn-dihk-ah*, (F), (S), prosperous, happy, pleasing, **

Nandini, *Nuhn-dihn-ee*, (F), (S), daughter, happy, pleasing, another name for Durga, **

Nandita, *Nuhn-diht-ah*, (F), (S), pleasing, delighted, **

Nar, *Nuhr*, (M), (S), male, hero, husband, another name for Brahman or the Supreme Spirit, ***

Naran, *Nuhr-uhn*, (M), (S), human, ***

Nargis, *Nuhr-gihs*, (F), (P), (A), eye, narcissus, ***

Narmada, *Nuhr-muhd-ah*, (M), (S), pleasing, a river, **

Narman, *Nuhr-muhn*, (M), (S), humour, play, ***

Narsi, *Nuhr-si*, (M), (S), poet, saint, ***

Narun, *Nuhr-un*, (M), (S), leader of men, ***

Natalya, *Nuhtt-ahl-yah*, (F), (O) – Russian, born on Christmas, ***

Natasha, *Nuhtt-ahsh-ah*, (F), (O) – Russian, born on Christmas, ★★★

Natesh, *Nuht-aesh*, (M), (S), another name for Shiva, ★★

Natraj, *Nuhtt-rahj*, (M), (S), lord of dance, Shiva as the cosmic dancer of destruction, ★★

Nathin, *Nahth-ihn*, (M), (S), protected, ★★

Naura, *Naw-rah*, (F), (A), flower, ★★★

Nav, *Nuhv*, (M), (S), new, praised, ★★★

Navaj, *Nuhv-uhj*, (M), (S), new, ★★★

Navaja, *Nuhv-uhj-ah*, (F), (S), new, ★★★

Naval, *Nuhv-uhl*, (M), (S), new, ★★★

Navam, *Nuhv-uhm*, (M), (S), new, ★★★

Navami, *Nuhv-uhm-ee*, (F), (S), new, ★★★

Navan, *Nuhv-uhn*, (M), (S), praise, ★★★

Navika, *Nuhv-ihk-ah*, (F), (S), new, ★★★

Navin, *Nuhv-een*, (M), (S), new, ★★★

Navina, *Nuhv-een-ah*, (F), (S), new, ★★★

Navya, *Nuhv-yah*, (F), (S), young, praiseworthy, ★★★

Navya, *Nuhv-yuh*, (M), (S), young, praiseworthy, ★★★

Nayaj, *Nuh-yuhj*, (M), (S), born of wisdom, ★★★

Nayaja, *Nuh-yuhj-ah*, (F), (S), born of wisdom, ★★★

Nayan, *Nuh-yuhn*, (M), (S), directing, eye, community, decorum, ★★★

Nayana, *Nuh-yuhn-ah*, (F), (S), the pupil of the eye, ★★★

Neera, *Neer-ah*, (F), (S), water, juice, liquor, ★★★

Nirad, *Neer-uhd*, (M), (S), cloud, ★★

Neeraj, *Neer-ahj*, (M), (S), to illuminate, irradiate, ★★★

Neerav, *Neer-uhv*, (M), (S), quiet, calm, ★★★★

Neeta, *Neet-ah*, (F), (S), guided, well-mannered, modest, ★★

Neeti, *Neet-ee*, (F), (S), policy, code, conduct, ★★

Neetika, *Neet-ihk-ah*, (F), (S), moral person, leader, ★★

Neha, *Nae-hah*, (F), (S), affectionate, ★★★

Neil, *Neel*, (M), (S), dark blue, sapphire, the Mynah bird, (O) – Gaelic, cloud, passionate, champion, ★★★

Nek, *Naek*, (M), (S), virtuous, (P), virtuous, lucky, ★★★

Neka, *Naek-ah*, (F), (S), virtuous, (P), good, beautiful, ★★★

Netra, Naet-rah, (F), (S), eye, leader, ★★

Netra, Naet-ruh, (M), (S), eye, leader, ★★

Nev, *Naev*, (M), (P), hero, courageous, ★★★

Nibha, *Nihbh-ah*, (F), (S), resembling, ★★

Nichika, *Nihch-ihk-ah*, (F), (S), entire, perfect, excellent, ★★★

Nichita, *Nihch-iht-ah*, (F), (S), covered, flowing, another name for the river Ganges, ★★

Niddha, *Nihddh-ah*, (F), (S), with a treasure, determined, assiduous, generous, ★★

Nidhan, *Nihdh-ahn*, (M), (S), with a treasure, receptacle, ★★

Nidhi, *Nihdh-ee*, (F), (S), treasure, wealth, ★★

Nidi, *Nihd-ee*, (F), (S), brilliant, to bestow, ★★

Nigam, *Nihg-uhm*, (M), (S), Vedic texts, teaching, town, victory, ★★★

Nihad, *Nih-hahd*, (M), (P), nature, mind, heart, resolution, ★★

Nihal, *Nih-hahl*, (M), (S), satisfied, (P), sapling, happy, successful, ★★★

Nihant, *Nih-hahnt*, (M), (S), boy, ★★

Nihar, *Nee-hahr*, (M), (S), mist, ★★★

Niharika, *Nee-hahr-ihk-ah*, (F), (S), misty, the Milky Way, ★★★

Nikam, *Nihk-ahm*, (M), (S), desire, joy, ★★★

Nikash, *Neek-ahsh*, (M), (S), appearance, ★★★

Nikash, *Nihk-ahsh*, (M), (S), horizon, ★★★

Nikash, *Nihk-uhsh*, (M), (S), touchstone, ★★★

Nikasha, *Nihk-uhsh-ah*, (F), (S), made, gold, ★★★

Niket, *Nihk-aet*, (M), (S), residence, home, ★★

Niketa, *Nihk-aet-ah*, (F), (S), residence, home, ★★

Nikhil, *Nihkh-ihl*, (M), (S), entire, perfect, ★★

Nikita, *Nihk-eett-ah*, (F), (O) – Greek, victorious,
    unconquerable, ★★★

Niksh, *Nihksh*, (M), (S), kiss, ★★★

Niksha, *Nihksh-ah*, (F), (S), kiss, ★★★

Nil, *Neel*, (M), (S), blue, indigo, sapphire, treasure, a mountain, ★★★

Nila, *Neel-ah*, (F), (S), blue, the Indigo plant, ★★★

Nilam, *Neel-uhm*, (F), (S), dark blue, sapphire, (P), sapphire, ★★★

Nilash, *Nihl-ahsh*, (M), (S), blue, ★★★

Nilasha, *Nihl-ahsh-ah*, (F), (S), blue, ★★★

Nilay, *Nihl-uhy*, (M), (S), refuge, home, ★★

Nilima, *Neel-eem-ah*, (F), (S), blue, ★★★

Nima, *Nihm-ah*, (F), (S), measure, to measure, (P),
    younger, smaller, ★★★

Nimal, *Nihm-uhl*, (M), (S), pure, brilliant, ★★★

Nimeya, *Nihm-ehy*, (M), (S), a known quantity, understood, ★★★

Nimish, *Nihm-ihsh*, (M), (S), transient, another name for Vishnu, ★★★

Nimisha, *Nihm-ihsh-ah*, (F), (S), transient, ★★★

Nimit, *Nihm-iht*, (M), (S), fixed, determined, ★★

Nimita, *Nihm-iht-ah*, (F), (S), fixed, determined, ★★

Nina, *Neen-ah*, (F), (S), bejewlled, slender, ★★★

Nipak, *Nihp-ahk*, (M), (S), wise, leader, ★★★

Nipun, *Nihp-un*, (M), (S), proficient, benevolent, talented, perfect,
    clever, ★★★

Nirad, *Neer-uhd*, (M), (S), cloud, ★★

Niraj, *Nihr-uhj*, (M), (S), pure, free from attachment, another name for Shiva, ★★★

Niraja, *Nihr-uhj-ah*, (F), (S), pure, lotus, another name for Lakshmi, ★★

Nirat, *Nihr-uht*, (M), (S), absorbed, satisfied, ★★★

Nirav, *Neer-uhv*, (M), (S), quiet, calm, ★★★★

Nirek, *Nihr-aek*, (M), (S), unique, best, unparalleled, ★★★

Niriksh, *Nihr-ihksh*, (M), (S), unique, anticipation, hope, ★★★

Niriksha, *Nihr-ihk-shah*, (F), (S), unique, anticipation, hope, ★★★

Nirmal, *Nihr-muhl*, (M), (S), pure, brilliant, ★★★

Nirmala, *Nihr-muhl-ah*, (F), (S), pure, brilliant, ★★★

Nirman, *Nihr-mahn*, (M), (S), free from pride, ★★★

Nirmay, *Nihr-mehy*, (M), (S), pure, brilliant, ★★★

Nirmit, *Nihr-miht*, (M), (S), created, ★★

Nirosh, *Nihr-oash*, (M), (S), calm, ★★★

Nirupam, *Nihr-up-uhm*, (M), (S), fearless, unique, incomparable, ★★★

Nirupama, *Nihr-up-uhm-ah*, (F), (S), fearless, unique, incomparable, ★★★

Nirva, *Nihr-vah*, (F), (S), refreshing, like the wind, ★★★

Nirval, *Nihr-vuhl*, (M), (S), sacred, devout, without a leader, ★★★

Nirvan, *Nihr-vahn*, (M), (S), salvation, liberated, ★★★

Nirvana, *Nihr-vahn-ah*, (F), (S), liberated, salvation, ★★★

Nirvani, *Nihr-vahn-ee*, (F), (S), goddess of bliss, ★★★

Nirvanin, *Nihr-vahn-ihn*, (M), (S), one who has attained nirvana, liberated, ★★★

Nirvar, *Nihr-vuhr*, (M), (S), best, unique, ★★★

Nisa, *Nihs-ah*, (F), (A), lady, (O) – Greek, goal, beginning, Hebrew, beloved, remembered, to test, ★★★

Nisam, *Nihs-ahm*, (M), (A), fresh air, ★★★

Nisama, *Nihs-ahm-ah*, (F), (S), matchless, ★★★

Nischal, *Nihs-chuhl*, (M), (S), immovable, steady, ★★★

Nischala, *Nihs-chuhl-ah*, (F), (S), immovable, the earth, ★★★

Nisha, *Nihsh-ah*, (F), (S), night, dream, ★★★

Nishad, *Nihsh-ahd*, (M), (S), a musical note, ★★

Nishank, *Nihsh-uhnk*, (M), (S), undoubting, fearless, ★★★

Nishant, *Nihsh-ahnt*, (M), (S), daybreak, peace, ★★★

Nishesh, *Nihsh-aesh*, (M), (S), perfect, complete, the moon, ★★★

Nishi, *Nihsh-ee*, (F), (S), invigorating, ★★★

Nishita, *Nihsh-iht-ah*, (F), (S), alert, fast, ★★

Nishk, *Nihshk*, (M), (S), gold, ★★★

Nishka, *Nihsh-kah*, (F), (S), pure, honest, gold, ★★★

Nishkam, *Nihsh-kahm*, (M), (S), selfless, ★★★

Nishkama, *Nihsh-kahm-ah*, (F), (S), selfless, ★★★

Nishna, *Nihsh-nah*, (F), (S), clever, talented, ★★★

Nishok, *Nih-shoak*, (M), (S), happy, satisfied, ★★★

Nishoka, *Nih-shoak-ah*, (F), (S), happy, satisfied, ★★★

Nishpar, *Nihsh-pahr*, (M), (S), limitless, ★★★

Nisit, *Nihs-iht*, (M), (S), sharp, invigorated, prepared, iron, steel, ★★

Nitin, *Niht-ihn*, (M), (S), master of the law, judge, ★★

Nitish, *Niht-ihsh*, (M), (S), master of the law, judge, ★★

Nitya, *Niht-yah*, (F), (S), eternal, another name for Durga, ★★

Nitya, *Niht-yuh*, (M), (S), eternal, ocean, ★★

Nivan, *Nihv-ahn*, (M), (S), bound, limited, ★★★

Nivat, *Nihv-aht*, (M), (S), secure, ★★

Nivedita, *Nihv-aed-iht-ah*, (F), (S), offered to god, ★

Nivid, *Nihv-ihd*, (M), (S), instruction, ★★

Niveet, *Nihv-eet*, (M), (S), adornment, the sacred thread worn by
   Brahma, ★★

Niyam, *Nih-yuhm*, (M), (S), rule, control, ★★★

Noor, *Noor*, (F), (A), light, brilliance, (P), moon, ★★★

Noora, *Noor-ah*, (F), (P), (O) – Latin, honourable, ★★★

Nora, *N-oh-rah*, (F), (O), Latin, Gaelic, honour, honourable, ★★★

Noya, *N-oh-yah*, (A), (O) – Hebrew, beautiful, bejewelled, ★★★

Nupur, *Noo-pur*, (F), (S), anklet, ★★

Nutan, *Noo-tuhn*, (F), (S), new, young, ★★

Nuti, *Nu-tee*, (F), (S), praise, prayer, ★★

Nyaayika, *Nyah-yihk-ah*, (F), (S), logician, ★★

Nysa, *Niy-sah*, (F), (O) – Greek, beginning, goal, Celtic, hunger,
   lamb, ★★★

O

Odati, *Oad-uht-ee*, (F), (S), refreshing, dawn, ★

Ojal, *Oaj-uhl*, (M), (S), splendid, sight, ★★★

Ojas, *Oaj-uhs*, (M), (S), virility, power, brilliance, light, appearance, water, ★★★

Ojasvi, *Oaj-uhs-vee*, (M), (S), brave, powerful, brilliant, active, ★★★

Ojasvi, *Oaj-uhs-vee*, (F), (S), brave, powerful, brilliant, active, ★★★

Ojasvin, *Oaj-uhs-vihn*, (M), (S), brave, powerful, brilliant, active, ★★★

Ojasvini, *Oaj-uhs-vihn-ee*, (F, (S), brave, brilliant, active, powerful, ★★★

Okaab, *Oak-ahb*, (M), (S), eagle, ★★★

Olivia, *Oal-ihv-ee-ah*, (F), (O) – Latin, peaceful, olive tree, ★★★

Om, *Oam*, (F), (S), 'so be it', sacred, god, the essence of life, the source of all mantras, symbolising Vishnu, Shiva and Brahma, ★★★

Om, *Oam*, (M), (S), 'so be it', sacred, god, the essence of life, the source of all mantras, symbolising Vishnu, Shiva and Brahma, ★★★

Oman, *Oam-uhn*, (M), (S), life giving, shelter, friend, ★★★

Omana, *Oam-uhn-ah*, (F), (S), life giving, shelter, friend, ★★★

Omar, *Oam-ahr*, (M), (A), flourishing, long-lived, orator, ★★★

Omesh, *Oam-aesh*, (M), (S), god of birth, life and death, ★★★

Omish, *Oam-eesh*, (M), (S), god of birth, life and death, ★★★

Omisha, *Oam-eesh-ah*, (F), (S), goddess of birth, life and death, ★★★

Omkar, *Oam-kahr*, (M), (S), Om, sacred, ★★★

Omkara, *Oam-kahr-ah*, (F), (S), Om, sacred, an auspicious
   beginning, ★★★

Opal, *Oap-uhl*, (F), (S), precious, gem, ★★★

Opash, *Oap-uhsh*, (F), (S), support, crown, ★★★

Oriana, *Oar-ee-ahn-ah*, (F), (O) – Latin, French, rising sun, gold,
   dawn, ★★★

P

Paajas, *Pah-juhs*, (M), (S), strength, brilliance, heaven and earth, ★★★

Paak, *Pahk*, (M), (S), simple, young, ignorant, (H), pure, clean, innocent, (O) – Urdu, pure, ★★★

Paal, *Pahl*, (M), (S), king, guardian, ★★★

Paalin, *Pahl-ihn*, (M), (S), guarding, ★★★

Paalit, *Pahl-iht*, (M), (S), protected, precious, ★★

Paalita, *Pahl-iht-ah*, (F), (S), protected, precious, ★★

Paaloma, *Pahl-oam-ah*, (F), (O) – Latin, dove, ★★★

Paanik, *Pahn-ihk*, (M), (S), hand, ★★★

Paaraj, *Pahr-uhj*, (M), (S), gold, ★★★

Paarak, *Pahr-uhk*, (M), (S), liberating, pleasant, ★★★

Paaras, *Pahr-uhs*, (M), (S), the mystical stone that is believed to convert base metals to gold, healthy, ★★★

Paarth, *Pahrth*, (M), (S), son of the earth, prince, ★★

Paarthiv, *Pahrth-ihv*, (M), (S), son of the earth, prince, brave, ★★

Paarthivi, *Pahrth-ihv-ee*, (F), (S), daughter of the earth, another name for Sita and Lakshmi, ★★

Paaru, *Pahr-u*, (M), (S), sun, fire, ★★★

Paarul, *Pahr-ul*, (F), (S), beautiful, practical, kind, ★★★

Paarvati, *Pahr-vuht-ee*, (F), (S), of the mountains, a goddess and wife of Shiva, ★

Paatav, *Paht-uhv*, (M), (S), clever, agile, ★★

Paavak, *Pahv-uhk*, (M), (S), purifying, fire, brilliant, ★★★

Paavaki, *Pahv-uhk-ee*, (F), (S), purifying, fire, another name for Saraswati, ★★★

Paavan, *Pahv-uhn*, (M), (S), purifying, pure, sacred, fire, incense, ★★★

Paavana, *Pahv-uhn-ah*, (F), (S), purifying, pure, sacred, ★★★

Paayal, *Pah-yuhl*, (F), (S), anklet, ★★★

Padam, *Puhd-uhm*, (M), (S), lotus, ★★

Padma, *Puhd-mah*, (F), (S), lotus, lotus coloured, another name for Lakshmi, ★★

Padma, *Puhd-muh*, (M), (S), lotus, a thousand billion, ★★

Padmini, *Puhd-mihn-ee*, (F), (S), lotus, a collection of lotuses, ★★

Pahal, *Puh-hehl*, (F), (S), initiative, beginning, ★★

Pahal, *Puh-hehl*, (M), (S), initiative, beginning, ★★

Pakshaj, *Puhk-shuhj*, (M), (S), moon, ★★★

Pakshil, *Puhk-shihl*, (M), (S), bird, logical, practical, ★★★

Pakshin, *Puhk-shihn*, (M), (S), bird, ★★

Pakshini, *Puhk-shihn-ee*, (F), (S), day of the full moon, bird, ★★

Palaksh, *Puhl-uhksh*, (M), (S), white, ★★★

Palakshi, *Puhl-uhksh-ee*, (F), (S), white, ★★★

Palank, *Puhl-uhnk*, (M), (P), leopard, panther, ★★★

Palash, *Puhl-ahsh*, (M), (S), greenery, (O) – Pahlavi, horse, ★★★

Palashini, *Puhl-ahsh-ihn-ee*, (F), (S), green, covered in greenery, a river, ★

Pallav, *Puhl-luhv*, (M), (S), sprout, blossom, ★★★

Pallavi, *Puhl-luhv-ee*, (F), (S), a shoot, young, ★★★

Panav, *Puhn-uhv*, (M), (S), prince, youthful, ★★★

Pancham, *Puhn-chuhm*, (M), (S), musical note, intelligent, attractive, ★★★

Panit, *Puhn-iht*, (M), (S), admired, ★★

Panita, *Puhn-iht-ah*, (F), (S), admired, ★★

Pankaj, *Puhn-kuhj*, (M), (S), lotus, another name for Brahma, ★★★

Pankaja, *Puhn-kuhj-ah*, (F), (S), lotus, ★★★

Panshul, *Puhn-shul*, (M), (S), fragrant, anointed in sandalwood, another name for Shiva, ★★

Parag, *Puhr-ahg*, (M), (S), pollen, fragrant, fame, ★★★

Param, *Puhr-uhm*, (M), (S), pre-eminent, best, ★★★

Parama, *Puhr-uhm-ah*, (F), (S), pre-eminent, best, ★★★

Parash, *Puhr-ahsh*, (M), (S), iron, ★★★

Paresh, *Puhr-aesh*, (M), (S), the highest lord, another name for Brahma, ★★★

Pari, *Puhr-ee*, (F), (H), (P), fairy, angel, beautiful, ★★★

Parimal, *Puhr-ihm-uhl*, (M), (S), fragrance, ★★★

Pariman, *Puhr-ihm-uhn*, (M), (S), quality, abundant, ★★★

Parimit, *Puhr-ihm-iht*, (M), (S), measured, moderate, ★★

Parinita, *Puhr-ihn-eet-ah*, (F), (S), complete, knowledge, married, ★

Parinut, *Puhr-ihn-ut*, (M), (S), praised, famous, ★

Parisa, *Puhr-ee-sah*, (F), (H), like a fairy or an angel, beautiful, ★★★

Parisi, *Puhr-ee-see*, (F), (H), like a fairy or an angel, beautiful, ★★★

Paritosh, *Puhr-iht-oash*, (M), (S), delight, ★★

Paroksh, *Puhr-oaksh*, (M), (S), beyond the horizon, mysterious, (H), absence, invisible, ★★

Parokshi, *Puhr-oaksh-ee*, (F), (S), mysterious, (H), invisible, out of sight, ★★

Parshav, *Puhr-shuhv*, (M), (S), warrior, ★★★

Paru, *Puhr-u*, (M), (S), limb, mountain, ocean, sky, paradise, ★★★

Parush, *Puhr-ush*, (M), (S), keen, sharp, knot, limb, violent, arrow, (H), cruel, pitiless, ★★★

Parvit, *Puhr-viht*, (M), (S), surrounded, protected, ★★

Patag, *Puht-uhg*, (M), (S), bird, the sun, ★★

Patush, *Puhtt-ush*, (M), (S), clever, ★★★

Paulomi, *Paul-oam-ee*, (F), (S), wife of Indra, ★★

Pav, *Puhv*, (M), (S), purification, air, ★★★

Pavan, *Puhv-uhn*, (M), (S), breeze, air, ★★★

Pavitra, *Puhv-iht-ruh*, (M), (S), pure, ★

Pehel, *Puh-hehl*, (F), (S), initiative, beginning, ★★

Pehel, *Puh-hehl*, (M), (S), initiative, beginning, ★★

Phaalguni, *Fahl-gun-ee*, (F), (S), the day of the full moon in the month of Phaalgun (February-March in the Hindu calendar), ★★

Phalak, *Fuhl-uhk*, (M), (S), shield, sky, ★★★

Phalya, *Fuhl-yah*, (F), (S), flower, bud, ★★★

Pinak, *Pihn-ahk*, (M), (S), bow, ★★★

Pinakin, *Pihn-ahk-ihn*, (M), (S), armed with a bow, another name for Shiva, ★★★

Pinakini, *Pihn-ahk-ihn-ee*, (F), (S), bow shaped, armed with a bow, a river, ★★★

Piya, *Pee-yah*, (F), (S), beloved, (O) – Greek, Latin, pious, ★★★

Piyush, *Pee-yoosh*, (M), (S), nectar, ★★★

Poonam, *Poo-nuhm*, (F), (S), full moon, ★★★

Poppy, *Pawp-pee*, (F), (O) – English, the poppy flower, ★★★

Poshit, *Poash-iht*, (M), (S), nourished, defended, loved, ★★

Poshita, *Poash-iht-ah*, (F), (S), nourished, defended, loved, ★★

Praachi, *Prahch-ee*, (F), (S), the east, orient, ★★★

Praachik, *Prahch-ihk*, (M), (S), driving, long-legged, ★★★

Praachika, *Prah-chihk-ah*, (F), (S), driving, falcon, long-legged, spider, ★★★

Praadha, *Prah-dhah*, (F), (S), supreme, prominent, ★★

Praakrit, *Prahk-riht*, (M), (S), natural, ★

Praakriti, *Prahk-riht-ee*, (M), (S), original, nature, the personification of Brahman or the Supreme Spirit, ★

Praan, *Prahn*, (M), (S), life, spirit, energy, might, another name for Brahma and Vishnu, ★★★

Praanad, *Prahn-uhd*, (M), (S), life giving, another name for Vishnu and Brahma, ★★

Praanak, *Prahn-uhk*, (M), (S), life giving, living, ★★★

Praanjal, *Prahn-juhl*, (M), (S), honest, self-respecting, sincere, ★★

Praanjali, *Prahn-juhl-ee*, (F), (S), self-respecting, respectful, ★★

Praanshu, *Prahn-shu*, (M), (S), tall, mighty, ★★★

Praapti, *Prahp-tee*, (F), (S), achievement, discovery, gain, ★

Praarthana, *Prahr-thuhn-ah*, (F), (S), prayer, ★

Praatar, *Praht-uhr*, (M), (S), bright, dawn, ★★

Praatika, *Prah-teek-ah*, (F), (S), image, beautiful, ★★

Prabal, *Puhb-uhl*, (M), (S), strong, powerful, ★★★

Prabha, *Pruhbh-ah*, (F), (S), light, brilliance, an apsara or celestial nymph, ★★

Prabhakar, *Pruhbh-ahk-uhr*, (M), (S), the sun, the moon, creating light, another name for Shiva, ★★

Prabhan, *Pruhbh-ahn*, (M), (S), light, brilliance, ★★

Prabhas, *Pruhbh-ahs*, (M), (S), brilliance, ★★

Prabhat, *Pruhbh-aht*, (M), (S), brilliant, dawn, ★★

Prabhata, *Pruhbh-aht-ah*, (F), (S), goddess of dawn, ★★

Prabhav, *Pruhbh-ahv*, (M), (S), eminent, excellent, origin, majesty, power, brilliance, attractiveness, ★★

Prabodh, *Pruhb-oadh*, (M), (S), consciousness, awareness, ★★

Prachet, *Pruh-chaet*, (M), (S), intelligent, ★★

Pradhi, *Pruhdh-ee*, (F), (S), intelligence, ★★

Pradip, *Pruh-deep*, (M), (S), lamp, brilliant, ★★

Pradosh, *Pruh-doash*, (M), (S), dusk, ★★

Pradyot, *Pruhd-yoat*, (M), (S), light, ★

Pradyut, *Pruhd-yut*, (M), (S), lit, brilliant, ★

Praful, *Pruhf-ul*, (M), (S), happy, blooming, expansive, playful, ★★★

Prafula, *Pruhf-ul-ah*, (F), (S), happy, blooming, expansive, playful, ★★★

Pragati, *Pruhg-uht-ee*, (F), (S), progress, ★★

Prahas, *Pruh-hahs*, (M), (S), laughter, colourful, brilliance, another name for Shiva, ★★★

Prahasit, *Pruh-huhs-iht*, (M), (S), laughing, a Buddha, ★

Prahlad, *Pruh-lahd*, (M), (S), happiness, ★★

Prahlav, *Pruh-luhv*, (M), (S), with a beautiful body, ★★★

Prajas, *Pruh-juhs*, (M), (S), born, ★★★

Prajin, *Pruh-jihn*, (M), (S), swift, air, ★★★

Prajit, *Pruh-jiht*, (M), (S), conquering, victorious, ★★

Prajna, *Pruhj-nah*, (F), (S), wisdom, information, another name for Saraswati, ★★★

Prajnan, *Pruhj-nahn*, (M), (S), intelligent, ★★★

Prakam, *Pruhk-ahm*, (M), (S), desire, achievement, joy, ★★★

Prakash, *Pruhk-ahsh*, (M), (S), light, brilliance, success, fame, appearance, ★★★

Praket, *Pruhk-aet*, (M), (S), understanding, intelligence, ★★

Prakul, *Pruhk-ul*, (M), (S), with a beautiful body, ★★★

Prakula, *Pruhk-ul-ah*, (F), (S), with a beautiful body, ★★★

Pralamb, *Pruhl-uhmb*, (M), (S), garland of flowers, ★★★

Prama, *Pruhm-ah*, (F), (S), foundation, knowledge, ★★★

Pramad, *Pruhm-uhd*, (M), (S), joy, ★★

Pramada, *Pruhm-uhd-ah*, (F), (S), delightful, beautiful, ★★

Pramat, *Pruhm-uht*, (M), (S), wise, prudent, ★★

Pramik, *Pruhm-ihk*, (F), (S), best, fulfilling desires, ★★★

Pramika, *Pruhm-ihk-ah*, (F), (S), best, fulfilling desires, ★★★

Pramit, *Pruhm-iht*, (M), (S), sensible, moderate, ★★

Pramiti, *Pruhm-iht-ee*, (F), (S), understanding, wisdom, ★★

Pramod, *Pruhm-oad*, (M), (S), pleasure, ★★

Pranav, *Pruhn-uhv*, (M), (S), sacred, auspicious, Om, ★★★

Pranay, *Pruhn-uhy*, (M), (S), leader, leadership, love, ★★

Pranit, *Pruhn-eet*, (M), (S), likeable, led, sanctified, ★★

Pranita, *Pruhn-eet-ah*, (F), (S), led, created, grown, holy water, a cup used in rituals, ★★

Pranod, *Pruhn-oad*, (M), (S), leader, ★★

Pranut, *Pruhn-ut*, (M), (S), praised, ★★

Prasad, *Pruhs-ahd*, (M), (S), devotional offering, purity, ★★

Prasal, *Pruhs-uhl*, (M), (S), cool, calm, winter, ★★★

Prasang, *Pruhs-uhng*, (M), (S), devotion, union, affection, ★★★

Prasann, *Pruhs-uhnn*, (M), (S), pure, clear, brilliant, peaceful, pleasant, happy, ★★★

Prasanna, *Pruhs-uhnn-ah*, (F), (S), pleasant, ★★★

Praasha, *Prahsh-ah*, (F), (S), desire, ★★★

Prasham, *Pruhhs-uhm*, (M), (S), cool, peaceful, autumn, ★★★

Prashami, *Pruhhs-uhm-ee*, (F), (S), peaceful, an apsara or celestial nymph, ★★★

Prashan, *Pruhhs-uhn*, (M), (S), successful, ★★★

Prashansa, *Pruhsh-uhn-sah*, (M), (F), praise, ★★

Prashant, *Pruhhs-ahnt*, (M), (S), calm, peace, ★★

Prastav, *Pruhs-tuhv*, (M), (S), hymn, song, ★★

Prasun, *Pruhs-oon*, (M), (S), born, created, blossom, ★★★

Prasut, *Pruhs-oot*, (M), (S), born, created, flower, ★★★

Prasvar, *Pruhs-vahr*, (M), (S), sacred, Om, ★★★

Pratan, *Pruht-ahn*, (M), (S), branch, a shoot, ★★

Pratap, *Pruht-ahp*, (M), (S), warmth, brilliance, eminence, vigour, majestic, ★★

Pratapi, *Pruht-ahp-ee*, (F), (S), brilliant, majestic, eminent, ★★

Pratik, *Pruh-teek*, (M), (S), appearance, image, ★★

Pratika, *Pruh-teek-ah*, (F), (S), appearance, image, ★★

Pratima, *Pruht-ihm-ah*, (F), (S), picture, sign, idol, ★★

Pratinav, *Pruht-ihn-uhv*, (M), (S), new, youthful, ★★

Pratir, *Pruht-eer*, (M), (S), shore, bank, ★★

Pratit, *Pruht-eet*, (M), (S), known, wise, ★★

Pratosh, *Pruht-oash*, (M), (S), satisfaction, ★★

Pratul, *Pruht-ul*, (M), (S), abundance, ★★

Pratush, *Pruht-ush*, (M), (S), happy, ★★

Praval, *Puhv-uhl*, (M), (S), strong, powerful, ★★★

Pravan, *Pruhv-uhn*, (M), (S), to defeat, ★★★

Pravar, *Pruhv-uhr*, (M), (S), best, eminent, ★★★

Pravara, *Pruhv-uhr-ah*, (F), (S), best, ★★★

Pravek, *Pruhv-aek*, (M), (S), excellent, greatest, ★★★

Pravin, *Pruhv-een*, (M), (S), talented, clever, ★★★

Pravir, *Pruhv-eer*, (M), (S), prince, best, better than the heroes, ★★★

Pravit, *Pruhv-iht*, (M), (S), hero, ★★

Pravita, *Pruhv-iht-ah*, (F), (S), heroine, ★★

Pravrit, *Pruhv-riht*, (M), (S), determined, ★★

Pravrita, *Pruhv-riht-ah*, (F), (S), determined, ★★

Prayag, *Pruh-yahg*, (M), (S), the city of holy sacrifices, the confluence of the holy rivers Ganges, Yamuna and Saraswati, ★★★

Prayas, *Pruh-yuhs*, (M), (S), pleasure, ★★★

Prayuj, *Pruh-yuj*, (M), (S), impulse, ★★★

Preet, *Preet*, (M), (S), pleased, ★★

Preeti, *Preet-ee*, (F), (S), love, happiness, ★★

Preetika, *Preet-ihk-ah*, (F), (S), beloved, ★★

Preksha, *Praek-shah*, (F), (S), seeing, ★★★

Prem, *Praem*, (M), (S), love, ★★★

Prema, *Praem-ah*, (F), (S), beloved, love, benevolence, ★★★

Prerana, *Praer-uhn-ah*, (F), (S), impulse, passion, drive, inspiration, command, ★★★

Preshtha, *Praesh-tthah*, (F), (S), dearest, ★★

Priank, *Pree-uhnk*, (M), (S), distinguished, bee, deer, saffron, ★★★

Priya, *Pree-yuh*, (M), (S), beloved, ★★★

Priya, *Pree-yah*, (F), (S), beloved, wife, ★★★

Priyam, *Pree-yuhm*, (M), (S), beloved, ★★★

Priyanka, *Pree-yahnk-ah*, (F), (S), beloved, ★★★

Puja, *Puj-ah*, (F), (S), worship, respect, ★★★

Pujan, *Puj-uhn*, (M), (S), worship, ★★★

Pujit, *Puj-iht*, (M), (S), respected, worshipped, ★★

Pujita, *Puj-iht-ah*, (F), (S), respected, worshipped, a goddess, ★★

Pulak, *Pul-uhk*, (M), (S), delight, jewel, ★★★

Pulin, *Pul-ihn*, (M), (S), river bank, ★★★

Pulish, *Pul-ihsh*, (M), (S), a sage, ★★★

Puloma, *Pul-oam-ah*, (F), (S), delighted, ★★★

Puloman, *Pul-oam-uhn*, (M), (S), delighted, ★★★

Punan, *Pun-ahn*, (M), (S), bright, pure, ★★★

Punish, *Poon-eesh*, (M), (S), lord of the pious, ★★★

Punit, *Pun-eet*, (M), (S), sacred, devout, pure, ★★

Punita, *Pun-eet-ah*, (F), (S), sacred, devout, ★★

Punya, *Pun-yah*, (F), (S), virtue, purity, Tulsi or Holy Basil, ★★★

Punya, *Pun-yuh*, (M), (S), sacred, auspicious, fair, worthy, pure, ★★★

Puran, *Poor-ahn*, (M), (S), complete, abundant, (P), successors, momento, ★★★

Puravi, *Pur-uhv-ee*, (F), (S), eastern, existing, welcoming, a musical raagini, ★★★

Purna, *Pur-nah*, (F), (S), complete, content, ★★★

Purnak, *Pur-nahk*, (M), (P), youth, ★★★

Purnima, *Poor-nihm-ah*, (F), (S), night of the full moon, ★★★

Purtab, *Pur-tahb*, (M), (P), powerful, ★★

Puru, *Pur-u*, (M), (S), heaven, mountain, abundant, ★★★

Purush, *Pur-ush*, (M), (S), man, the pupil of the eye, Brahman or the Supreme Spirit, ★★★

Puruva, *Pur-oov-ah*, (F), (S), eastern, elder, ★★★

Puruvi, *Pur-oov-ee*, (F), (S), achiever, eastern, a musical raagini, ★★★

Pushan, *Poosh-uhn*, (M), (S), provider, protector, ★★★

Pushana, *Poosh-uhn-ah*, (F), (S), provider, protector, ★★★

Pushkal, *Push-kuhl*, (M), (S), abundant, perfect, mighty, loud, pure, another name for Shiva, ★★★

Pushkar, *Push-kuhr*, (M), (S), Lotus, sky, heaven, sun, another name
   for Krishna and Shiva, ★★★
Pushkara, *Push-kuhr-ah*, (F), (S), like a lotus, ★★★
Pushp, *Pushp*, (M), (S), flower, fragrance, topaz, ★★★
Pushpa, *Push-pah*, (F), (S), flower, ★★★
Pushpaj, *Push-puhj*, (M), (S), nectar, ★★★
Pushpaja, *Push-puhj-ah*, (F), (S), nectar, ★★★

Q

Qaabil, *Kahb-ihl*, (M), (A), capable, ★★★
Qarar, Kuhr-ahr, (M), (A), comfort, succour, promise, ★★★

R

Raadha, *Rahdh-ah*, (F), (S), wealth, success, lightning, Krishna's love, Krishna's intellectual energy and inspiration, ★★

Raadhak, *Rahdh-uhk*, (M), (S), generous, ★★

Raadhana, *Rahdh-uhn-ah*, (F), (S), speech, ★★

Raadhani, *Rahdh-uhn-ee*, (F), (S), worship, ★★

Raadhi, *Rahdh-ee*, (F), (S), achievement, perfection, success, ★★

Raadhik, *Rahdh-ihk*, (M), (S), successful, wealthy, ★★

Raadhika, *Rahdh-ihk-ah*, (F), (S), successful, wealthy, another name for Raadha, ★★

Raag, *Rahg*, (M), (S), to bring to life, love, beauty, vigour, passion, desire, the colour red, melody, king, sun, moon, a form of Indian classical music, ★★★

Raaga, *Rahg-ah*, (F), (S), bringing to life, emotion, beauty, melody, passionate, desire, the colour red, a form of Indian classical music, ★★★

Raaghav, *Rahg-huhv*, (M), (S), another name for Raam, ★★

Raagini, *Rahg-ihn-ee*, (F), (S), melody, love, an apsara or celestial nymph, a form of Indian classical musical, another name for Lakshmi, ★★★

Raahi, *Rah-hee*, (M), (P), (H), traveller, ★★★

Raahul, *Rah-hul*, (M), (S), competent, efficient, ★★★

Raajak, *Rahj-uhk*, (M), (S), brilliant, ruler, ★★★

Raajan, *Rahj-uhn*, (M), (S), king, royal, ★★★

Raajas, *Rahj-uhs*, (M), (S), passionate, endowed with zest for life and its pleasures, ★★★

Raajasi, *Rahj-uhs-ee*, (F), (S), passionate, endowed with zest for life
and its pleasures, another name for Durga, ★★★

Raajavi, *Rahj-uhv-ee*, (F), (S), royal, bird, ★★★

Raajin, *Rahj-ihn*, (M), (S), moonlight, ★★★

Raajita, *Rahj-iht-ah*, (F), (S), bright, brilliant, ★★

Raajiv, *Rahj-eev*, (M), (S), distinguished, deer, lotus, crane, ★★★

Raajni, *Rahj-nee*, (F), (S), princess, queen, that which contains the
soul of the universe, the wife of the sun, ★★★

Raaka, *Rahk-ah*, (F), (S), full moon, the day of the full moon,
a river, ★★★

Raakesh, *Rahk-aesh*, (M), (S), lord of the full moon, another name
for Shiva, ★★★

Raakhi, *Rahk-hee*, (F), (S), symbol of protection, ★★

Raakini, *Rahk-ihn-ee*, (F), (S), night, ★★★

Raam, *Rahm*, (M), (S), soothing, captivating, omnipresent, happiness,
dark, an incarnation of Vishnu, ★★★

Raana, *Rahn-ah*, (F), (S), murmering, a goddess, (A), attractive, ★★★

Raani, *Rahn-ee*, (F), (S), queen, ★★★

Raania, *Rahn-ee-ah*, (F), (A), attractive, (O) – Hebrew, song, joy, ★★★

Raano, *Rahn-oh*, (F), (S), peacock's tail, ★★★

Raas, *Rahs*, (M), (S), noise, play, lively, emotional, ★★★

Raashi, *Rahsh-ee*, (F), (S), wealth, zodiac sign, ★★★

Raayika, *Rah-yihk-ah*, (F), (P), beloved, desired, ★★★

Rachit, *Ruhch-iht*, (M), (S), created, ★★★

Rachita, *Ruhch-iht-ah*, (F), (S), created, ★★★

Rachna, *Ruhch-nah*, (F), (S), achievement, creation, ★★★

Raghu, *Ruh-ghu*, (M), (S), swift, light, ★★

Rahas, *Ruh-huhs*, (M), (S), solitude, privacy, the act of physical
love, ★★★

135

Raibhya, *Raebh-yuh*, (M), (S), praise, Hindu religious
verses, ★

Raisa, *Rae-sah*, (F), (O) – Greek, adaptable, easy–going,
Yiddish, rose, ★★★

Raivat, *Raeh-vuht*, (M), (S), prosperous, from a wealthy family,
another name for Shiva, ★★

Raj, *Rahj*, (M), (S), rule, kingdom, ★★★

Rajani, *Ruhj-uhn-ee*, (F), (S), night, turmeric, royal, an apsara or
celestial nymph, another name for Durga, ★★★

Rajas, *Ruhj-uhs*, (M), (S), horizon, mist, pollen, darkness, autumn,
passion, anger, ★★★

Rajat, *Ruhj-uht*, (M), (S), bright, pleasant, mind, ★★

Rajit, *Ruhj-iht*, (M), (S), attracted, enchanted, ★★

Rak, *Ruhk*, (M), (S), crystal, ★★★

Raksh, *Ruhk-sh*, (M), (S), protector, ashes, ★★★

Raksha, *Ruhk-shah*, (F), (S), protection, ★★★

Rakshak, *Ruhk-shuhk*, (M), (S), protector, amulet, ★★★

Rakshan, *Ruhk-shuhn*, (M), (S), protector, another name
for Vishnu, ★★★

Rakshana, *Ruhk-shuhn-ah*, (F), (S), protection, ★★★

Rakshik, *Ruhk-shihk*, (M), (S), protector, ★★★

Rakshika, *Ruhk-shihk-ah*, (F), (S), protector, ★★★

Rakshit, *Ruhk-shiht*, (M), (S), protected, ★★

Rakshita, *Ruhk-shiht-ah*, (F), (S), protected, an apsara or
celestial nymph, ★★

Rakta, *Ruhk-tah*, (F), (S), blood, painted, pleasant, ★★

Rama, *Ruhm-ah*, (F), (S), beautiful, captivating, red, fortune,

brilliance, an apsara or celestial nymph, another name for
Mahalakshmi, ★★★

Raman, *Ruhm-uhn*, (M), (S), pleasant, lover, another name for the
love god Kaama, ★★★

Ramana, *Ruhm-uhn-ah*, (F), (S), enchanting, attractive, beloved, ★★★

Ramani, *Ruhm-uhn-ee*, (F), (S), beautiful, affectionate, pleasant,
happy, ★★★

Rambh, *Ruhm-bh*, (M), (S), support, bamboo, ★★

Rambha, *Ruhm-bhah*, (F), (S), lovable, pleasant, support, an apsara or
celestial nymph, ★★

Ramit, *Ruhm-iht*, (M), (S), loved, happy, ★★

Ramita, *Ruhm-iht-ah*, (F), (S), loved, happy, ★★

Ramona, *Ruhm-oan-ah*, (F), (O) – German, Spanish, counsel,
protector, ★★★

Ramya, *Ruhm-yah*, (F), (S), captivating, lovely, night, ★★★

Ramya, *Ruhm-yuh*, (M), (S), captivating, handsome, ★★★

Ramyak, *Ruhm-yuhk*, (M), (S), lover, ★★★

Ran, *Ruhn*, (M), (S), war, joy, noise, ★★★

Ranak, *Ruhn-uhk*, (M), (S), ruler, warrior, ★★★

Rangan, *Ruhn-guhn*, (M), (S), pleasing, cheerful, ★★★

Rangana, *Ruhn-guhn-ah*, (F), (S), pleasing, cheerful, ★★★

Rangati, *Ruhn-guht-ee*, (F), (S), lovable, passionate, a musical raag, ★★

Rangit, *Ruhn-giht*, (M), (S), handsome, ★★

Rangita, *Ruhn-giht-ah*, (F), (S), happy, ★★

Ranhit, *Ruhn-hiht*, (M), (S), quick, ★★

Ranhita, *Ruhn-hiht-ah*, (F), (S), quick, ★★

Ranit, *Ruhn-iht*, (M), (S), voice, audible, ★★

Ranita, *Ruhn-iht-ah*, (F), (S), voice, audible, ★★

Ranjan, *Ruhn-juhn*, (M), (S), pleasant, fun, ★★★

Ranjana, *Ruhn-juhn-ah*, (F), (S), pleasant, fun, ★★★

Ranjik, *Ruhn-jihk*, (M), (S), pleasant, exciting, loveble, ★★★

Ranjika, *Ruhn-jihk-ah*, (F), (S), pleasant, exciting, loveble, ★★★

Ranjini, *Ruhn-jihn-ee*, (F), (S), fun, pleasant, ★★★

Ranjit, *Ruhn-jeet*, (M), (S), victorious, ★★

Ranjita, *Ruhn-jeet-ah*, (F), (S), victorious, ★★

Ranjita, *Ruhn-jiht-ah*, (F), (S), coloured, delighted, ★★

Ranva, *Ruhn-vah*, (F), (S), pleasant, happy, lovely, ★★★

Ranvit, *Ruhn-viht*, (M), (S), pleasant, happy, ★★

Ranvita, *Ruhn-viht-ah*, (F), (S), happy, ★★

Ranya, *Ruhn-yah*, (F), (S), pleasant, assertive, aggressive, ★★★

Rashad, *Ruhsh-uhd*, (M), (A), with integrity, sensible, ★★

Rasik, *Ruhs-ihk*, (M), (S), passionate, elegant, handsome, entertaining, discerning, ★★★

Rasika, *Ruhs-ihk-ah*, (F), (S), discerning, elegant, beautiful, passionate, ★★★

Rashmi, *Ruhsh-mee*, (F), (S), rope, ray of light, ★★★

Rashmin, *Ruhsh-mihn*, (M), (S), sun, moon, ★★★

Rasna, *Ruhs-nah*, (F), (S), relishing, taste, the tongue, ★★★

Rasul, *Ruhs-ool*, (M), (H), prophet, divine messenger, ★★★

Rasya, *Ruhs-yah*, (F), (S), emotional, juicy, ★★★

Ratan, *Ruht-uhn*, (M), (S), best, gift, riches, jewel, ★★

Rati, *Ruht-ee*, (F), (S), love, pleasure, desire, an apsara or celestial nymph, ★★

Ratik, *Ruht-ihk*, (M), (S), happy, loved, ★★

Ratika, *Ruht-ihk-ah*, (F), (S), happy, loved, ★★

Ratish, *Ruht-ihsh*, (M), (S), the god of love Kaama, ★★

Ratna, *Ruht-nuh*, (M), (S), best, gift, riches, jewel, ★★

Ratna, *Ruht-nah*, (F), (S), jewel, ★★

Raveena, *Ruhv-een-ah*, (F), (S), sunny, fair, ★★★

Ravi, *Ruhv-ee*, (M), (S), sun, fire, ★★★

Ravij, *Ruhv-ihj*, (M), (S), born of the sun, another name for Karan
    and Saturn, ★★★

Ravija, *Ruhv-ihj-ah*, (M), (S), born of the sun, another name for the
    river Yamuna, ★★★

Ravish, *Ruhv-eesh*, (M), (S), desiring the sun, another name for the
    god of love Kaama, ★★★

Ravit, *Ruhv-iht*, (M), (S), sun, fire, ★★★

Rayya, *Ruh-yah*, (F), (A), fragrance, breeze, ★★★

Rayna, *Rae-nah*, (F), (O) – Latin, queen, Yiddish, pure, clean, ★★★

Rebh, *Raebh*, (M), (S), singer of praise, ★★

Rebha, *Rae-bhah*, (F), (S), singer of praise, ★★

Reema, *Reem-ah*, (F), (S), a prayer, another name for Durga, ★★★

Reena, *Reen-ah*, (F), (S), melted, dissolved, (O) – Latin, rebirth,
    clear, bright, ★★★

Reeti, *Reet-ee*, (F), (S), method, wealth, protection, conduct,
    auspiciousness, ★★

Reetika, *Reet-ihk-ah*, (F), (S), brass, ★★

Rekha, *Rae-khah*, (F), (S), line, ★★

Renu, *Rae-nu*, (F), (S), an atom, dust, sand, pollen, ★★★

Renuk, *Rae-nuk*, (M), (S), born of dust, ★★★

Renuka, *Rae-nuk-ah*, (F), (S), born of dust, ★★★

Rev, *Raev*, (M), (S), moving, ★★★

Reva, *Rae-vah*, (F), (S), agile, quick, another name for Kaali and the river Narmada, ★★★

Revat, *Rae-vuht*, (M), (S), wealthy, attractive, brilliant, ★★

Revati, *Rae-vuht-ee*, (F), (S), wealth, constellation, musical raagini, ★★

Reya, *Rae-yah*, (F), (S), singer, ★★★

Rhea, *Rih-yah*, (F), (S), singer, (O) – Greek, river, to flow, (O) –
    Latin, poppy flower, ★★★

Rhianna, *Rhee-ahn-ah*, (F), (O) – Welsh, maiden, young, queen, ★★★

Rianna, *Ree-ahn-ah*, (F), (O) – Welsh, maiden, young, queen, ★★★

Ribhya, *Rihbh-yah*, (F), (S), worshipped, ★★

Richa, *Rihch-ah*, (F), (S), the collected body of the Vedas, brilliance,
    hymn, ★★★

Richak, *Rihch-uhk*, (M), (S), created by a hymn, desire, ★★★

Richik, *Rihch-ihk*, (M), (S), one who praises, one who knows
    hymns, ★★★

Richika, *Rihch-ihk-ah*, (F), (S), one who praises, one who knows
    hymns, ★★★

Riddhi, *Rihdd-hee*, (F), (S), wealth, success, superiority, supernatural
    power, another name for Lakshmi and Paarvati, ★★

Rig, *Rihg*, (M), (S), a Vedic text, ★★★

Rijul, *Rih-jul*, (M), (S), innocent, honest, ★★★

Rijut, *Rih-jut*, (M), (S), innocence, honesty, ★★

Rijuta, *Rih-jut-ah*, (F), (S), innocence, honesty, ★★

Riona, *Rai-oan-ah*, (F), (O) – Latin, Celtic, queen, ★★★

Rishabh, *Rihsh-uhbh*, (M), (S), bull, excellent, a musical note, ★★

Rishabha, *Rihsh-uhbh-ah*, (F), (S), excellent, ★★

Rishan, *Rihsh-ahn*, (M), (S), strong, good, ★★★

Rishi, *Rihsh-ee*, (M), (S), sage, wise, pious, light, ★★★

Rishik, *Rihsh-ihk*, (M), (S), pious, learned, ★★★

Rishika, *Rihsh-ihk-ah*, (F), (S), pious, learned, ★★★

Rishit, *Rihsh-iht*, (M), (S), best, learned, ★★

Rishita, *Rihsh-iht-ah*, (F), (S), best, learned, ★★

Rishma, *Rihsh-mah*, (F), (S), lustrous, moonbeam, ★★★

Rishva, *Rihsh-vah*, (F), (S), noble, great, ★★★

Rit, *Rihtt*, (M), (S), truth, ★★★

Rit, *Riht*, (M), (S), appropriate, respected, brilliant, truth, ★★

Rita, *Reet-ah*, (F), (H), empty, ★★

Rita, *Reett-ah*, (F), (O) – Greek, pearl, precious, honoured, ★★

Ritam, *Riht-uhm*, (M), (S), true, stable, law, justice, duty, ★★

Ritap, *Riht-uhp*, (M), (S), guarding divine truth, ★★

Riti, *Riht-ee*, (F), (S), welfare, ★★

Ritu, *Riht-u*, (F), (S), period of time, season, ★★

Ritvik, *Riht-vihk*, (M), (S), timely, priest, ★★

Riwa, *Rih-wah*, (F), (P), fruitfulness, plenty, ★★★

Riya, *Rih-yah*, (F), (S), singer, (O) – Greek, river, to flow, (O) –
    Latin, poppy flower, ★★★

Rochak, *Roach-uhk*, (M), (S), illuminating, pleasant, tasty, ★★★

Rochan, *Roach-uhn*, (M), (S), brilliant, pleasant, ★★★

Rochana, *Roach-uhn-ah*, (F), (S), light, brilliant, attractive,
    blossom, ★★★

Rochit, *Roach-iht*, (M), (S), wonderous, delightful, ★★

Rohak, *Roa-huhk*, (M), (S), ascending, ★★★

Rohan, *Roa-huhn*, (M), (S), rising, a blossom, another name for
    Vishnu, (P), finest Indian steel, ★★★

Rohi, *Roa-hee*, (F), (S), ascending, red, doe, ★★★

Rohil, *Roa-hihl*, (M), (S), ascended, ★★★

Rohin, *Roa-hihn*, (M), (S), ascending, another name for Vishnu, ★★★

Rohini, *Roa-hihn-ee*, (F), (S), ascending, tall, (P), Indian steel, ★★★

Rohit, *Roa-hiht*, (M), (S), red, the sun, jewellery, a rainbow, blood, saffron, another name for Surya and Agni, ★★

Rohita, *Roa-hiht-ah*, (F), (S), red, ★★

Roma, *Roam-ah*, (F), (S), hairy, ★★★

Romik, *Roam-ihk*, (M), (S), salt, magnet, ★★★

Romir, *Roam-ihr*, (M), (S), pleasant, ★★

Romna, *Roam-nah*, (F), (P), pomegranate, ★★★

Romola, *Roam-oal-ah*, (F), (S), hairy, charming, (O) – Latin, the female form of Romulus, ★★★

Romona, *Roam-oan-ah*, (F), (O) – German, Spanish, counsel, protector, ★★★

Ronak, *Raw-nuhk*, (M), (H), elegance, brilliance, (O) – Urdu, celebration, cheer, decoration, ★★★

Ronit, *Roan-ihtt*, (M), (O) – Hebrew, song, tune, ★★★

Roshan, *Raw-shuhn*, (F), (P), (H), (O) – Urdu, brilliant, celebrated, ★★★

Roshan, *Raw-shuhn*, (M), (P), (H), (O) – Urdu, brilliant, celebrated, ★★★

Roshana, *Raw-shuhn-ah*, (F), P), (H), (O) – Urdu, light, brilliance, ★★★

Roshani, *Raw-shuhn-ee*, (F), (P), (H), (O) – Urdu, light, brilliance, law, ★★★

Roshank, *Raw-shuhnk*, (M), (P), (H), (O) – Urdu, light, brilliance, ★★★

Roshansa, *Raw-shuhn-sah*, (F), (S), desire, ★★★

Royina, *Roh-yihn-ah*, (F), (S), ascending, growing, ★★★

Rubina, *Rub-een-ah*, (F), (A), (O) – English, ruby, red, Hebrew, to have seen, ★★★

Ruby, *Ru-bee*, (F), (O) – English, ruby, red, jewel, precious, ★★★

Ruch, *Ru-ch*, (M), (S), bright, brilliant, good, attractive, ★★★

Rucha, *Ru-chah*, (F), (S), light, brilliance, desire, melodious, the voice of the Mynah bird, ★★★

Ruchak, *Ru-chuhk*, (M), (S), pleasant, melodious, attractive, golden, auspicious, ★★★

Ruchi, *Ru-chee*, (F), (S), beauty, taste, desire, joy, brilliance, an apsara or celestial nymph, ★★★

Ruchika, *Ru-chihk-ah*, (F), (S), brilliance, attractive, ★★★

Ruchir, *Ru-chihr*, (M), (S), handsome, pleasant, brilliant, ★★★

Ruchira, *Ru-chihr-ah*, (F), (S), beautiful, pleasant, brilliant, ★★★

Ruchit, *Ru-chiht*, (M), (S), brilliant, happy, pleasant, ★★

Ruchita, *Ru-chiht-ah*, (F), (S), brilliant, happy, pleasant, ★★

Rudra, *Ru-drah*, (F), (S), thunderous, another name for Paarvati, ★★

Rudra, *Ru-druh*, (M), (S), god of storms, fearsome, thunder and lightning, another name for Shiva, ★★

Rudraaksh, *Ru-drah-ksh*, (M), (S), auspicious, fruit dried and used for making rosaries, ★

Ruh, *Rooh*, (M), (P), good behaviour, purity, (A), (H), soul, spirit, essence, ★★★

Ruha, *Ru-hah*, (F), (S), grown, ascended, ★★★

Ruhaan, *Ru-hahn*, (M), (S), spiritual, ★★★

Ruhaani, *Ru-hahn-ee*, (F), (S), spiritual, (A), spiritual, holy, ★★★

Ruhi, *Roo-hee*, (F), (S), ascending, essence, soul, (A), spiritual, beloved, ★★★

Ruhika, *Ru-hihk-ah*, (F), (S), ascending, desire, ★★★

Rukh, *Rukh*, (M), (P), face, point, crown, ★★

Rukmat, *Ru-kmuht*, (M), (S), brilliant, another name for Agni, ★★

Rukmin, *Ru-kmihn*, (M), (S), wearing gold, ★★★

Rukmini, *Ru-kmihn-ee*, (F), (S), consort of Krishna, an incarnation of Lakshmi, ★★★

Ruma, *Ru-mah*, (F), (S), hymn, salty, ★★★

Rup, *Roop*, (M), (S), shape, beauty, ★★★

Rupa, *Roop-ah*, (F), (S), shaped, the earth, silver, ★★★

Rupali, *Roop-ahl-ee*, (F), (S), beautiful, shapely, ★★★

Rupik, *Roop-ihk*, (M), (S), shapely, gold or silver coin, ★★★

Rupika, *Roop-ihk-ah*, (F), (S), shapely, gold or silver coin, ★★★

Rushabh, *Rush-uhbh*, (M), (S), bull, excellent, a musical note, ★★

Rusham, *Ru-shuhm*, (M), (S), calm, ★★★

Rushama, *Ru-shuhm-ah*, (F), (S), calm, ★★★

Rushat, *Ru-shuht*, (M), (S), brilliant, white, ★★

Rushati, *Ru-shuht-ee*, (F), (S), fair skinned, ★★

Rushil, *Rush-ihl*, (M), (S), charming, polite, aimable, ★★★

Rustam, *Rust-uhm*, (M), (P), (O) – Urdu, originating from steel, strong, large, tall, well-built, ★★

Ruvan, *Ruv-ahn*, (M), (O) – Pahlavi, soul, ★★★

Ruwa, *Ruw-ah*, (F), (A), beautiful countenance, comely, prettiness, ★★

Ryan, *Ruhy-uhn*, (M), (O) – Celtic, royal, descended from a little king, ★★★

S

Saachar, *Sahch-ahr*, (M), (S), appropriate, well-mannered, ★★★

Saachi, *Sahch-ee*, (M), (S), following, companion, another name for Agni, ★★★

Saadar, *Sahd-uhr*, (M), (S), attached, respectful, thoughtful, ★★

Saadhaka, *Sahd-uhk-ah*, (F), (S), proficient, magical, another name for Durga, ★★

Saadhan, *Sahdh-uhn*, (M), (S), work, achievement, worship, ★★

Saadhana, *Sahdh-uhn-ah*, (F), (S), work, achievement, worship, ★★

Saadhik, *Sahd-ihk*, (M), (S), pious, proficient, ★★

Saadhika, *Sahd-ihk-ah*, (F), (S), pious, proficient, another name for Durga, ★★

Sadhil, *Sahdh-ihl*, (M), (S), perfect, leader, ruler, ★★

Saadhin, *Sahdh-ihn*, (M), (S), achievement, work, ★★

Saadhav, *Sahdh-uhv*, (M), (S), simple, loyal, decent, worthy, chaste, devout, right, noble, peaceful, ★★

Saadhvi, *Sahdh-vee*, (F), (S), simple, loyal, decent, worthy, chaste, devout, right, noble, peaceful, ★★

Saadhya, *Sahdh-yah*, (F), (S), feasible, to be accomplished, ascetic, seeking salvation, ★★

Saadhya, *Sahdh-yuh*, (M), (S), feasible, to be accomplished, ascetic, seeking salvation, ★★

Saagar, *Sahg-uhr*, (M), (S), ocean, ★★★

Saagarik, *Sahg-uhr-ihk*, (M), (S), belonging to the ocean, ★★

Saagarika, *Sahg-uhr-ihk-ah*, (F), (S), wave, born in the ocean, ★★

Saagnik, *Sahg-nihk*, (M), (S), fiery, passionate, married, ★★

Saagnika, *Sahg-nihk-ah*, (F), (S), fiery, passionate, married, ★★

Saahas, *Sah-huhs*, (M), (S), valour, ★★★

Saahasya, *Sah-huhs-yuh*, (M), (S), powerful, ★★

Saahat, *Sah-huht*, (M), (S), powerful, ★★

Saahil, Sah-hihl, (M), (P), (O) – Urdu, shore, bank, ★★★

Saahib, Sah-hihb, (M), (A), master, gentleman, ★★★

Saahiba, Sah-hihb-ah, (F), (A), lady, wife, friend, ★★★

Saahir, Sah-hihr, (M), (A), alert, nocturnal, ★★★

Saahira, Sah-hihr-ah, (F), (A), alert, nocturnal, ★★★

Saakar, *Sahk-ahr*, (M), (S), shapely, concrete, formal, attractive, ★★★

Saakash, *Sahk-ahsh*, (M), (S), one with a light shone upon him, ★★★

Saaket, *Sahk-aet*, (M), (S), city, home, another name for Ayodhya, ★★

Saaksh, *Sahksh*, (M), (S), witness, with eyes, ★★★

Saakshi, *Sahk-shee*, (F), (S), witness, evidence, ★★★

Saam, *Sahm*, (M), (S), a Vedic text, ★★★

Saaman, *Sahm-uhn*, (M), (S), soothing, purifying, hymn, plentiful, prosperous, universal, ★★★

Saamant, *Sahm-uhnt*, (M), (S), bordering, leader, ★★

Saamar, *Sahm-uhr*, (M), (S), accompanied by the eternal gods, ★★★

Saamiya, *Sahm-ee-yah*, (F), (A), exalted, praised, ★★★

Saamod, *Sahm-oad*, (M), (S), happy, fragrant, ★★

Saanal, *Sahn-uhl*, (M), (S), fiery, energetic, powerful, ★★★

Saanik, *Sahn-ihk*, (M), (S), melodious, ★★★

Saanika, *Sahn-ihk-ah*, (F), (S), melodious, flute, ★★★

Saanjya, *Sahn-jyuh*, (M), (S), unique, incomparable, ★★

Saanjali, *Sahn-juhl-ee*, (F), (S), hand clasped in prayer, ★★★

Saara, *Sahr-ah*, (F), (S), firm, precious, (P), pure, excellent, sweet smelling, (A), princess, veil, ★★★

Saaran, *Sahr-uhn*, (M), (S), causing to flow, perfume,
the autumn wind, ★★★

Saarang, *Sahr-uhng*, (M), (S), musical instrument, distinguished,
brilliance, light, jewel, gold, sandalwood, the earth, a musical
raag, another name for the love god Kaama and Shiva, ★★

Saarangi, *Sahr-uhng-ee*, (F), (S), distinguished, doe,
a musical raagini, ★★

Saaras, *Sahr-uhs*, (M), (S), the moon, ★★★

Saarik, *Sahr-ihk*, (M), (S), the Mynah bird, ★★★

Saarika, *Sahr-ihk-ah*, (F), (S), the Mynah bird, beauty, friend, another
name for Durga, ★★★

Saasha, *Sah-shah*, (F), (O) – Russian, defender of men, helper of
humankind, ★★★

Saatvik, *Saht-vihk*, (M), (S), worthy, important, pure, good, ★

Saavan, *Sahv-uhn*, (M), (S), the fifth month of the Hindu year, one
who offers a sacrifice to god, ★★★

Saavant, *Sahv-uhnt*, (M), (S), employer, ★★

Saavini, *Sahv-ihn-ee*, (F), (S), pertaining to the month of Saavan,
nectar giving, ★★★

Saavitra, *Sahv-iht-ruh*, (M), (S), of the sun, offering, fire, ★

Saavitri, *Sahv-iht-ree*, (F), (S), a ray of light, hymn, ★

Saaya, Sah-yah, (F), (H), (O) – Urdu, shelter, shade, influence,
evening, ★★★

Saayak, *Sah-yuhk*, (M), (S), weapon, ★★★

Saayan, *Sah-yuhn*, (M), (S), friend, ★★★

Saayir, *Sah-yihr*, (M), (A), voyager, ★★★

Saaz, *Sahz*, (F), (A), melody, ★★★

Saaz, *Sahz*, (M), (A), melody, ★★★

Sabah, *Suhb-ah*, (F), (P), morning breeze, (A), morning, dawn, beautiful, ★★★

Sabal, *Suhb-uhl*, (M), (S), strong, ★★★

Sabar, *Suhb-uhr*, (M), (S), milk, nectar, ★★★

Sabha, *Suhbh-ah*, (F), (A), fair, beautiful, ★★★

Sabhya, *Suhb-yuh*, (M), (S), polite, well-born, gracious, ★★

Sabina, *Suhb-een-ah*, (F), (O) – Latin, a woman of the Sabine tribe that inhabited ancient Italy, catlike, ★★★

Sabrina, *Suhb-reen-ah*, (F), (O) – Latin, Gaelic, original Welsh name of the river Severn, a princess in Celtic legend, ★★★

Sachan, *Suhch-uhn*, (M), (S), friendly, kind, ★★★

Sachet, *Suhch-aet*, (M), (S), alert, attentive, ★★

Sachil, *Suhch-ihl*, (M), (S), virtuous, respectable, ★★★

Sachin, *Suhch-ihn*, (M), (S), consciousness, caring, another name for Shiva, ★★★

Sachint, *Suhch-ihnt*, (M), (S), thoughtful, ★★★

Sachit, *Suhch-iht*, (M), (S), consciousness, wise, another name for Brahma, ★★

Sachiv, *Suhch-ihv*, (M), (S), secretary, companion, friend, adviser, ★★★

Sadar, *Suhd-uhr*, (M), (S), afraid, ★★

Sadhan, *Suhdh-uhn*, (M), (S), wealthy, ★★

Sadiv, *Suhd-ihv*, (M), (S), eternal, ★★

Safa, *Suhf-ah*, (F), (A), pure, friendship, delight, (H), pure, a page, ★★★

Safal, *Suhf-uhl*, (M), (S), fruitful, effective, (H), (O) – Urdu, successful, ★★★

Sagan, *Suhg-uhn*, (M), (S), leader, general, another name for Shiva, ★★★

Sagar, *Suhg-uhr*, (M), (S), atmosphere, air, ★★★

Sagun, *Suhg-un*, (M), (S), virtuous, ★★★

Saguna, *Suhg-un-ah*, (F), (S), virtuous, ★★★

Sah, *Suh*, (M), (S), mighty, tolerant, victorious, prevailing, enduring, ★★★

Saha, *Suh-ah*, (F), (S), tolerant, the earth, an apsara or celestial nymph, ★★★

Sahab, *Suh-hahb*, (M), (A), mercury, cloud, ★★★

Sahah, *Suh-hah*, (F), (A), perfect, complete, healthy, ★★★

Sahaj, *Suh-huhj*, (M), (S), natural, ★★★

Sahar, *Suh-huhr*, (M), (S), another name for Shiva, (A), dawn, ★★★

Saharsh, *Suh-huhrsh*, (M), (S), happy, ★★★

Sahas, *Suh-huhs*, (M), (S), laughing, happy, ★★★

Sahay, *Suh-hahy*, (M), (S), friend, helpful, another name for Shiva, ★★★

Saheli, *Suh-hael-ee*, (F), (S), friend, ★★★

Sahir, *Suh-hihr*, (M), (S), mountain, ★★★

Sahit, *Suh-hiht*, (M), (S), near, ★★

Sahita, *Suh-hiht-ah*, (F), (S), near, ★★

Sahlad, *Sae-huhl-ahd*, (M), (S), happy, ★★

Sahoj, *Suh-hoaj*, (M), (S), strong, ★★★

Sahuri, *Suh-hur-ee*, (F), (S), war, powerful, victorious, the earth, ★★★

Sahvan, *Seh-vuhn*, (M), (S), strong, important, ★★

Sajal, *Suhj-uhl*, (M), (H), clouds, containing water, tearful, ★★★

Sajala, *Suhj-uhl-ah*, (F), (H), clouds, containing water, tearful, ★★★

Sajiv, *Suh-jeev*, (M), (S), lively, alive, ★★★

Sajjan, *Suhj-juhn*, (M), (S), noble, from a good family, respectable, guard, ★★★

Sakal, *Suhk-uhl*, (M), (S), perfect, entire, universe, ★★★

Sakash, *Suh-kahsh*, (M), (S), brilliance, an enlightened soul, ★★★

Sakina, *Suhk-een-ah*, (F), (A), peace, dignity, comfort, presence of god, ★★★

Saksham, *Suhk-shuhm*, (M), (S), competent, powerful, ★★★

Salil, *Suhl-ihl*, (M), (S), water, ★★★

Salila, *Suhl-ihl-ah*, (F), (S), water, ★★★

Saloni, *Suhl-oan-ee*, (F), (H), beautiful, charming, ★★

Sam, *Suhm*, (M), (S), equal, honest, equitable, peace, smooth, ★★★

Sama, *Suhm-ah*, (F), (S), peaceful, evenness, comparable, a year, (A), sky, heavens, ★★★

Samaira, *Suhm-aer-ah*, (F), (A), (O) – Hebrew, protected by god, guardian, ★★★

Saman, *Suhm-ahn*, (M), (S), comparable, honourable, ★★★

Samant, *Suhm-uhnt*, (M), (S), near, omnipresent, ★★

Samar, *Suhm-ahr*, (M), (A), fruit, possessions, ★★★

Samar, *Suhm-uhr*, (M), (S), encounter, conflict, (A), son, fruit, wealth, ★★★

Samara, *Suhm-ahr-ah*, (F), (A), (O) – Hebrew, protected by god, guardian, Latin, elm seed, ★★★

Samara, *Suhm-uhr-ah*, (F), (S), encounter, conflict, (A), fruit, result, ★★★

Samarchit, *Suhm-uhr-chiht*, (M), (S), worshipped, loved, ★

Samarth, *Suhm-uhrth*, (M), (S), powerful, smooth, multi-talented, another name for Krishna, ★★

Samartha, *Suhm-uhrth-ah*, (F), (S), powerful, smooth, multi-talented, ★★

Samasti, *Suhm-uhst-ee*, (F), (S), achieving, the universe, ★★

Samat, *Suhm-uht*, (M), (S), justice, peace, kindness, ★★

Samata, *Suhm-uht-ah*, (F), (S), justice, peace, kindness, ★★

Samay, *Suhm-ehy*, (M), (S), time, rule, oath, code, direction, season, understanding, ★★

Sambhav, *Suhm-bhuhv*, (M), (S), possible, practicable, meeting, creation, ★★

Sambhavan, *Suhm-bhahv-uhn*, (M), (S), respect, honour, possibility, fitness, affection, ★

Sambhavna, *Suhm-bhahv-uhn-ah*, (F), (S), togetherness, honour, esteem, possibility, ★

Sambit, *Suhm-biht*, (M), (S), consciousness, ★★

Sambita, *Suhm-biht-ah*, (F), (S), consciousness, ★★

Sambodh, *Suhm-boadh*, (M), (S), consciousness, ★★

Samedh, *Suhm-aedh*, (M), (S), strong, ★★

Samesh, *Suhm-aesh*, (M), (S), lord of equality, god-like, ★★★

Samhit, *Suhm-hiht*, (M), (S), a Vedic composition, ★★

Samhita, *Suhm-hiht-ah*, (F), (S), a Vedic composition, ★★

Samich, *Suhm-eech*, (M), (S), ocean, ★★★

Samichi, *Suhm-eech-ee*, (F), (S), praise, doe, an apsara or celestial nymph, ★★

Samih, *Suhm-eeh*, (M), (S), desire, ★★★

Samiha, *Suhm-eeh-ah*, (F), (S), desire, ★★★

Samin, *Suhm-ihn*, (M), (S), pacifist, peaceful, consoler, ★★★

Samina, *Suhm-ihn-ah*, (F), (S), pacifist, peaceful, ★★★

Samina, Suhm–een-ah, (F), (A), healthy, plump, ★★★

Samir, *Suhm-eer*, (M), (S), breeze, air, creator, another name for Shiva, (A), companion, friend of the night, era, ★★★

Samira, *Suhm-eer-ah*, (F), (S), breeze, air, (A), companion, friend of
the night, ★★★

Samish, *Suhm-ihsh*, (M), (S), javelin, ★★★

Samit, *Suhm-iht*, (M), (S), collected, ★★

Samita, *Suhm-iht-ah*, (F), (S), collected, ★★

Sammad, *Suhm-muhd*, (M), (S), happiness, excitement, ★★

Sammat, *Suhm-muht*, (M), (S), agreed, respected, ★★

Sammit, *Suhm-miht*, (M), (S), balanced, ★★

Sammita, *Suhm-miht-ah*, (F), (S), balanced, ★★

Sammod, *Suhm-moad*, (M), (S), perfume, ★★

Sammud, *Suhm-mud*, (M), (S), delight, ★★

Sampad, *Suhm-puhd*, (F), (S), perfection, achievement, destiny,
blessing, ★★

Sampada, *Suhm-puhd-ah*, (F), (S), perfection, achievement, destiny,
blessing, ★★

Sampar, *Suhm-pahr*, (M), (S), accomplished, ★★★

Sampat, *Suhm-puht*, (M), (S), fortune, success, welfare, ★★

Sampati, *Suhm-puht-ee*, (F), (S), fortune, success, welfare, ★★

Samra, *Suhm-rah*, (F), (A), light, tanned, (O) – Hebrew, guardian, ★★★

Samrat, *Suhm-rahtt*, (M), (S), ruler, universal, ★★★

Samridh, *Suhm-rihdh*, (M), (S), accomplished, prosperous, perfect, ★

Samridhi, *Suhm-rihdh-ee*, (F), (S), perfection, wealth,
accomplishment, welfare, ★

Samrudh, *Suhm-rudh*, (M), (S), accomplished, perfect, prosperous, ★

Samud, *Suhm-ud*, (M), (S), happy, ★★

Samvar, *Suhm-vuhr*, (M), (S), content, best, ★★★

San, *Suhn*, (M), (S), long-lived, old, ★★★

Sana, *Suhn-ah*, (F), (A), lustre, majesty, silk, ★★★

Sanam, *Suhn-uhm*, (F), (S), favour, benevolence, (A), beloved, mistress, image, ★★★

Sanan, *Suhn-uhn*, (M), (S), acquiring, ★★★

Sanas, *Suhn-uhs*, (M), (S), cheerful, ★★★

Sanat, *Suhn-uht*, (M), (S), immortal, another name for Brahma, ★★

Sanatan, *Suhn-aht-uhn*, (M), (S), immortal, constant, ancient, another name for Brahma, Vishnu and Shiva, ★★

Sanatani, *Suhn-aht-uhn-ee*, (F), (S), immortal, constant, ancient, another name for Durga, Lakshmi and Saraswati, ★★

Sanaya, *Suhn-ah-yah*, (F), (A), eminent, ★★★

Sanchal, *Suhn-chuhl*, (F), (S), movement, water, ★★★

Sanchal, *Suhn-chuhl*, (M), (S), movement, water, ★★★

Sanchala, *Suhn-chuhl-ah*, (F), (S), movement, water, ★★★

Sanchali, *Suhn-chuhl-ee*, (F), (S), movement, ★★★

Sanchay, *Suhn-chaey*, (M), (S), mass, riches, collection, ★★★

Sanchaya, *Suhn-chaey-ah*, (F), (S), mass, riches, collection, ★★

Sanchit, *Suhn-chiht*, (M), (S), collected, gathered, ★★

Sanchita, *Suhn-chiht-ah*, (F), (S), collected, gathered, ★★

Sandhya, *Suhn-dhyah*, (F), (S), dusk, union, thought, ★★

Sandip, *Suhn-deep*, (M), (S), brilliant, ablaze, ★★

Sangat, *Suhn-guht*, (M), (S), union, appropriate, constant, ★★

Sangav, *Suhn-guhv*, (M), (S), afternoon, ★★

Sangit, *Suhn-geet*, (M), (S), music, ★★

Sangita, *Suhn-geet-ah*, (F), (S), musical, ★★

Sani, *Suhn-ee*, (F), (S), gift, reward, a portion of the sky, (O) – English, same pronunciation as sunny meaning bright, ★★★

Sani, *Suhn-ee*, (M), (S), gift, reward, a quarter of the sky, (O) – English, same pronunciation as sunny meaning bright ★★★

Sanil, *Suhn-ihl*, (M), (S), gifted, rewarded, ★★★

Sanj, *Suhnj*, (M), (S), creator, another name for Brahma
and Shiva, ★★★

Sanjan, *Suhn-juhn*, (M), (S), creator, ★★★

Sanjana, *Suhn-juhn-ah*, (F), (S), creator, ★★★

Sanjar, *Suhn-juhr*, (M), (O) – Turkish, hawk, ruler, ★★★

Sanjay, *Suhn-jehy*, (M), (S), victorious, ★★

Sanjit, *Suhn-jiht*, (M), (S), victorious, ★★

Sanjiti, *Suhn-jiht-ee*, (F), (S), victory, ★★

Sanjiv, *Suhn-jeev*, (M), (S), alive, existing, ★★★

Sankalp, *Suhnk-uhlp*, (M), (S), conviction, idea, determination, ★★

Sankalpa, *Suhnk-uhlp-ah*, (F), (S), conviction, determination, ★★

Sanket, *Suhn-kaet*, (M), (S), indication, sign, stipulation,
agreement, ★★

Sankil, *Suhn-kihl*, (M), (S), fiery, torch, ★★★

Sankila, *Suhn-kihl-ah*, (F), (S), fiery, torch, ★★★

Sankram, *Suhn-kruhm*, (M), (S), change, progress, bridge, a
shooting star, ★★★

Sankul, *Suhn-kul*, (M), (S), fiery, torch, ★★★

Sankula, *Suhn-kul-ah*, (F), (S), fiery, torch, ★★★

Sanmati, *Suhn-muht-ee*, (F), (S), nobleminded, ★★

Sanoj, *Suhn-oaj*, (M), (S), immortal, ★★★

Sanoja, *Suhn-oaj-ah*, (F), (S), immortal, ★★★

Sanoli, *Suhn-oal-ee*, (F), (S), introspective, ★★★

Sanraj, *Suhn-rahj*, (M), (S), supreme rule, ruler, ★★★

Sanrakt, *Suhn-ruhkt*, (M), (S), red, pleasant, ★★

Sanrakta, *Suhn-ruhk-tah*, (F), (S), red, pleasant, beautiful, ★★

Sansar, *Suhn-sahr*, (M), (S), the world, ★★★

Sanskar, *Suhns-kahr*, (M), (S), culture, consecration, purity, purification, sacrament, impressions on the mind, ★★★

Sanskriti, *Suhns-kriht-ee*, (F), (S), culture, refinement, purification, civilisation, perfection, determination, dedication, ★

Sanskriti, *Suhns-kriht-ee*, (M), (S), culture, refinement, purification, civilisation, perfection, determination, dedication, another name for Krishna, ★

Sant, *Suhnt*, (M), (S), calm, saint, ★★

Santap, *Suhn-tahp*, (M), (S), heat, another name for Agni, ★★

Santosh, *Suhn-toash*, (M), (S), satisfaction, ★★

Santushti, *Suhn-tush-ttee*, (F), (S), satisfaction, ★

Sanyam, *Suhn-yuhm*, (M), (S), effort, restraint, ★★★

Sanyukt, *Suhn-yukt*, (M), (S), connected, bonded, united, ★

Sanyukta, *Suhn-yukt-ah*, (F), (S), connected, bonded, united, ★

Sapan, *Suhp-uhn*, (M), (S), dream, ★★★

Sapna, *Suhp-nah*, (F), (S), dream, ★★★

Sarab, *Suhr-ahb*, (M), (P), illusion, ★★★

Saraj, *Suhr-uhj*, (M), (S), born in water, lotus, ★★★

Saral, *Suhr-uhl*, (M), (S), simple, honest, ★★★

Saran, *Suhr-uhn*, (M), (S), running, (P), lily, yard of a sail, ★★★

Saransh, *Suhr-ahnsh*, (M), (S), summary, precise, result, ★★★

Sarat, *Suhr-uht*, (M), (S), autumn, ★

Sarik, *Suhr-ihk*, (M), (S), precious, ★★★

Sarika, *Suhr-ihk-ah*, (F), (S), precious, pearl necklace, the sky, ★★★

Saril, *Suhr-ihl*, (M), (S), water, ★★★

Sarin, *Suhr-een*, (M), (S), helpful, ★★★

Sarina, *Suhr-een-ah*, (F), (S), helpful, ★★★

Sarish, *Suhr-ihsh*, (M), (S), equal, (O) – Urdu, morning, ★★★

Sarit, *Suhr-iht*, (M), (S), stream, river, ★★

Sarita, *Suhr-iht-ah*, (F), (S), stream, river, ★★

Saroj, *Suhr-oaj*, (M), (S), born in lakes, lotus, ★★★

Sarosh, *Suhr-oash*, (M), (P), hearing, inspiration, auspicious
    messenger, ★★★

Saruh, *Suhr-u-h*, (M), (S), successful, wealthy, ★★★

Sashang, *Suhsh-ahng*, associated, connected, ★★

Sashangi, *Suhsh-ahn-gee*, associated, connected, ★★

Sarv, *Suhrv*, (M), (S), perfect, complete, another name for Krishna
    and Shiva, ★★★

Sarva, *Suhr-vah*, (F), (S), perfect, complete, ★★★

Sarvag, *Suhr-vuhg*, (M), (S), soul, omnipresent, another name for
    Shiva, ★★★

Sarvak, *Suhr-vuhk*, (M), (S), complete, universal, ★★★

Sarvaka, *Suhr-vuhk-ah*, (F), (S), complete, universal, ★★★

Sarvika, *Suhr-vihk-ah*, (F), (S), complete, universal, ★★★

Sasang, *Suhs-uhng*, (M), (S), attached, ★★★

Sasmit, *Suhs-miht*, (M), (S), smiling, cheerful, ★★

Sasmita, *Suhs-miht-ah*, (F), (S), smiling, cheerful, ★★

Sat, *Suht*, (M), (S), truth, essence, worthy, honest, handsome, strength,
    enduring, existing, real, learned, a sage, ★★

Satkar, *Suht-kahr*, (M), (S), respect, worthy, ★★

Satvi, *Suht-vee*, (F), (S), real, ★★

Satvik, *Suht-vihk*, (M), (S), virtuous, real, ★★

Satya, *Suht-yah*, (F), (S), truthful, real, another name for Durga
    and Sita, ★★

Satya, *Suht-yuh*, (M), (S), true, real, worthy, another name for Vishnu
    and Krishna, ★★

Satyaj, *Suht-yuhj*, (M), (S), true, honest, ★★

Satyak, *Suht-yuhk*, (M), (S), honest, ★★

Satyam, *Suht-yuhm*, (M), (S), the truth, honest, worthy, ★★

Saubal, *Sohb-uhl*, (M), (S), powerful, ★★

Saubhagya, *Sohb-ahg-yah*, (F), (S), welfare, fortune, beauty, ★

Saubhagya, *Sohb-ahg-yuh*, (M), (S), welfare, fortune, attractiveness, ★

Saugat, *Soh-guht*, (M), (S), enlightened, a Buddhist, ★

Saumya, *Soh-myah*, (F), (S), linked to the moon, gentle, calm, charming, beautiful, auspicious, jasmine, a pearl, another name for Durga, ★★

Saumya, *Soh-myuh*, (M), (S), linked to the moon, gentle, calm, charming, handsome, auspicious, brilliant, ★★

Saur, *Sohr*, (M), (S), divine, another name for the planet Saturn, ★★

Saurabh, *Sohr-uhbh*, (M), (S), fragrant, saffron, aroma, ★★

Saurav, *Sohr-uhv*, (M), (S), melodious, ★★

Saurik, *Sohr-ihk*, (M), (S), divine, another name for the planet Saturn, ★★

Savir, *Suhv-eer*, (M), (S), leader, a general, ★★★

Savit, *Suhv-iht*, (M), (S), the sun, ★★

Savita, *Suhv-iht-ah*, (F), (S), the sun, ★★

Savya, *Suhv-yuh*, (M), (S), southern, another name for Vishnu, ★★

Savya, *Suhv-yah*, (F), (S), southern, ★★★

Sayali, *Suh-yahl-ee*, (F), (O) – Marathi, flower, ★★★

Sayam, *Suh-yuhm*, (M), (H), afternoon, early evening, ★★★

Sayyal, *Suhy-yahl*, (M), (A), fluid, precious, perfect, fish, ★★★

Sayyar, *Suhy-yahr*, (M), (A), voyager, ★★★

Sera, *Sihr-ah*, (F), (O) – Hebrew, fiery, ★★★

Serena, *Sehr-een-ah*, (F), (O) – Latin, clear, bright, serene, ★★★

Seva, *Saev-ah*, (F), (S), prayer, effort, devotion, ★★★

Sevit, *Saev-iht*, (M), (S), cherished, ★★

Sevita, *Saev-iht-ah*, (F), (S), cherished, ★★

Seyan, *Seh-yuhn*, (M), (S), achiever, ★★

Shaahak, *Shah-huhk*, (M), (O) – Pahlavi, prince, ★★★

Shaahid, *Shah-hihd*, (M), (A), martyr, witness, another name for god, (P), handsome, beloved, ★★

Shaak, *Shahk*, (M), (S), might, help, vegetation, ★★★

Shaaka, *Shahk-ah*, (F), (S), might, help, ★★★

Shaakin, *Shahk-ihn*, (M), (S), helpful, mighty, god of herbs, ★★★

Shaakini, *Shahk-ihn-ee*, (M), (S), helpful, mighty, goddess of herbs, another name for Paarvati, ★★★

Shaakir, *Shah-kihr*, (M), (A), grateful, another name for god, ★★★

Shaalin, *Shah-lihn*, (M), (S), homeowner, praiseworthy, ★★★

Shaalina, *Shah-lihn-ah*, (F), (S), polite, ★★★

Shaalini, *Shah-lihn-ee*, (F), (S), shy, humble, stable, homely, ★★★

Shaam, *Shahm*, (M), (S), calm, (P), master, supper, ★★★

Shaamak, *Shahm-uhk*, (M), (O) – Pahlavi, drop, ★★★

Shaamani, *Shahm-uhn-ee*, (F), (S), calm, peace, ★★★

Shaamik, *Shahm-ihk*, (M), (O) – Pahlavi, drop, ★★★

Shaan, *Shahn*, (M), (A), grandeur, dignity, power, glory, respect, (P), honey, science, mystery, ★★★

Shaant, *Shahnt*, (M), (S), calm, friendly, ★★

Shaanta, *Shahnt-ah*, (F), (S), calm, ★★

Shaantanu, *Shahn-tuhn-u*, (M), (S), wholesome, a king of the Lunar dynasty in the Mahabharata, ★

Shaanti, *Shahnt-ee*, (F), (S), peace, ★★

Shaantiv, *Shahnt-ihv*, (M), (S), peaceful, ★★

Shaantiva, *Shahnt-ihv-ah*, (F), (S), peaceful, friendly, benevolent, a deity, ★★

Shaarav, *Shah-ruhv*, (M), (S), innocent, pure, ★★★

Shaaravi, *Shah-ruhv-ee*, (F), (S), innocence, purity, ★★★

Shaarini, *Shahr-ihn-ee*, (F), (S), the earth, ★★★

Shaast, *Shahst*, (M), (S), ruler, one who commands, ★★

Shaasti, *Shahs-tee*, (F), (S), command, royal authority, hymn, ★★

Shaayar, Shah-yuhr, (M), (A), (O) – Urdu, poet, knowledgeable, ★★

Shaayara, Shah-yuhr-ah, (F), (A), (O) – Urdu, poetess, ★★

Shaba, *Shuhb-ah*, (F), (A), image, young, ★★★

Shabana, *Shuhb-ahn-ah*, (F), (A), nocturnal, ★★★

Shabar, *Shuhb-uhr*, (M), (S), distinguished, ★★★

Shabara, *Shuhb-uhr-ah*, (F), (S), distinguished, marked, ★★★

Shabast, *Shuhb-uhst*, (M), (S), armoured, protected, ★★

Shabnam, *Shuhb-nuhm*, (F), (P), dew, ★★★

Shachi, *Shuhch-ee*, (F), (S), power, agility, help, kindness, talent, elegance, ★★★

Shachika, *Shuhch-ihk-ah*, (F), (S), kind, agile, elegant, talented, ★★★

Shagun, *Shuhg-un*, (M), (S), auspicious, ★★★

Shahnaz, *Sheh-nahz*, (F), (A), glory of a king, bride, ★★

Shail, *Shael*, (M), (S), rocky, mountain, ★★

Shaila, *Shael-ah*, (F), (S), living in the mountains, ★★

Shailaj, *Shael-uhj*, (M), (S), daughter of the mountains, ★★

Shailaja, *Shael-uhj-ah*, (F), (S), daughter of the mountains, wife of Shiva, ★★

Shaili, *Shael-ee*, (F), (S), carved in rock, face, habit, ★★

Shaiv, *Shaev*, (M), (S), holy, a sect worshipping Shiva, ★★

Shaivi, *Shaev-ee*, (F), (S), wealth, auspiciousness, ★★

Shaivya, *Shaev-yuh*, (M), (S), auspicious, wealthy, the cult of
Shiva, ★★

Shakira, *Shuhk-eer-ah*, (F), (A), grateful, ★★★

Shakt, *Shuhkt*, (M), (S), able, ★★

Shakti, *Shuhk-tee*, (F), (S), power, vigour, ability, the female
energy of a god, another name for Lakshmi, Saraswati,
Durga and Kaali, ★★

Shakti, *Shuhk-tee*, (M), (S), power, aid, sword, gift, ★★

Shal, *Shuhl*, (M), (S), weapon, spear, ★★★

Sham, *Shuhm*, (M), (S), peace, calm, ★★★

Shama, *Shuhm-ah*, (F), (S), peaceful, lamp, an apsara or celestial
nymph, (P), lamp, ★★★

Shamak, *Shuhm-uhk*, (M), (S), peaceful, ★★★

Shamani, *Shuhm-uhn-ee*, (F), (S), calming, night, ★★★

Shamas, *Shuhm-uhs*, (M), (A), sunny, ★★★

Shamath, *Shuhm-uhth*, (M), (S), peaceful, calm, ★★

Shamen, *Shuhm-aen*, (M), (S), happy, auspicious, security, wealthy, ★★

Shami, *Shuhm-ee*, (M), (S), work, ★★★

Shamik, *Shuhm-eek*, (M), (S), peaceful, restrained, ★★★

Shamika, *Shuhm-eek-ah*, (F), (S), peaceful, ★★★

Shamin, *Shuhm-ihn*, (M), (S), peaceful, restrained, ★★★

Shamira, *Shuhm-ihr-ah*, (F), (S), a chameli flower, ★★★

Shamit, *Shuhm-iht*, (M), (S), peaceful, calmed, prepared, ★★

Shamita, *Shuhm-iht-ah*, (F), (S), peaceful, calmed, prepared, ★★

Shammad, *Shuhm-muhd*, (M), (S), one who has conquered
his ego, ★★

Shampak, *Shuhm-puhk*, (M), (S), brilliant, ★★★

Shamvat, *Shuhm-vuht*, (M), (S), wealthy, auspicious, ★★

Shani, *Shuhn-ee*, (M), (S), slow, Saturn, ★★★

Shania, *Shuhn-ai-yah*, (F), (O) – Native American, on my way, Yiddish, beautiful, ★★★

Shankan, *Shuhnk-uhn*, (M), (S), wonderous, awe-inspiring, ★★★

Shankana, *Shuhnk-uhn-ah*, (F), (S), wonderous, awe-inspiring, ★★★

Shankar, *Shuhnk-uhr*, (M), (S), auspicious, another name for Shiva, ★★★

Shankara, *Shuhnk-uhr-ah*, (F), (S), auspicious, a musical raag, ★★★

Shankh, *Shuhnkh*, (M), (S), auspicious, conch shell, a number equivalent to 10 billion crores, ★★

Shankha, *Shuhn-khah*, (F), (S), flute, ★★

Shansita, *Shuhn-siht-ah*, (F), (S), desired, celebrated, ★★

Shanyu, *Shuhn-yu*, (M), (S), kind, lucky, happy, ★★★

Shar, *Shuhr*, (M), (S), arrow, ★★★

Sharad, *Shuhr-uhd*, (M), (S), autumn, ★

Sharaf, *Shuhr-uhf*, (M), (A), honour, dignity, nobility, (O) – Hebrew, faithful, 'God is my judge', ★★★

Sharan, *Shuhr-uhn*, (M), (S), shelter, ★★★

Sharat, *Shuhr-uht*, (M), (S), autumn, breeze, cloud, ★★

Sharaya, *Shehr-ai-yah*, (F), (O) – Hebrew, princess, singer, Greek, delight, ★★★

Sharif, *Shuhr-eef*, (M), (H), (O) – Urdu, gentleman, noble, virtuous, pure, holy, ★★★

Sharifa, *Shuhr-eef-ah*, (F), (H), (O) – Urdu, lady, noble, virtuous, pure, holy, ★★★

Sharman, *Shuhr-muhn*, (M), (S), shelter, happiness, ★★★

Sharmin, *Shuhr-mihn*, (M), (S), auspicious, fortunate, happy, ★★★

2

3

Sharv, *Shuhrv*, (M), (S), killing with an arrow, another name for
   Shiva and Vishnu, ★★★

Sharva, *Shuhr-vah*, (F), (S), consort of Shiva, ★★★

Shashaank, *Shuhsh-ahnk*, (M), (S), the moon, ★★

Shashi, *Shuhsh-ee*, (F), (S), the moon, an apsara or celestial
   goddess, ★★★

Shashi, *Shuhsh-ee*, (M), (S), the moon, ★★★

Shasti, *Shuhs-tee*, (F), (S), hymn, another name for Durga, ★★

Shauchin, *Shoh-chihn*, (M), (S), pure, ★★

Shaunak, *Shohn-uhk*, (M), (S), wise, a famous sage and teacher, ★★★

Shaurav, *Shohr-uhv*, (M), (S), of the brave, ★★

Shaurya, *Shohr-yuh*, (M), (S), bravery, power, heroism, ★

Shavas, *Shuhv-uhs*, (M), (S), bravery, power, heroism, ★★★

Sheel, *Sheel*, (M), (S), character, worth, custom, ★★★

Sheela, *Sheel-ah*, (F), (S), calm, with a good character, ★★★

Sheelin, *Sheel-ihn*, (M), (S), moral, worthy, ★★★

Sheena, *Sheen-ah*, (F), (O) – Hebrew, Gaelic, god's gracious gift, ★★★

Sheerak, *Sheer-uhk*, (M), (S), plough, the sun, ★★★

Sheerin, *Sheer-ihn*, (M), (S), ploughman, grass, ★★★

Sheetal, *Sheet-uhl*, (F), (S), cool, calm, gentle, the wind, the moon, ★★

Sheetal, *Sheet-uhl*, (M), (S), cool, calm, gentle, the wind,
   the moon, ★★

Shefali, *Shaef-ahl-ee*, (F), (S), perfumed, the jasmine tree, ★★

Shekhar, *Shaekh-uhr*, (M), (S), pinnacle, ultimate, best, crown
   of the head, ★★

Shehnaz, *Sheh-nahz*, (F), (A), glory of a king, bride, ★★

Shephar, *Shaef-uhr*, (M), (S), delightful, ★★★

Shev, *Shaev*, (M), (S), fortune, joy, homage, ★★★

Sheva, *Shaev-ah*, (F), (S), fortune, joy, homage, ★★★

Shevar, *Shaev-ahr*, (M), (S), treasury, ★★★

Shikh, *Shihkh*, (M), (S), peak, ★★

Shikha, *Shihkh-ah*, (F), (S), peak, flame, light, ★★

Shikhar, *Shihk-huhr*, (M), (S), peak, ultimate, ★★

Shilin, *Shihl-ihn*, (M), (S), rocky, ★★★

Shilish, *Shihl-eesh*, (M), (S), lord of the mountain, determined, ★★★

Shilp, *Shihlp*, (M), (S), shapely, multi-coloured, ★★★

Shilpa, *Shihl-pah*, (F), (S), shapely, multi-coloured, ★★★

Shilpi, *Shihl-pee*, (F), (S), artist, ★★★

Shilpika, *Shihl-pihk-ah*, (F), (S), artist, ★★★

Shipra, *Shihp-rah*, (F), (S), cheeks, jaw, the nose, a holy river, ★★★

Shiprak, *Shihp-ruhk*, (M), (S), full cheeked, ★★★

Shirina, *Shihr-ihn-ah*, (F), (S), night, ★★★

Shishay, *Shihsh-uhy*, (M), (S), generous, ★★

Shishir, *Shihsh-ihr*, (M), (S), cold, winter, frost, ★★★

Shishul, *Shihsh-ul*, (M), (S), infant, child, ★★★

Shiv, *Shihv*, (M), (S), all encompassing, auspicious, lovely, welfare, water, joy, merciful, saving, friendly, beloved, divine, the third god of the Hindu trinity, ★★★

Shiva, *Shihv-ah*, (F), (S), auspicious, all-encompassing, lovely, welfare, water, joy, graceful, salvation, the energy of Shiva in the form of his wife Paarvati, ★★★

Shivali, *Shihv-ahl-ee*, (F), (S), beloved of Shiva, another name for Paarvati, ★★★

Shivam, *Shihv-uhm*, (M), (S), of Shiva, fortunate, elegant, auspicious, ★★★

Shivangi, *Shihv-ahng-ee*, (F), (S), beautiful, ★★

Shivani, *Shihv-ahn-ee*, (F), (S), another name for Paarvati, ★★★

Shivank, *Shihv-ahnk*, (M), (S), the mark of Shiva, ★★★

Shivanshi, *Shihv-ahn-shee*, (F), (S), a part of Shiva, ★★

Shive, *Shihv-aeh*, (M), (S), Shiva, the third god of the
Hindu trinity, ★★★

Shivika, *Shihv-ihk-ah*, (F), (S), palanquin, ★★★

Shlok, *Shloak*, (M), (S), Hindu mantra or verse of praise, ★★★

Shloka, *Shloaka*, (F), (S), Hindu mantra or verse of praise, ★★★

Shobha, *Shoabh-ah*, (F), (S), brilliance, beauty, elegance, ★★

Shobhak, *Shoabh-uhk*, (M), (S), brilliant, handsome, ★★

Shobhan, *Shoabh-uhn*, (M), (S), excellent, handsome, another name
for Shiva and Agni, ★★

Shobhana, *Shoabh-uhn-ah*, (F), (S), beautiful, turmeric, ★★

Shobhika, *Shoabh-ihk-ah*, (F), (S), brilliant, beautiful, ★★

Shobhin, *Shoabh-ihn*, (M), (S), brilliant, handsome, ★★

Shobhini, *Shoabh-ihn-ee*, (F), (S), graceful, brilliant, ★★

Shobhit, *Shoabh-iht*, (M), (S), brilliant, handsome, ★★

Shobhita, *Shoabh-iht-ah*, (F), (S), brilliant, beautiful, ★★

Shon, *Shoan*, (M), (S), fire, ★★★

Shona, *Shoan-ah*, (F), (S), heat, fiery, ★★★

Shraav, *Shrahv*, (M), (S), attentive, ★★★

Shraavan, *Shrahv-uhn*, (M), (S), monsoon season, ★★★

Shraavani, *Shrahv-uhn-ee*, (F), (S), the day of the full moon in the
month of Shraavan, ★★★

Shraddha, *Shruhdh-ah*, (F), (S), worship, confidence, fidelity, ★★

Shravya, *Shruhv-yah*, (F), (S), a musical note, worthy of being
heard, ★★

Shravya, *Shruhv-yuh*, (M), (S), a musical note, worthy of
being heard, **

Shreshth, *Shraesh-tth*, (M), (S), best, ultimate, another name
for Vishnu, *

Shreya, *Shrae-yah*, (F), (S), excellent, best, beautiful, ***

Shreyas, *Shrae-yuhs*, (M), (S), best, excellent, handsome, auspicious,
fortunate, ***

Shri, *Shree*, (F), (S), prosperity, beauty, grace, power, brilliance,
dignity, majesty, another name for Lakshmi and Saraswati, ***

Shri, *Shree*, (M), (S), sacred, auspicious, a musical raag, ***

Shrida, *Shree-dah*, (F), (S), bestowed by Lakshmi, auspicious,
bringing fortune, **

Shrika, *Shrih-kah*, (F), (S), fortune, beauty, ***

Shrila, *Shrih-lah*, (F), (S), bestowed by Lakshmi, happy, beautiful,
fortunate, wealthy, eminent, ***

Shrina, *Shree-nah*, (F), (S), night, ***

Shrinika, *Shree-nihk-ah*, (F), (S), night, ***

Shriya, *Shri-yah*, (F), (S), wealth, success, joy, ***

Shrut, *Shrut*, (M), (S), knowledge, celebrated, scriptures, **

Shruta, *Shrut-ah*, (F), (S), known, glorious, celebrated, **

Shruti, *Shrut-ee*, (F), (S), insight, knowledge of the Vedas, **

Shuban, *Shub-uhn*, (M), (S), brilliant, ***

Shubh, *Shubh*, (M), (S), brilliant, attractive, auspicious, fortunate,
wealthy, worthy, **

Shubha, *Shubh-ah*, (F), (S), brilliance, beauty, desire, **

Shubhad, *Shubh-uhd*, (M), (S), auspicious, fortunate, *

Shubhada, *Shubh-uhd-ah*, (F), (S), auspicious, fortunate, *

Shubham, *Shubh-uhm*, (M), (S), auspicious, **

Shubhika, *Shubh-ihk-ah*, (F), (S), auspicious, a garland of flowers, ★★

Shubhra, *Shubh-rah*, (F), (S), brilliant, another name for the
river Ganges, ★★

Shubhra, *Shubh-ruh*, (M), (S), attractive, brilliant, white, heaven, ★★

Shuchi, *Shuch-ee*, (F), (S), bright, holy, worthy, ★★★

Shuchika, *Shuch-ihk-ah*, (F), (S), pure, sacred, virtuous, an apsara or
celestial nymph, ★★

Shuchit, *Shuch-iht*, (M), (S), purity, ★★

Shuchita, *Shuch-iht-ah*, (F), (S), purity, ★★

Shuk, *Shuk*, (M), (S), bright, parrot, ★★★

Shukla, *Shuk-lah*, (F), (S), white, bright, pure, another name for
Saraswati, ★★★

Shukra, *Shuk-ruh*, (M), (S), bright, pure, white, another name
for Agni, ★★

Shulank, *Shool-ahnk*, (M), (S), distinguished, marked by a spear,
another name for Shiva, ★★★

Shun, *Shun*, (M), (S), auspicious, another name for Vaayu
and Indra, ★★★

Shur, *Shoor*, (M), (S), mighty, brave, lion, tiger, ★★★

Shuraj, *Shoor-uhj*, (M), (S), son of a hero, ★★★

Shuraja, *Shoor-uhj-ah*, (F), (S), daughter of a hero, ★★★

Shwet, *Shwaet*, (M), (S), white, the planet Venus, an incarnation of
Shiva and Vishnu, ★

Shweta, *Shwaet-ah*, (F), (S), white, ★

Shweti, *Shwaet-ee*, (F), (S), silver, ★

Shyaam, *Shyahm*, (M), (S), dark, cloud, a bird, a musical raag, another
name for Krishna, ★★

Shyaama, *Shyahm-ah*, (F), (S), dark, attractive, consort of Krishna, ★★

Shyaamal, *Shyahm-uhl*, (M), (S), dark, ★★

Sia, *See-yah*, (F), (S), another name for Sita, the wife of Raam, ★★

Siddh, *Sihdh*, (M), (S), accomplished, meditative, successful, holy, pure, another name for Shiva, ★★

Siddha, *Sihdh-ah*, (F), (S), accomplished, meditative, ★★

Siddhant, *Sihdh-ahnt*, (M), (S), doctrine, ★

Siddharth, *Sihdh-ahrth*, (M), (S), accomplished, Gautam Buddha as a boy, ★

Siddhesh, *Sihdh-aesh*, (M), (S), entire, perfect, ★

Siddhi, *Sihdh-ee*, (F), (S), accomplishment, fortune, success, magic, another name for Durga, ★★

Sidhra, *Sihdh-ruh*, (M), (S), perfect, successful, ★★

Siddhran, *Sihdh-rahn*, (M), (S), perfection, ★

Sidhya, *Sihdh-yuh*, (M), (S), auspicious, ★★

Sienna, *See-ehn-ah*, (F), (O) – Italian, reddish brown, a city in Italy, ★★★

Sierra, *See-ehr-ah*, (F), (O) – Spanish, mountain range, beauty of nature, ★★★

Sikat, *Sihk-uht*, (M), (S), sand, ★★

Sima, *Seem-ah*, (F), (S), limit, peak, shore, horizon, moral code, (O) – Hebrew, treasure★★★

Simant, *Seem-uhnt*, (M), (S), boundary, ★★★

Simra, *Sihm-rah*, (F), (A), princess, ★★★

Simran, *Sihm-ruhn*, (F), (S), (O) – Punjabi, meditation, god's gift, ★★★

Sinha, *Sihn-hah*, (M), (S), ruler, lion, brave, mighty, Leo, ★★★

Sinhi, *Sihn-hee*, (F), (S), lioness, ★★★

Siraj, *Sihr-ahj*, (M), (A), lamp, sun, ★★★

Sit, *Siht*, (M), (S), bright, white, pure, Venus, ★★

Sita, *Seet-ah*, (F), (S), the wife of Raam, the divine incarnation of
    Mahalakshmi, ★★

Sitara, *Siht-ahr-ah*, (F), (S), star, the pupil of the eye, meteor, perfume,
    (P), star, pupil of the eye, ★★

Siya, *See-yah*, (F), (S), the wife of Raam, the divine incarnation of
    Mahalakshmi, ★★

Smaran, *Smuhr-uhn*, (M), (S), memory, ★★

Smarani, *Smuhr-uhn-ee*, (F), (S), memory, rosary, ★★

Smera, *Smaer-ah*, (F), (S), cheerful, friendly, apparent, in bloom, ★★★

Smit, *Smiht*, (M), (S), cheerful, blooming, ★★

Smita, *Smiht-ah*, (F), (S), cheerful, blooming, ★★

Smiti, *Smiht-ee*, (F), (S), smile, cheer, ★★

Smrit, *Smriht*, (M), (S), remembered, ★★

Smrita, *Smriht-ah*, (F), (S), remembered, ★★

Smriti, *Smriht-ee*, (F), (S), memory, desire, a code of laws, ★★

Sneh, *Snaeh*, (M), (S), love, tenderness, ★★★

Sneha, *Snae-hah*, (F), (S), love, tenderness, ★★★

Soham, *Soa-huhm*, (M), (S), 'I am none other but Brahman', 'I am
    the same', the divine in every soul, ★★★

Sohan, *Soa-huhn*, (M), (H), handsome, ★★★

Sohana, *Soa-hahn-ah*, (F), (H), beautiful, graceful, ★★★

Sohani, *Soa-hahn-ee*, (F), (H), beautiful, a musical raag, ★★★

Sohel, *Soa-hael*, (F), (H), handsome, ★★

Sohela, *Soa-hael-ah*, (F), (H), beautiful, ★★

Sohin, *Soa-hihn*, (M), (S), handsome, ★★★

Sohini, *Soa-hihn-ee*, (F), (S), beautiful, ★★★

Som, *Soam*, (M), (S), nectar, ambrosia, the moon, juice of the Soma plant that grants immortality, another name for Shiva, ★★★

Soma, *Soam-ah*, (F), (S), the Soma plant, beautiful, gentle, derived from the moon, an apsara or celestial nymph, ★★★

Somak, *Soam-uhk*, (M), (S), little moon, ★★★

Somali, *Soam-ahl-ee*, (F), (S), loved by the moon, ★★★

Soman, *Soam-uhn*, (M), (S), the moon, ★★★

Somil, *Soam-ihl*, (M), (S), calm, ★★★

Somila, *Soam-ihl-ah*, (F), (S), calm, moonlike, ★★★

Sona, *Soan-ah*, (F), (H), gold, ★★★

Sonakshi, *Soan-ahk-shee*, (F), (H), golden eyed, another name for Paarvati, ★★★

Sonal, Soan-uhl, (F), (H), golden, ★★★

Sonal, Soan-uhl, (M), (H), golden, ★★★

Sonali, *Soan-ahl-ee*, (F), (H), golden, ★★★

Sonalika, *Soan-ahl-ihk-ah*, (F), (H), golden, ★★★

Sonam, *Soan-uhm*, (F), (H), golden, auspicious, beautiful, ★★★

Sonam, *Soan-uhm*, (M), (H), golden, auspicious, handsome, ★★★

Soni, *Soan-ee*, (F), (H), with golden beauty, ★★★

Sonia, *Soan-yah*, (F), (H), golden, (O) – Greek, wisdom, ★★★

Sonika, *Soan-ihk-ah*, (F), (H), golden, beautiful, ★★★

Sova, *Soav-ah*, (M), (S), one's own, ★★★

Soval, *Soav-uhl*, (M), (S), powerful, ★★★

Soven, *Soav-aen*, (M), (S), beautiful, ★★★

Sparsh, *Spuhrsh*, (M), (S), touch, ★★★

Spring, *Sprih-ng*, (F), (O) – Old English, lively, entertainer, from a stream or a spring, the spring season, ★★★

Srishti, *Srihsh-tthee*, (F), (S), creation, ★

Stav, *Stuhv*, (M), (S), praise, ★★

Stavit, *Stuhv-iht*, (M), (S), praised, ★★

Stavita, *Stuhv-iht-ah*, (F), (S), praised, ★★

Stavya, *Stuhv-yuh*, (M), (S), praiseworthy, god, ★

Stuti, *Stut-ee*, (F), (S), praise, another name for Durga, ★★

Stuvat, *Stuhv-uht*, (M), (S), pious, one who praises, ★

Subal, *Sub-ahl*, (M), (S), good, boy, divine, ★★★

Subal, *Sub-uhl*, (M), (S), powerful, another name for Shiva, ★★★

Subha, *Subh-ah*, (F), (S), fortunate, auspicious, ★★

Subhas, *Subh-ahs*, (M), (S), brilliant, ★★

Subhash, *Subh-ahsh*, (M), (S), articulate, soft–spoken★★

Subhashani, *Subh-ahsh-uhn-ee*, (F), (S), soft–spoken, articulate ★

Subodh, *Sub-oadh*, (M), (S), intelligent, ★★

Suchara, *Such-ahr-ah*, (F), (S), talented, performer, ★★★

Suchet, *Such-aet*, (M), (S), intelligent, sharp, alert, ★★

Sucheta, *Such-aet-ah*, (F), (S), intelligent, sharp, alert, ★★

Suchetan, *Such-aet-uhn*, (M), (S), conscious, alert, distinguished, ★

Suchetas, *Such-aet-uhs*, (M), (S), intelligent, kind, ★

Suchir, *Such-ihr*, (M), (S), eternity, ★★★

Suchit, *Such-iht*, (M), (S), sensible, intelligent, informed, pure, focussed, another name for Brahma, ★★

Suchita, *Such-iht-ah*, (F), (S), holy, auspicious, informed, sensible, ★★

Suchitra, *Such-iht-rah*, (F), (S), distinguished, beautiful, picture, ★★

Suchitra, *Such-iht-ruh*, (M), (S), distinguished, ★★

Sudarsh, *Sud-uhrsh*, (M), (S), apparent, handsome, ★★

Sudarshini, *Sud-uhrsh-ihn-ee*, (F), (S), beautiful, ★

Suday, *Sud-aey*, (M), (S), auspicious gift, ★★

Suddh, *Sud-dh*, (M), (S), true, pure, white, ★★

Suddha, *Sud-dhah*, (F), (S), sacred, pure, ★★

Sudesh, *Sud-aesh*, (M), (S), a beautiful country, elegant, handsome, ★★

Sudeshna, *Sud-aesh-nah*, (F), (S), well-born, ★★

Sudha, *Sudh-ah*, (F), (S), welfare, lightning, nectar, ambrosia, water, another name for the river Ganges, ★★

Sudhakar, *Sudh-ahk-uhr*, (M), (S), the moon, ★

Sudhanya, *Sudh-uhn-yuh*, (M), (S), blessed, celebrated, ★

Sudhar, *Sudh-uhr*, (M), (S), home of the good, ★★

Sudhi, *Sudh-ee*, (F), (S), sense, wisdom, ★★

Sudhir, *Sudh-eer*, (M), (S), determined, thoughtful, wise, ★★

Sudhit, *Sudh-iht*, (M), (S), benevolent, like nectar, ★★

Sudiksha, *Sud-eek-shah*, (F), (S), beautiful, offering, another name for Lakshmi, ★★

Sudip, *Sud-eep*, (M), (S), brilliant, ★★

Sudipa, *Sud-eep-ah*, (F), (S), brilliant, ★★

Sudiv, *Sud-ihv*, (M), (S), brilliant, ★★

Sugat, *Sug-uht*, (M), (S), fortunate, ★★

Sugati, *Sug-uht-ee*, (F), (S), solution, fortune, ★★

Sugeshna, *Sug-aesh-nah*, (F), (S), good singer, ★★★

Sugriv, *Sug-reev*, (M), (S), weapon, hero, swan, ★★★

Suha, *Su-hah*, (F), (S), celebration, a musical raag, ★★★

Suhas, *Su-hahs*, (M), (S), beautiful smile, ★★★

Suhasini, *Su-hahs-ihn-ee*, (F), (S), smiling beautifully, ★★★

Suhav, *Su-huhv*, (M), (S), religious, ★★★

Suhit, *Su-hiht*, (M), (S), appropriate, good, ★★

Suhita, *Su-hiht-ah*, (F), (S), appropriate, good, ★★

Suhrab, *Su-h-rahb*, (M), (P), illustrious, ★★★

Sujal, *Su-juhl*, (M), (S), lotus, ★★★

Sujan, *Su-juhn*, (M), (S), good, virtuous, respectable, kind, ★★★

Sujat, *Su-jaht*, (M), (S), well-born, handsome, ★★

Sujata, *Su-jaht-ah*, (F), (S), well-born, beautiful, ★★

Sujay, *Su-juhy*, (M), (S), victory, ★★

Sujaya, *Su-juhy-ah*, (F), (S), victory, ★★

Sujit, *Su-jiht*, (M), (S), victorious, ★★

Sukam, *Su-kahm*, (M), (S), ambitious, desired, handsome, ★★★

Sukama, *Su-kahm-ah*, (F), (S), ambitious, desired, beautiful, ★★★

Sukant, *Su-kahnt*, (M), (S), handsome, ★★

Suket, *Suk-aet*, (M), (S), kind, well-meaning, ★★

Suketu, *Suk-aet-u*, (M), (S), brilliant, another name for Vishnu, ★

Sukh, *Sukh*, (M), (S), happiness, (P), happy, joy, good, auspicious, ★★

Sukha, *Sukh-ah*, (F), (S), happiness, piety, virtue, prosperity, welfare, ★★

Sukhin, *Sukh-ihn*, (M), (S), happy, ★★

Sukirti, *Suk-eer-tee*, (F), (S), praised, hymn, ★

Sukrit, *Suk-riht*, (M), (S), devout, kind, auspicious, worthy, wise, ★

Sukrita, *Suk-riht-ah*, (F), (S), devout, worthy, ★

Sukriti, *Suk-riht-ee*, (F), (S), worth, benevolence, auspiciousness, ★

Sukul, *Suk-ul*, (M), (S), noble, ★★

Sulabh, *Su-lahbh*, (M), (S), natural, ★★

Sulabha, *Su-lahbh-ah*, (F), (S), natural, jasmine, ★★

Sulaksh, *Sul-uhksh*, (M), (S), distinguished, fortunate, ★★★

Sulakshana, *Sul-uhksh-uhn-ah*, (F), (S), distinguished, fortunate, ★★★

Sulek, *Sul-aek*, (M), (S), the sun, ★★★

Sulekha, *Sul-aekh-ah*, (M), (S), distinguished, fortunate, ★★

Sulochan, *Sul-oach-uhn*, (M), (S), with beautiful eyes, deer, ★★

Sulochana, *Sul-oach-uhn-ah*, (M), (S), with beautiful eyes, an apsara or celestial nymph, ★★

Suloma, *Sul-oam-ah*, (F), (S), with beautiful hair, a tree, ★★★

Sumaira, *Sum-aer-ah*, (F), (P), celebrated, a famous woman, ★★★

Suman, *Sum-uhn*, (F), (S), cheerful, pleasant, considerate, kind, beautiful, (P), jasmine, (A), fame, ★★★

Suman, *Sum-uhn*, (M), (S), cheerful, pleasant, considerate, handsome, (P), jasmine, (A), fame, ★★★

Sumana, *Sum-uhn-ah*, (F), (S), pleasant, beautiful, jasmine, ★★★

Sumant, *Sum-uhnt*, (M), (S), friendly, ★★

Sumantra, *Sum-uhnt-ruh*, (M), (S), good adviser, well-advised, ★

Sumat, *Sum-uht*, (M), (S), good natured, wise, ★★

Sumay, *Sum-ahy*, (M), (S), wise, ★★★

Sumaya, *Sum-ahy-ah*, (F), (S), wise, ★★★

Sumed, *Sum-aed*, (M), (S), wise, ★★

Sumeda, *Sum-aed-ah*, (F), (S), wise, ★★

Sumedh, *Sum-aedh*, (M), (S), sensible, wise, ★★

Sumedha, *Sum-aedh-ah*, (F), (S), sensible, wise, ★★

Sumeet, *Sum-eet*, (M), (S), good friend, ★★

Sumer, *Sum-aer*, (M), (S), a divine mountain, (O) – English, a region in modern day Iraq that was the home of the Sumerians, ★★★

Sumera, *Sum-aer-ah*, (F), (S), a divine mountain, ★★★

Sumeru, *Sum-aeru*, (M), (S), high, emintent, excellent, a divine mountain, another name for Shiva, ★★★

Sumira, *Sum-ihr-ah*, (F), (S), memorable, celebrated, ★★★

Sumit, *Sum-iht*, (M), (S), shapely, ★★

Sumita, *Sum-iht-ah*, (F), (S), shapely, ★★

Summer, *Suhm-muhr*, (F), (O) – English, the summer season, ★★★

Sumona, *Sum-oan-ah*, (F), (S), calm, ★★★

Sunar, *Soo-nuhr*, (M), (S), happy, ★★★

Sunay, *Sun-uhy*, (M), (S), just, well-behaved, ★★

Sunaya, *Sun-uhy-ah*, (F), (S), just, well-behaved, ★★

Sunetra, *Sun-aet-rah*, (F), (S), with beautiful eyes, ★★

Sunil, *Sun-eel*, (M), (S), blue, sapphire, ★★★

Sunishka, *Sun-ihsh-kah*, (F), (S), bejewelled, ★★★

Sunit, *Sun-eet*, (M), (S), well-mannered, sensible, ★★

Sunita, *Sun-eet-ah*, (F), (S), well-mannered, ★★

Suniti, *Sun-eet-ee*, (F), (S), morality, good behaviour, ★★

Suparn, *Sup-uhrn*, (M), (S), with beautiful leaves, with beautiful
   wings, a ray of the sun, another name for Mahavishnu, ★★

Suparna, *Sup-uhr-nah*, (F), (S), lotus, another name for Paarvati, ★★★

Supash, *Sup-ahsh*, (M), (S), another name for Ganesha, ★★★

Suposh, *Sup-oash*, (M), (S), wealthy, ★★★

Supriya, *Sup-rih-yah*, (F), (S), beautiful, loved, an apsara or
   celestial nymph, ★★★

Supun, *Sup-un*, (M), (S), auspicious, worthy, one who earns
   blessings, ★★★

Supunya, *Sup-un-yah*, (F), (S), auspicious, worthy, meritorious, one
   who earns blessings, ★★★

Sur, *Sur*, (M), (S), divine, wise, sage, the sun, ★★★

Sura, *Sur-ah*, (F), (S), wine, ★★★

Surabhi, *Sur-uhbh-ee*, (F), (S), fragrant, pleasant, brilliant, beautiful,
   famous, beloved, wise, virtuous, jasmine, the earth, ★★

Suraj, *Soo-ruhj*, (M), (S), the sun, illuminating, ★★★

Suraja, *Sur-uhj-ah*, (F), (S), born of the gods, an apsara or celestial nymph, ★★★

Suramya, *Sur-uhm-yah*, (F), (S), beautiful, gorgeous, extremely charming, ★★★

Suran, *Sur-uhn*, (M), (S), happy, cheery, ★★★

Surana, *Sur-uhn-ah*, (F), (S), happy, cheery, ★★★

Suravi, *Sur-ahv-ee*, (M), (S), sacred, the sun, ★★

Suravi, *Sur-ahv-ee*, (F), (S), sacred, the sun, ★★

Surayya, *Sur-uhy-yah*, (F), (P), prosperous, light, brilliant, ★★

Surebh, *Sur-aebh*, (M), (S), with a good voice, ★★

Surebha, *Sur-aebh-ah*, (F), (S), with a good voice, ★★

Surejya, *Sur-aej-yah*, (F), (S), sacred to the gods, Tulsi or the holy Basil, ★★

Surejya, *Sur-aej-yuh*, (F), (S), instructor of the gods, ★★

Suri, *Soor-ee*, (F), (S), consort of the sun, (P), beautiful red rose, happiness, ★★★

Suri, *Soor-ee*, (M), (S), learned, pious, the sun, another name for Krishna, ★★★

Suri, *Sur-ee*, (F), (S), goddess, ★★★

Suri, Sur-ee, (M), (S), learned, sage, ★★★

Surin, *Soor-ihn*, (M), (S), wise, learned, ★★★

Surina, *Soor-ihn-ah*, (F), (S), wise, a goddess, ★★★

Surochan, *Sur-oach-uhn*, (M), (S), amiable, brilliant, illuminating, ★★

Surochana, *Sur-oach-uhn-ah*, (F), (S), amiable, brilliant, illuminating, ★★

Suruch, *Sur-uch*, (M), (S), with refined tastes, glorious, taking great delight, ★★

Surucha, *Sur-uch-ah*, (F), (S), light, brilliant, with refined tastes, ★★

Suruchi, *Sur-uch-ee*, (F), (S), taking great delight in, with
    refined tastes, ★★

Surush, *Sur-oosh*, (M), (S), brilliant, ★★★

Surya, *Soor-yah*, (F), (S), wife of Surya, ★★

Surya, *Soor-yuh*, (M), (S), the sun, one of the original Vedic triad
    with Agni and Indra, ★★

Suryaj, *Soor-yuhj*, (M), (S), child of the sun, Saturn, ★★

Susham, *Sush-uhm*, (M), (S), extremely handsome, extremely
    smooth, ★★★

Sushant, *Sush-ahnt*, (M), (S), calm, ★★

Sushanta, *Sush-ahnt-ah*, (F), (S), calm, ★★

Sushim, *Su-sheem*, (M), (S), cold, pleasant, moonstone, ★★★

Sushir, *Sush-eer*, (M), (S), sensible, ★★★

Sushit, *Sush-iht*, (M), (S), white, brilliant, ★★

Sushil, *Sush-eel*, (M), (S), good natured, likeable, ★★★

Sushila, *Sush-eel-ah*, (F), (S), good natured, ★★★

Sushma, *Sush-mah*, (F), (S), beauty, brilliance, charm, ★★★

Sushmit, *Sush-miht*, (M), (S), with a lovely smile, ★★

Sushmita, *Sush-miht-ah*, (F), (S), with a lovely smile, ★★

Sushok, *Sush-oak*, (M), (S), brilliant, ★★★

Sushon, *Sush-oan*, (M), (S), dark red, ★★★

Suvach, *Suv-ahch*, (M), (S), laudable, melodious,
    keeper of the Som, ★★★

Suvah, *Suv-aeh*, (M), (S), patient, ★★

Suvak, *Suv-ahk*, (M), (S), soft-spoken, melodious, learned, ★★★

Suvama, *Suv-ahm-ah*, (F), (S), beautiful, ★★★

Suvan, *Suv-uhn*, (M), (S), the sun, the moon, fire, ★★★

Suvansh, *Suv-uhnsh*, (M), (S), from a good family, ★★★

Suvar, *Suv-uhr*, (M), (S), light, the sun, heaven, ★★★

Suvir, *Suv-eer*, (M), (S), hero, brave, another name for Shiva, ★★★

Suvit, *Suv-iht*, (M), (S), welfare, fortune, luck, ★★

Suviti, *Suv-iht-ee*, (F), (S), divine, knowledge, ★★

Swaaha, *Swah-ah*, (F), (S), auspicious word uttered when pouring offerings to the gods on a fire, the goddess presiding over burnt offerings, ★★★

Swaamin, *Swahm-ihn*, (M), (S), ruler, owner, another name for Vishnu and Shiva, ★★★

Swaati, *Swaht-ee*, (F), (S), star, ★★

Swajit, *Swuh-jeet*, (M), (S), victory, ★★

Swapan, *Swuhp-uhn*, (F), (S), dream, ★★

Swapna, *Swuhp-nah*, (F), (S), dream, ★★

Swapnil, *Swuhp-nihl*, (M), (S), dreamlike, ★★

Swarg, *Swuhrg*, (M), (S), heaven, paradise, ★★

Swaran, *Swuhr-uhn*, (M), (S), gold, ★★

Swarit, *Swuhr-iht*, (M), (S), a Vedic tone, ★★

Swarna, *Swuhr-nah*, (F), (S), golden, an apsara or celestial nymph, ★★

Swarnik, *Swuhr-nihk*, (M), (S), golden, ★★

Swarnika, *Swuhr-nihk-ah*, (F), (S), golden, ★★

Swarup, *Swuhr-oop*, (M), (S), pleasant, handsome, wise, ★★

Swarupa, *Swuhr-oop-ah*, (F), (S), pleasant, beautiful, wise, ★★

Swastik, *Swuhst-ihk*, (M), (S), an auspicious Hindu symbol, ★

Syon, *Syoan*, (M), (S), gentle, pleasant, auspicious, a ray of light, the sun, ★★

Syum, *Syoom*, (M), (S), a ray of light, happiness, water, ★★

Syun, *Syoon*, (M), (S), a ray of light, ★★

Syuna, *Syoon-ah*, (F), (S), a ray of light, ★★

Taahir, *Tah-hihr*, (M), (A), (O) – Urdu, holy, pure, chaste, ★★

Taahira, *Tah-hihr-ah*, (F), (A), (O) – Urdu, holy, pure, chaste, ★★

Taaj, *Tahj*, (M), (H), (O) – Urdu, crown, the Taaj Mahal, ★★

Taalank, *Tahl-uhnk*, (M), (S), auspicious, another name for Shiva, ★★

Taalika, *Tahl-ihk-ah*, (F), (S), palm, calm, nightingale, (H), key, a list, table, ★★

Taalin, *Tahl-ihn*, (M), (S), musical, another name for Shiva, ★★

Taalish, *Tahl-eesh*, (M), (S), lord of the earth, mountain, ★★

Taamas, *Tahm-uhs*, (M), (S), dark, ★★

Taamasi, *Tahm-uhs-ee*, (F), (S), night, rest, a river, another name for Durga, ★★

Taanaya, *Tahn-yah*, (F), (S), daughter, born of the body, ★★

Taania, *Tahn-yah*, (F), (S), daughter, born of the body, ★★

Taania, *Ttahn-yah*, (F), (O) – Latin, from the house of Tatius, ★★★

Taantav, *Tahn-tuhv*, (M), (S), a woven cloth, son, ★

Taara, *Tahr-ah*, (F), (S), star, the pupil of the eye, meteor, fragrance, (P), star, pupil of the eye, ★★

Taarak, *Tahr-uhk*, (M), (S), planet, star, guardian, boat, pupil of the eye, (P), helmet, ★★

Taaraka, *Tahr-uhk-ah*, (F), (S), star, meteor, pupil of the eye, palms, ★★

Taaraksh, *Tahr-ahksh*, (M), (S), star eyed, ★

Taarik, *Tahr-ihk*, (M), (S), divine, ★★

Taarika, *Tahr-ihk-ah*, (F), (S), divine, of the stars, (H), film actress, ★★

Taarini, *Tahr-ihn-ee*, (F), (S), saviour, she who frees, she who delivers from sin, another name for Durga, ★★★

Taatiana, *Ttahtt-iahn-ah*, (F), (O) – Latin, from the house of Tatius, a saint, ★★★

Taayin, *Tah-yihn*, (M), (S), guardian, ★★

Tabassum, *Tuhb-uhs-sum*, (F), (A), blossoming, smile, ★

Taksh, *Tuhksh*, (M), (S), chopping, to make from wood, ★★

Takshak, *Tuhk-shuhk*, (M), (S), carpenter, divine architect, ★★

Taksheel, Tuhk–sheel, (M), (S), with a strong character, ★★

Takshin, *Tuhk-shihn*, (M), (S), carpenter, woodcutter, ★★

Talat, *Tuhl-uht*, (M), (A), face, vision, ★★

Talav, *Tuhl-uhv*, (M), (S), musician, ★★

Talun, *Tuhl-un*, (M), (S), young, wind, ★★

Taluni, *Tuhl-un-ee*, (F), (S), young, ★★

Tama, *Tuhm-ah*, (F), (S), night, ★★

Tamanna, *Tuhm-uhn-nah*, (F), (A), (H), (O) – Urdu, ambition, desire, ★★

Tamara, *Ttuhm-ahr-ah*, (F), (O) – Hebrew, palm tree, ★★★

Tamas, *Tuhm-uhs*, (M), (S), darkness, ★★

Tamasa, *Tuhm-uhs-ah*, (F), (S), dark, ★★

Tanak, *Tuhn-uhk*, (M), (S), reward, ★★

Tanas, *Tuhn-uhs*, (M), (S), child, ★★

Tanav, *Tuhn-uhv*, (M), (S), attractive, slender, ★★

Tanavi, *Tuhn-uhv-ee*, (F), (S), attractive, slender, ★★

Tanay, *Tuhn-uhy*, (M), (S), son, ★★

Tanaya, *Tuhn-uhy-ah*, (F), (S), daughter, ★★

Tanika, *Tuhn-ihk-ah*, (F), (H), rope, ★★

Tanima, *Tuhn-ihm-ah*, (F), (S), slender, ★★

Tanish, *Tuhn-ihsh*, (M), (S), ambition, god of physique, ★★

Tanisha, *Tuhn-ihsh-ah*, (F), (S), ambition, goddess of physique, ★★

Tanmay, *Tuhn-muhy*, (M), (S), absorbed in, identical, ★

Tanmaya, *Tuhn-muhy-ah*, (F), (S), absorbed in, identical, ★

Tanshu, *Tuhn-shu*, (M), (S), attractive, ★★

Tanu, *Tuhn-u*, (F), (S), slender, minute, delicate, ★★

Tanu, *Tuhn-u*, (F), (S), delicate, thin, ★★

Tanu, *Tuhn-u*, (M), (S), delicate, thin, ★★

Tanuj, *Tuhn-ooj*, (M), (S), son, ★★

Tanuja, *Tuhn-ooj-ah*, (F), (S), daughter, ★★

Tanuka, *Tuhn-uk-ah*, (F), (S), slender, delicate, ★★

Tanushree, *Tuhn-ush-ree*, (F), (S), shapely, with a divine body, ★★

Tanvi, *Tuhn-vee*, (F), (S), delicate, beautiful, thin, ★★

Tapan, *Tuhp-uhn*, (M), (S), brilliant, fiery, the sun, ★★

Tapas, *Tuhp-uhs*, (M), (S), heat, fervour, fire, worth, austerity, meditation, sage, bird, the sun, the moon, another name for Agni, ★★

Tapasi, *Tuhp-uhs-ee*, (F), (S), ascetic, ★★

Tapat, *Tuh-uht*, (M), (S), warming, born of the sun, ★★

Tapati, *Tuh-uht-ee*, (F), (S), heat, born of the sun, one who has undergone penance, ★★

Tapit, *Tuhp-iht*, (M), (S), purified, ★★

Taral, *Tuhr-uhl*, (M), (S), ruby, gem, brilliant, shining, a wave, ★★

Tarala, *Tuhr-uhl-ah*, (F), (S), bee, ★★

Taran, *Tuhr-uhn*, (M), (S), thunder, heaven, earth, another name for Vishnu, (P), rose, field, ★★

Tarana, *Tuhr-ahn-ah*, (F), (S), (P), song, voice★★

Tarang, *Tuhr-uhng*, (M), (S), (P), a wave, ★★

Tarangini, *Tuhr-uhng-ihn-ee*, (F), (S), river, ★

Tarant, *Tuhr-uhnt*, (M), (S), ocean, ★★

Tarish, *Tuhr-eesh*, (M), (S), competent, ocean, boat, ★★

Tarit, *Tuhr-iht*, (M), (S), lightning, ★★

Tarita, *Tuhr-iht-ah*, (F), (S), leader, forefinger, another name
   for Durga, ★★

Tarpan, *Tuhr-puhn*, (M), (S), delightful, satisfying, ★★

Tarpani, *Tuhr-puhn-ee*, (F), (S), satisfying, offering oblations, ★★

Tarpini, *Tuhr-pihn-ee*, (F), (S), satisfying, offering oblations, ★★

Tarsh, *Tuhrsh*, (M), (S), shapely, desire, profit, boat, ocean, sun, ★★

Tarshit, *Tuhr-shiht*, (M), (S), thirsty, desirous, ★★

Tarshita, *Tuhr-shiht-ah*, (F), (S), thirsty, desirous, ★★

Taru, *Tuhr-u*, (F), (S), fast, guardian, tree, ★★

Taru, *Tuhr-u*, (M), (S), fast, guardian, tree, ★★

Tarun, *Tuhr-un*, (M), (S), young, gentle, ★★

Taruna, *Tuhr-un-ah*, (F), (S), young, ★★

Tarunak, *Tuhr-un-uhk*, (M), (S), young, ★

Taruni, *Tuhr-un-ee*, (F), (S), young, ★★

Tarush, *Tuhr-ush*, (M), (S), victor, ★★

Tarushi, *Tuhr-ush-ee*, (F), (S), victory, ★★

Taulik, *Toh-lihk*, (M), (S), painter, ★★

Taulika, *Toh-lihk-ah*, (F), (S), painter, ★★

Tavalin, *Tuhv-uhl-een*, (M), (S), religious, meditative, ★★

Tavasya, *Tuhv-uhs-yuh*, (M), (S), strength, ★

Tavish, *Tuhv-ihsh*, (M), (S), strong, brave, vigorous, ocean,
   heaven, gold, ★★

Tavisha, *Tuhv-ihsh-ah*, (F), (S), strong, brave, vigorous, divine, ★★

Tavishi, *Tuhv-ihsh-ee*, (F), (S), divine, strength, bravery, virgin, river,
   the earth, ★★

Tej, *Taej*, (M), (S), brilliance, glory, security, ★★

Teja, *Taej-ah*, (F), (S), brilliant, ★★

Tejal, *Taej-uhl*, (F), (S), brilliant, ★★

Tejal, *Taej-uhl*, (M), (S), brilliant, ★★

Tejas, *Taej-uhs*, (M), (S), tip of the flame, fire, light, brilliance,
gold, spirit, vigour, power, might, honour, ★★

Tejashree, *Taej-uhsh-ree*, (F), (S), endowed with divine power
and grace, ★

Tejasvini, *Taej-uhs-vihn-ee*, (F), (S), brilliant, brave, powerful,
celebrated, energetic, noble, honourable, ★

Tejasvin, *Taej-uhs-vihn*, (M), (S), brilliant, brave, powerful, celebrated,
energetic, noble, honourable, ★

Teji, *Taej-ee*, (F), (S), brilliant, ★★

Tejini, *Taej-ihn-ee*, (F), (S), brilliant, energetic, ★★

Tejit, *Taej-iht*, (M), (S), sharpened, ★★

Tevan, *Taev-uhn*, (M), (S), play, pastime, a pleasure garden, ★★

Tia, *Tee-yah*, (F), (O) – English, tiara, Latin, joy, Spanish, aunt, ★★★

Tiara, *Tee-ahr-ah*, (F), (O) – English, Latin, decorative, tiara worn on
the head typically by royalty, ★★★

Tilak, *Tihl-uhk*, (M), (S), auspicious ritualistic mark applied on the
forehead, a flowering tree, ★★

Tilaka, *Tihl-uhk-ah*, (F), (S), necklace, ★★

Tilika, *Tihl-ihk-ah*, (F), (S), a small mark of sandalwood, ★★

Timit, *Tihm-iht*, (M), (S), calm, constant, ★★

Timita, *Tihm-iht-ah*, (F), (S), calm, constant, ★★

Tina, *Teen-ah*, (F), (O) – Latin, largely a short form of European
names ending with it Tina such as Christina and Augustina,
dignified, august, ★★★

Tishya, *Tihsh-yuh*, (M), (S), auspicious, lucky, ★★

Titiksha, *Tiht-ihk-shah*, (F), (S), patience, ★

Titikshu, *Tiht-ihk-shu*, (M), (S), patience, ★

Tiya, *Tee-yah*, (F), (O) – English, tiara, Latin, joy, Spanish, aunt, ★★★

Tosh, *Toash*, (M), (S), satisfaction, ★★

Toshan, *Toash-uhn*, (M), (S), satisfied, ★★

Toshani, *Toash-uhn-ee*, (F), (S), satisfying, another name
    for Durga, ★★

Toshin, *Toash-ihn*, (M), (S), satisfied, ★★

Toshit, *Toash-iht*, (M), (S), satisfied, ★★

Traaman, *Trahm-uhn*, (M), (S), protection, ★★

Traanan, *Trahm-uhn*, (M), (S), guarding, ★★

Trayi, *Truh-yee*, (F), (S), intellect, ★★

Treya, *Trae-yah*, (F), (S), walking in three paths, trinity, ★★

Triaksh, *Tree-ahksh*, (M), (S), three eyed, another name for Shiva, ★

Triambak, *Tree-uhm-uhk*, (M), (S), three eyed, another name
    for Shiva, ★

Triambika, *Tree-uhm-ihk-ah*, (F), (S), another name for Paarvati, ★

Tridiva, *Trih-dihv-ah*, (F), (S), heaven, ★

Trijna, *Trihj-nuh*, (M), (S), all-knowing, divine, sage, a Buddha, ★

Tripan, *Trihp-uhn*, (M), (S), pleasant, refreshing, ★★

Tripat, *Trihp-uht*, (M), (S), pleasant, the moon, ★★

Tript, *Trihpt*, (M), (S), satisfied, ★★

Tripta, *Trihp-tah*, (F), (S), satisfied, another name for the river
    Ganges, ★★

Tripti, *Trihp-tee*, (F), (S), satisfaction, water, ★★

Trisha, *Trihsh-ah*, (F), (S), thirst, ★★

Trishla, *Trihsh-lah*, (F), (S), desirous, causing thirst, ★★

Trishna, *Trihsh-nah*, (F), (S), thirst, ★★

Triya, *Trih-yah*, (F), (S), young, ★★

Tuhar, *Tu-huhr*, (M), (S), enlightening, ★★

Tuhin, *Tu-hihn*, (M), (S), snow, moonlight, ★★

Tuhina, *Tu-hihn-ah*, (F), (S), snow, ★★

Tuk, *Tuk*, (M), (S), young, ★★

Tul, *Tul*, (M), (S), balance, Libra, ★★

Tulak, *Tul-uhk*, (M), (S), thinker, ★★

Tulasi, *Tul-uhs-ee*, (F), (S), unmatched, unique, a sacred leaf thought
    to be the incarnation of Mahalakshmi, ★★

Tulika, *Tul-ihk-ah*, (F), (S), painter's brush, pencil, collyrium stick, ★★

Tulya, *Tul-yuh*, (M), (S), alike, similar, equivalent, ★★

Turab, *Tur-ahb*, (M), (A), earth, dust, ★★

Turag, *Tur-uhg*, (M), (S), agile, thought, mind, ★★

Turanya, *Tur-uhn-yah*, (F), (S), quick, ★

Turanya, *Tur-uhn-yuh*, (M), (S), quick, ★

Turashat, *Tur-ahsh-uht*, (M), (S), overpowering the mighty, another
    name for Indra, ★

Turi, *Tur-ee*, (F), (S), paint brush, ★★

Turni, *Toor-nee*, (F), (S), fast, clever, the mind, ★★

Turvash, *Tur-vuhsh*, (M), (S), victorious, ★★

Turvi, *Tur-vee*, (F), (S), superior, victorious, ★★

Turya, *Tur-yah*, (F), (S), superior, one fourth, ★★

Turya, *Tur-yah*, (F), (S), a musical instrument, ★★

Turya, *Toor-yuh*, (M), (S), musical instrument, ★★

Tushar, *Tush-ahr*, (M), (S), cold, snow, ★★

Tushit, *Tush-iht*, (M), (S), satisfied, an incarnation of Vishnu, ★★

Tushita, *Tush-iht-ah*, (F), (S), satisfied, ★★

Tushti, *Tush-tee*, (F), (S), satisfaction, ★★

Tushya, *Tush-yuh*, (M), (S), satisfied, another name for Shiva, ★

Tuviksh, *Tuv-ihk-sh*, (M), (S), strong, ★

Tuyam, *Too-yuhm*, (M), (S), strong, rapid, water, ★★

Tvesha, *Tvae-shah*, (F), (S), brilliant, beautiful, impulsive, ★

Tveshin, *Tvaesh-ihn*, (M), (S), impulsive, ★

Tvisha, *Tvihsh-ah*, (F), (S), light, brilliance, ★★

Tvishi, *Tvihsh-ee*, (F), (S), determination, impulsiveness,
    rays of light, brilliance, ★★

U

Uchak, *Uch-uhk*, (M), (S), fearless, ruler, ★★

Uchal, *Uch-uhl*, (M), (S), the mind, understanding, ascending, ★★

Ucharya, *Uch-ahr-yuh*, (M), (S), uttered, articulated, ★

Uchat, *Uch-uht*, (M), (S), excellence, supremacy, ★

Uchata, *Uch-uht-ah*, (F), (S), excellence, supremacy, ★

Uchit, *Uch-iht*, (M), (S), appropriate, right, agreeable, ★★

Uchita, *Uch-iht-ah*, (F), (S), appropriate, right, agreeable, ★★

Udaj, *Ud-uhj*, (M), (S), born in water, lotus, ★★

Udam, *Ud-ahm*, (M), (S), unbound, proud, substantial, excessive, impulsive, ★★

Udamay, *Ud-uhm-uhy*, (M), (S), made of water, ★

Udanchit, *Ud-uhn-chiht*, (M), (S), elevated, worshipped, ★

Udant, *Ud-ahnt*, (M), (S), humble, vigorous, pure, worthy, elevated, ★★

Udant, *Ud-uhnt*, (M), (S), virtuous, excellent, respite, news, story, ★★

Udantika, *Ud-uhnt-ihk-ah*, (F), (S), satisfaction, ★★

Udap, *Ud-ahp*, (M), (S), success, ★★

Udapi, *Ud-ahp-ee*, (M), (S), successful, ★★

Udar, *Ud-ahr*, (M), (S), high, best, munificent, gentle, dignified, eminent, ★★

Udarak, *Ud-ahr-uhk*, (M), (S), excellent, ★★

Udarsh, *Ud-uhrsh*, (M), (S), delighted, enjoyment, ★★

Udat, *Ud-aht*, (M), (S), great, eminent, liberal, loved, gift, ★★

Uday, *Ud-uhy*, (M), (S), sunrise, creation, wealth, brilliance, success, ★★

Udaya, *Ud-uhy-ah*, (F), (S), sunrise, success, brilliance, ★★

Udayanjali, *Ud-uhy-ahn-juhl-ee*, (F), (S), offering to the rising sun, prayer to the sun, ★

Udayanti, *Ud-uhy-uhnt-ee*, (F), (S), ascended, worthy, excellent, ★

Udayin, *Ud-ahy-ihn*, (M), (S), ascending, successful, another name for Vishnu, ★

Udbal, *Ud-buhl*, (M), (S), powerful, ★★

Udbala, *Ud-buhl-ah*, (F), (S), powerful, ★★

Udbhash, *Ud-bhahsh*, (M), (S), brilliance, ★

Udbhav, *Ud-bhuhv*, (M), (S), existence, origin, birth, ★

Udbhavna, *Ud-bhahv-uhn-ah*, (F), (S), birth, thought, ★

Udbhid, *Ud-bhihd*, (M), (S), sprout, shott, tree, germinating, ★

Udesh, *Ud-aesh*, (M), (S), region, direction, explanation, distinction, ★★

Udeshna, *Ud-aesh-nah*, (F), (S), born, distinguished, ★★

Udeshni, *Ud-aesh-nee*, (F), (S), born, distinguished, ★★

Udeshya, *Ud-aesh-yah*, (F), (S), aim, purpose, ★★

Udeshya, *Ud-aesh-yuh*, (M), (S), aim, purpose, ★★

Udgam, *Ud-guhm*, (M), (S), ascension, ★★

Udgat, *Ud-guht*, (M), (S), ascended, leader, wise, ★★

Udgati, *Ud-guht-ee*, (F), (S), birth, rise, ★★

Udharsh, *Ud-dhuhr-sh*, (M), (S), courage, ★

Udhav, *Ud-dhuhv*, (M), (S), uplifting, sacrificial fire, festival, pleasure, ★★

Udit, *Ud-iht*, (M), (S), sunrise, ascended, brilliant, ★★

Udita, *Ud-iht-ah*, (F), (S), sunrise, ascended, brilliant, ★★

Uditi, *Ud-iht-ee*, (F), (S), sunrise, ★★

Udojas, *Ud-oaj-uhs*, (M), (S), powerful, efficient, ★★

Udrek, *Ud-raek*, (M), (S), blossoming of a thought, passion, abundance, superiority, ★★

Udu, *Udu*, (F), (S), water, star, ★★

Udvah, *Ud-vuh*, (M), (S), son, best, descendent, ★★

Udvaha, *Ud-vuh-ah*, (F), (S), descendent, daughter, ★★

Udvahni, *Ud-vuhn-ee*, (F), (S), brilliant, ★

Udvansh, *Ud-vuhnsh*, (M), (S), noble, ★★

Udyam, *Ud-yuhm*, (M), (S) effort, exertion, preparation, diligence, enterprise, ★★

Udyami, *Ud-yuhm-ee*, (M), (H) active, hardworking, entrepreneur, ★★

Udyan, *Ud-yahn*, (M), (S), going out, park, purpose, motive, ★★

Udyat, *Ud-yuht*, (M), (S), ascending, a star, ★★

Udyati, *Ud-yuht-ee*, (F), (S), ascended, ★★

Udyot, *Ud-yoat*, (M), (S), brilliance, ★★

Ugam, *Ug-uhm*, (M), (S), ascending, ★★

Ugan, *Ug-uhn*, (M), (S), army, ★★

Ugrak, *Ug-ruhk*, (M), (S), courageous, powerful, ★★

Ujala, *Uj-ahl-ah*, (F), (S), brilliance, ★★

Ujas, *Uj-ahs*, (M), (S), light before dawn, ★★

Ujay, *Uj-juhy*, (M), (S), archer, ★★

Ujayan, *Uj-juhy-uhn*, (M), (S), conqueror, ★

Ujayant, *Uj-juhy-uhnt*, (M), (S), conqueror, ★

Ujayati, *Uj-juhy-uht-ee*, (F), (S), conqueror, ★

Ujesh, *Uj-jaesh*, (M), (S), conquering, ★★

Ujesha, *Uj-jaesh-ah*, (F), (S), conquering, ★★

Ujval, *Uj-vuhl*, (M), (S), lit, brilliant, attractive, sunshine, ★★

Ujvala, *Uj-vuhl-ah*, (F), (S), brilliance, ★★

Ulban, *Ul-buhn*, (M), (S), abundant, dense, brilliant, powerful, ★★

Ulka, *Ul-kah*, (F), (S), meteor, fire, lamp, brilliant, ★★

Ullas, *Ul-lahs*, (M), (S), joy, celebration, light, brilliance, progress, ★★

Ullasin, *Ul-lahs-ihn*, (M), (S), playful, celebrating, ★★

Ullasit, *Ul-lahs-iht*, (M), (S), brilliant, joyous, ★★

Uma, *Um-ah*, (F), (S), light, brilliance, night, celebrity, calm, turmeric, another name for Paarvati and Durga, ★★★

Umang, *Um-uhng*, (M), (H), joy, zeal, aspiration, ambition, ★★★

Umed, *Um-aed*, (M), (P), hope, desire, trust, greed, ★★

Umesh, *Um-aesh*, (M), (S), another name for Shiva, ★★

Umid, *Um-eed*, (M), (H), (P), hope, desire, trust, greed, ★★

Umika, *Um-ihk-ah*, (F), (S), another name for Paarvati, ★★★

Unmada, *Un-muhd-ah*, (F), (S), beautiful, enchanting, passionate, an apsara or celestial nymph, ★★

Unmaj, *Un-muhj*, (M), (S), ascending, progressing, ★★

Unmesh, *Un-maesh*, (M), (S), blossoming, progressing, ★★

Unmil, *Un-meel*, (M), (S), to appear, ★★

Unabh, *Un-ahbh*, (M), (S), elevated, eminent, ruler, ★★

Unnat, *Un-nuht*, (M), (S), eminent, elevated, tall, regal, a Buddha, ★★

Unnati, *Un-nuht-ee*, (F), (S), progress, wealth, success, ★★

Unni, *Un-nee*, (M), (S), to lift up, to support, help, redeem, ★★

Upada, *Up-uhdd-ah*, (F), (S), gift, generous, ★★

Upahar, *Up-uh-hahr*, (M), (S), gift, offering, oblation to a deity, ★★

Upal, *Up-uhl*, (M), (S), rock, jewel, sugar, ★★★

Upala, *Up-uhl-ah*, (F), (S), rock, jewel, sugar, ★★★

Upam, *Up-uhm*, (M), (S), highest, best, next, first, ★★

Upama, *Up-uhm-ah*, (F), (S), comparison, similar, equality, ★★

Upanay, *Up-uhn-ahy*, (M), (S), leader, ★

Upanayik, *Up-uhn-ahy-ihk*, (M), (S), fit for an offering, a character
next in importance to the hero,*

Upang, *Up-ahng*, (M), (S), the act of anointing, **

Upanshu, *Up-ahn-shu*, (M), (S), a murmured prayer, **

Upasana, *Up-ahs-uhn-ah*, (F), (S), devotion, worship, **

Updesh, *Up-daesh*, (M), (S), sermon, counsel, **

Upeksh, *Up-aeksh*, (M), (S), to expect patiently, to disregard,
to neglect, **

Upeksha, *Up-aeksh-ah*, (F), (S), awaiting, disregard, neglect, **

Upjas, *Up-juhs*, (M), (S), produced, divine, **

Upjay, *Up-juhy*, (M), (S), to help, to support, **

Upjit, *Up-jiht*, (M), (S), to acquire by victory, **

Upkar, *Up-kahr*, (M), (S), favour, kindness, **

Upkash, *Up-kahsh*, (M), (S), dawn, **

Upkosh, *Up-koash*, (M), (S), treasure, **

Upkosha, *Up-koash-ah*, (F), (S), treasure, **

Urj, *Oorj*, (M), (S), powerful, **

Urja, *Oor-jah*, (F), (S), affectionate, daughter, nutrition, energy,
breath, another name for Paarvati, **

Urjit, *Oor-jiht*, (M), (S), powerful, handsome, noble, excellent, **

Urjita, *Oor-jiht-ah*, (F), (S), powerful, excellent, **

Urmi, *Ur-mee*, (F), (S), wave, light, **

Urmika, *Ur-mihk-ah*, (F), (S), wave, **

Urmila, *Ur-mihl-ah*, (F), (S), wave, beautiful, **

Urmya, *Urm-yah*, (F), (S), wavy, night, **

Urusha, *Ur-ush-ah*, (F), (S), generous, bountiful, **

Uruvi, *Ur-uv-ee*, (F), (S), substantial, excellent, the earth, **

Urvang, *Ur-vahng*, (M), (S), substantial, mountain, ocean, **

Urvaksh, *Ur-vuhksh*, (M), (S), joyful, ★★

Urvan, *Ur-vuhn*, (M), (P), soul according to the
Zoroastrian faith, ★★★

Urvan, *Uhr-vuhn*, (M), (O) – Latin, city dweller, urban, ★★★

Urvana, *Ur-vuhn-ah*, (F), (P), soul, ★★★

Urvara, *Ur-vuhr-ah*, (F), (S), fertile, the earth, an apsara or celestial
nymph, ★★

Urvashi, *Ur-vuhsh-ee*, (F), (S), unearthly, an apsara or celestial nymph
considered to be the most beautiful in the three worlds, ★★

Urvi, *Ur-vee*, (F), (S), substantial, the earth, river, both heaven
and earth, ★★

Urvish, *Ur-veesh*, (M), (S), king, lord of the earth, ★★

Usha, *Ush-ah*, (F), (S), dawn, ★★

Ushana, *Ush-ahn-ah*, (F), (S), desire, the Som plant that
produces Soma, ★★

Ushana, *Ush-uhn-ah*, (F), (S), desirous, ★★

Ushas, *Uhsh-uhs*, (F), (S), dawn, daybreak, the goddess of dawn, ★★★

Ushasi, *Ush-uhs-ee*, (F), (S), dawn, ★★

Ushenya, *Ush-aen-yuh*, (M), (S), desirable, ★

Ushi, *Ush-ee*, (F), (S), desire, ★★

Ushij, *Ush-ihj*, (M), (S), born of desire, energetic, pleasant, desirous,
fire, ghee, ★★

Ushija, *Ush-ihj-ah*, (F), (S), born of desire, desirous, energetic,
pleasant, ★★

Ushik, *Ush-ihk*, (M), (S), dawn worshipper, early riser, ★★

Ushika, *Ush-ihk-ah*, (F), (S), dawn worshipper, early riser, ★★

Ushman, *Oosh-muhn*, (M), (S), heat, passion, ★★

Ushra, *Ush-rah*, (F), (S), dawn, the earth, ★★

Utkal, *Ut-kuhl*, (M), (S), wonderful country, carrying a burden, another name for Orissa, ★★

Utkala, *Ut-kuhl-ah*, (F), (S), coming from Utkal, ★★

Utkalika, *Ut-kuhl-ihk-ah*, (F), (S), longing for glory, curiousity, a bud, a wave, ★

Utkalita, *Ut-kuhl-iht-ah*, (F), (S), brilliant, blossoming, ★

Utkarsh, *Ut-kuhrsh*, (M), (S), supreme, handsome, wealth, eminence, glorious, progress, ★★

Utkarsha, *Ut-kuhrsh-ah*, (F), (S), supreme, beautiful, wealth, eminence, glorious, progress, ★★

Utkash, *Ut-kahsh*, (M), (S), to shine forth, to come forth, ★★

Utkashana, *Ut-kahsh-uhn-ah*, (F), (S), commanding, ★

Utpal, *Ut-puhl*, (M), (S), blossoming, lotus blossom, ★★

Utpala, *Ut-puhl-ali*, (F), (S), a river, ★★

Utpar, *Ut-pahr*, (M), (S), infinite, ★★

Utsah, *Ut-sah*, (M), (S), happiness, excitement, energy, courage, determination, ★

Utsarg, *Ut-suhrg*, (M), (S), emission, giving, gift, donation, sacrifice, ★

Utsav, *Ut-suhv*, (M), (S), celebration, festival, occasion, desire, ★★

Uttal, *Ut-tahl*, (M), (S), powerful, quick, best, mighty, tall, loud, impetuous, ★

Uttam, *Ut-tuhm*, (M), (S), best, most eminent, ★★

Uttama, *Ut-tuhm-ah*, (F), (S), best, loving, most eminent, ★★

Uttank, *Ut-tuhnk*, (M), (S), cloud, ★★

Uttar, *Ut-tuhr*, (M), (S), north, better, another name for Shiva, ★★

Uttara, *Ut-tuhr-ah*, (F), (S), north, better, outcome, ★★

V

Vaadin, *Vahd-ihn*, (M), (S), orator, ★★

Vaadish, *Vahd-ihsh*, (M), (S), peace-maker, arbitrator, worthy, learned, sage, ★★

Vaagar, *Vahg-uhr*, (M), (S), scholar, hero, ★★★

Vaaghat, *Vahg-huht*, (M), (S), institutor of a sacrifice, ★★

Vaagish, *Vahg-eesh*, (M), (S), lord of speech, another name for Brahma, ★★★

Vaagmin, *Vahg-mihn*, (M), (S), articulate, ★★★

Vaahak, *Vah-huhk*, (M), (S), porter, bearer, carrier, charioteer, ★★★

Vaahik, *Vah-hihk*, (M), (S), carrying, ★★★

Vaahin, *Vah-hihn*, (M), (S), driving, bearing, causing, carrying, another name for Shiva, ★★★

Vaahini, *Vah-hihn-ee*, (F), (S), one who carries, army, river, ★★

Vaaj, *Vahj*, (M), (S), wing, body, energy, might, speed, race, impulsiveness, gain, ★★★

Vaajin, *Vahj-ihn*, (M), (S), heroic, quick, strong, spirited, arrow, horse, ★★★

Vaak, *Vahk*, (M), (S), word, speech, voice, ocean, ★★★

Vaaka, *Vahk-ah*, (F), (S), word, speech, voice, ocean, goddess of speech, ★★★

Vaakini, *Vahk-ihn-ee*, (F), (S), one who recites, ★★★

Vaakmya, *Vahk-myuh*, (M), (S), praiseworthy, ★★

Vaam, *Vahm*, (M), (S), pleasant, brilliant, noble, another name for Shiva and the love god Kaama, ★★★

Vaama, *Vahm-ah*, (F), (S), beautiful, another name for Durga, Lakshmi and Saraswati, ★★★

Vaamani, *Vahm-uhn-ee*, (F), (S), auspicious, short, mare, ★★

Vaamika, *Vahm-ihk-ah*, (F), (S), aligned to the left, another name for Durga, ★★★

Vaan, *Vahn*, (M), (S), intelligent, flow of water, perfume, woven mat, another name for Yama, ★★★

Vaani, *Vahn-ee*, (F), (S), speech, music, praise, another name for Saraswati, ★★★

Vaanini, *Vahn-ihn-ee*, (F), (S), soft-spoken, enchanting, intelligent, ★★★

Vaanishri, *Vahn-ee-shree*, (F), (S), divine speech, another name for Saraswati, ★★

Vaanya, *Vahn-yah*, (F), (S), sylvan, inhabiting the woods, ★★★

Vaari, *Vahr-ee*, (F), (S), generous, water, modesty, speech, goddess of speech, another name for Saraswati, ★★★

Vaarip, *Vahr-ihp*, (M), (S), lord of water, ★★★

Vaarish, *Vahr-ihsh*, (M), (S), lord of water, ocean, ★★★

Vaasak, *Vahs-uhk*, (M), (S), inhabitant, ★★★

Vaasan, *Vahs-uhn*, (M), (S), imagination, experience, passion, ★★

Vaasana, *Vahs-uhn-ah*, (F), (S), imagination, experience, idea, passion, desire, another name for Durga, ★★

Vaasav, *Vahs-uhv*, (M), (S), descended from or relating to the Vaasus or Indra, another name for Indra, ★★★

Vaasavi, *Vahs-uhv-ee*, (F), (S), divine, daughter of the all-pervading, ★★

Vaashi, *Vahsh-ee*, (M), (S), roaring, another name for Agni, ★★★

Vaatik, *Vaht-ihk*, (M), (S), airy, a talker, ★★

Vaayav, *Vah-yuhv*, (M), (S), scared to the wind god, breath, related to wind, ★★★

Vaayu, *Vah-yu*, (M), (S), wind, divine, ★★★

Vaayun, *Vah-yun*, (M), (S), god, ★★★

Vachan, *Vuhch-uhn*, (M), (S), declaration, vow, ★★★

Vachasya, *Vuhch-uhs-yuh*, (M), (S), praiseworthy, famous, ★★

Vadanya, *Vuhd-ahn-yuh*, (M), (S), generous, prosperous, articulate, ★★

Vaibhav, *Vaeh-bhuhv*, (M), (S), power, eminence, ★★

Vaibudh, *Vaeh-budh*, (M), (S), divine, ★★

Vaidat, *Vaeh-duht*, (M), (S), knowledgable, ★★

Vaidhav, *Vaeh-dhuhv*, (M), (S), born of the moon, another
    name for Mercury, ★★

Vaidhyat, *Vaeh-dhyuht*, (M), (S), supporter of the law, ★

Vaidurya, *Vaeh-door-yuh*, (M), (S), excellent, ★

Vaidya, *Vaeh-dyuh*, (M), (S), erudite, physician, ★★

Vaidyut, *Vaeh-dyut*, (M), (S), brilliant, ★★

Vairag, *Veh-rahg*, (M), (S), detached, free from desire and
    attachment, ★★★

Vairagi, *Veh-rahg-ee*, (F), (S), detached, free from desire and
    attachment, ★★

Vairaj, *Vaeh-rahj*, (M), (S), divine glory, belonging to Brahma, ★★

Vaishak, *Vaeh-shahk*, (M), (S), the Hindu months of April and May,
    churning rod, ★

Vaishaka, *Vaeh-shahk-ah*, (F), (S), lioness, ★

Vaishakhi, *Vaeh-shahkh-ee*, (F), (S), the day of the full moon in the
    month of Vaishakh, ★

Vaishali, *Vaeh-shahl-ee*, (F), (S), great, princess, ★

Vaishnav, *Vaehsh-nuhv*, (M), (S), worshipper of Vishnu, ★

Vaishnavi, *Vaehsh-nuhv-ee*, (F), (S), worshipper of Vishnu, the
    personified energy of Vishnu, ★

Vajra, *Vuhj-rah*, (F), (S), powerful, another name for Durga, ★★★

Vajra, *Vuhj-ruh*, (M), (S), powerful, hard, thunderbolt, diamond, ★★★

Vajrin, *Vuhj-rihn*, (M), (S), another name for Indra, ★★★

Vaksh, *Vuhksh*, (M), (S), chest, strengthening, to grow, ★★★

Vakshan, *Vuhk-shuhn*, (M), (S), nourishing, chest, ★★★

Vakshana, *Vuhk-shuhn-ah*, (F), (S), nourishing, river bed, stomach, oblation, flame, ★★★

Vakshani, *Vuhk-shuhn-ee*, (F), (S), nourishing, ★★

Vakshi, *Vuhk-shee*, (F), (S), nutrition, flame, ★★★

Vakshu, *Vuhk-shu*, (M), (S), refreshing, ★★★

Vakti, *Vuhk-tee*, (F), (S), speech, ★★

Vakul, *Vuhk-ul*, (M), (S), crooked, curved, ★★★

Vallabh, *Vuhll-uhbh*, (M), (S), first, beloved, cowherd, lover, ★★

Vallabha, *Vuhll-uhbh-ah*, (F), (S), beloved, ★★

Vallaki, *Vuhl-uhk-ee*, (F), (S), lute, ★★

Vallari, *Vuhl-uhr-ee*, (F), (S), cluster of blossoms, creeper, another name for Sita, ★★

Vallav, *Vuhll-uhv*, (M), (S), cowherd, ★★★

Vallik, *Vuhll-ihk*, (M), (S), edge of a thatched roof, ★★★

Vallika, *Vuhll-ihk-ah*, (F), (S), greenery, the earth, ★★★

Vallur, *Vuhll-ur*, (M), (S), cluster of blossoms, ★★

Vanad, *Vuhn-uhd*, (M), (S), cloud, ★★

Vanaj, *Vuhn-uhj*, (M), (S), natural, born of the forest, born of the water, lotus, ★★★

Vanaja, *Vuhn-uhj-ah*, (F), (S), natural, born of the forest, born of the water, lotus, ★★★

Vanan, *Vuhn-uhn*, (M), (S), desire, ★★★

Vanas, *Vuhn-uhs*, (M), (S), handsome, desire, ★★★

Vanchit, *Vuhn-chiht*, (M), (S), desired, precious, loved, ★★

Vanchita, *Vuhn-chiht-ah*, (F), (S), desired, precious, loved, ★★

Vandan, *Vuhn-duhn*, (M), (S), worship, praise, ★★

Vandana, *Vuhn-duhn-ah*, (F), (S), worship, praise, ★★

Vandin, *Vuhn-dihn*, (M), (S), bard, a class of poets and scholars who sing songs of praise in the royal courts, ★★

Vandit, *Vuhn-diht*, (M), (S), praised, worshipped, ★

Vandita, *Vuhn-diht-ah*, (F), (S), praised, worshipped, ★

Vandya, *Vuhn-dyah*, (F), (S), amiable, praiseworthy, ★★

Vanit, *Vuhn-iht*, (M), (S), loved, desired, ★★

Vanita, *Vuhn-iht-ah*, (F), (S), loved, desired, ★★

Vanjul, *Vuhn-jul*, (M), (S), of the beauty of the forest, the Ashoka tree, ★★

Vanmayi, *Vuhn-muh-yee*, (F), (S), goddess of speech, another name for Saraswati, ★★

Vansh, *Vuhnsh*, (M), (S), cane, bamboo, backbone, lineage, ★★★

Vansha, *Vuhn-shah*, (F), (S), cane, bamboo, backbone, lineage, an apsara or celestial nymph, ★★★

Vanshaj, *Vuhn-shuhj*, (M), (S), well-born, ★★★

Vanshaja, *Vuhn-shuhj-ah*, (F), (S), well-born, ★★★

Vanshi, *Vuhn-shee*, (F), (S), flute, ★★★

Vanshika, *Vuhn-shihk-ah*, (F), (S), flute, ★★★

Vanu, *Vuhn-u*, (M), (S), friend, ★★★

Vapra, *Vuhp-rah*, (F), (S), garden bed, ★★★

Vapun, *Vuhp-un*, (M), (S), formless, a god, knowledge, ★★

Vapus, *Vuhp-us*, (M), (S), beauty, shapely, appearance, ★★

Vapush, *Vuhp-ush*, (M), (S), embodied, wonderful, admirable, ★★

Vapush, *Vuhp-ush*, (M), (S), embodied, wonderful, admirable, ★★

Vapusha, *Vuhp-ush-ah*, (F), (S), beautiful, embodied, nature, an apsara or celestial nymph, ★★

Var, *Vuhr*, (M), (S), blessing, choice, best, noble, ★★★

Vara, *Vuhr-ah*, (F), (S), blessing, choice, best, another name for Paarvati, ★★★

Varalika, *Vuhr-ahl-ihk-ah*, (F), (S), goddess of power, another name for Durga, ★★

Varana, *Vuhr-uhn-ah*, (F), (S), river, ★★

Varasya, *Vuhr-uhs-yah*, (F), (S), request, desire, ★★

Varatam, *Vuhr-uht-uhm*, (M), (S), best, ★★

Varatar, *Vuhr-uht-uhr*, (M), (S), best, excellent, ★

Varchas, *Vuhr-chuhs*, (M), (S), light, energy, shape, ★★★

Vardhan, *Vuhr-dhuhn*, (M), (S), auspicious, increasing prosperity, strength, ★★

Vardhin, *Vuhr-dhihn*, (M), (S), auspicious, generous, growing, ★★

Vardhit, *Vuhr-dhiht*, (M), (S), increased, developed, ★

Vardhita, *Vuhr-dhiht-ah*, (F), (S), increased, developed, ★

Varenya, *Vuhr-aen-yah*, (F), (S), desirable, excellent, best, saffron, ★★

Varga, *Vuhr-gah*, (F), (S), class, group, an apsara or celestial nymph, ★★★

Varin, *Vuhr-ihn*, (M), (S), generous, ★★★

Varisha, *Vuhr-ihsh-ah*, (F), (S), the rainy season, ★★★

Varja, *Vuhr-jah*, (F), (S), water born, lotus, ★★★

Varnika, *Vuhr-nihk-ah*, (F), (S), pure, golded, ★★

Varsh, *Vuhrsh*, (M), (S), year, cloud, rain, strengthen, ★★★

Varsha, *Vuhr-shah*, (F), (S), rain, rainfall, ★★★

Varshit, *Vuhr-shiht*, (M), (S), strong, potent, ★★

Varshita, *Vuhr-shiht-ah*, (F), (S), strong, ★★

Varun, *Vuhr-un*, (M), (S), all enveloping sky, a Vedic god regarded as the supreme deity, he is seen as upholding heaven and earth and guarding immortality, ★★★

Varuna, *Vuhr-un-ah*, (F), (S), wife of Varun (see above), a river, ★★★

Varya, *Vuhr-yah*, (F), (S), treasure, ★★★

Varya, *Vuhr-yuh*, (M), (S), treasure, illustrious, excellent, another name for the love god Kaama, ★★★

Vasant, *Vuhs-uhnt*, (M), (S), spring, rich, generous, ★★

Vasanti, *Vuhs-uhnt-ee*, (F), (S), spring, name of a musical raagini, ★★

Vash, *Vuhsh*, (M), (S), authority, will, wish, power, divine, ★★★

Vasha, *Vuhsh-ah*, (F), (S), submissive, willing, dependent, ★★★

Vashin, *Vuhsh-ihn*, (M), (S), authoritative, lord, independent, in control of own passions, ★★★

Vashishth, *Vuhsh-ihsh-tth*, (M), (S), best, most prosperous, distinguished, dearest, master of all creation and desire, ★

Vasu, *Vuhs-u*, (F), (S), brilliance, wealth, light, ★★★

Vasu, *Vuhs-u*, (M), (S), divine, light, brilliance, prosperous, best, precious, god, gem, gold, water, sun, Brahman or the Supreme Spirit, another name for, Shiva, Vishnu and Agni, ★★★

Vasul, *Vuhs-ul*, (M), (S), a god, ★★★

Vasur, *Vuhs-ur*, (M), (S), prosperous, precious, ★★★

Vasushri, *Vuhs-ush-ree*, (F), (S), divine grace, ★★

Vasvi, *Vuhs-vee*, (F), (S), the divine night, ★★★

Vatsa, *Vuht-sah*, (F), (S), calf, girl, chest, ★★

Vatsa, *Vuht-suh*, (M), (S), calf, child, beloved, ★★

Vatsak, *Vuht-suhk*, (M), (S), young calf, term of endearment, ★★

Vatsal, *Vuht-suhl*, (M), (S), affectionate, gentle, ★★

Vatsala, *Vuht-suhl-ah*, (F), (S), affectionate, gentle, ★★

Vatsha, *Vuht-shah*, (F), (S), calf, daughter, breast, ★★

Vatsin, *Vuht-sihn*, (M), (S), fertile, one with many children, another name for Vishnu, ★★

Vatya, *Vuht-yah*, (F), (S), storm, hurricane, ★★

Vavan, *Vuhv-uhn*, (M), (O) – Avestan, conqueror, ★★★

Vaya, *Vuh-yah*, (F), (S), child, branch, energy, power, ★★★

Vayun, *Vuh-yun*, (M), (S), moving, active, alive, clear, ★★★

Vayuna, *Vuh-yun-ah*, (F), (S), agile, living, knowledge, aim, ★★★

Ved, *Vaed*, (M), (S), sacred knowledge, riches, precious, four philosophical scriptures underlying Hinduism, ★★

Veda, *Vaed-ah*, (F), (S), devout, celebrated, worthy, ★★

Vedang, *Vaed-ahng*, (M), (S), part of the Vedas, one of six sciences – chanting, ritual, grammar, vocabulary, speech interpretation, astrology, ★★

Vedant, *Vaed-ahnt*, (M), (S), absolute truth, theology, Hindu philosophy, ★★

Vedanti, *Vaed-ahnt-ee*, (F), (S), knowledgeable about the Vedas, theologian, ★★

Vedas, *Vaed-uhs*, (M), (S), knowledge, wealth, acquisition, ★★

Vedhas, *Vaedh-uhs*, (M), (S), worthy, courageous, wise, learned, religious, creator, preserver, disposer, Brahma, ★★

Vedi, *Vaed-ee*, (F), (S), science, knowledge, the wife of Brahma, ★★

Vedi, *Vaed-ee*, (M), (S), learned, teacher, ★★

Vedika, *Vaed-ihk-ah*, (F), (S), consciousness, an apsara or celestial nymph, ★★

Vedin, *Vaed-ihn*, (M), (S), knowledgeable, sensitive, another name for Brahma, ★★

Vedini, *Vaed-ihn-ee*, (F), (S), knowledgeable, sensitive, ★★

Vedish, *Vaed-eesh*, (M), (S), lord of the wise, another name for Brahma, ★★

Veduk, *Vaed-uk*, (M), (S), seeking knowledge, ★★

Vedya, *Vaed-yah*, (F), (S), knowledge, known, ★★

Vedya, *Vaed-yuh*, (M), (S), famous, knowledge, ★★

Vegin, *Vaeg-ihn*, (M), (S), rapid, hawk, falcon, another name for Vaayu, ★★★

Vegini, *Vaeg-ihn-ee*, (F), (S), rapid, a river, ★★★

Vela, *Vael-ah*, (F), (S), shore, ★★★

Ven, *Vaen*, (M), (S), desirous, affectionate, ★★★

Vena, *Vaen-ah*, (F), (S), desire, to move, discern, to play on an instrument, ★★★

Veni, *Vaen-ee*, (F), (S), a braid of hair, stream, bridge, the confluence of rivers, ★★★

Venika, *Vaen-ihk-ah*, (F), (S), stream, ★★★

Venkat, *Vehn-kuhtt*, (M), (S), existing, natural, divine, ★★

Venya, *Vaen-yuh*, (F), (S), beloved, desirable, ★★★

Vibali, *Vihb-ahl-ee*, (F), (S), young, ★★★

Vibha, *Vihbh-ah*, (F), (S), beauty, ray of light, brilliance, ★★

Vibhakar, *Vihbh-ahk-uhr*, (M), (S), brilliance, creator of light, sun, fire, moon, ruler, ★

Vibhas, *Vihbh-uhs*, (M), (S), light, ★★

Vibhat, *Vihbh-aht*, (M), (S), dawn, ascending, brilliant, ★

Vibhav, *Vihbh-ahv*, (M), (S), friend, another name for Shiva, ★★

Vibhav, *Vihbh-uhv*, (M), (S), power, riches, property, dignity, omnipresence, magnanimity, ★★

Vibhava, *Vihbh-ahv-ah*, (F), (S), friend, ★★

Vibhor, *Vihbh-oar*, (M), (S), delighted, ★★

Vibhu, *Vihbh-u*, (M), (S), eternal, omnipotent, ruler, powerful, great, another name for Brahma, Vishnu, Shiva and Buddha, ★★

Vibhush, *Vihbh-oosh*, (M), (S), attractive, light, brilliance, ★

Vibhusha, *Vihbh-oosh-ah*, (F), (S), attractive, light, brilliance, ★

Vibhuti, *Vihb-hoot-ee*, (F), (S), powerful, auspicious, greatness, properity, accomplishment, ash applied to the forehead, ★

Vibodh, *Vihb-oadh*, (M), (S), insight, intelligence, ★★

Vibudh, *Vihb-udh*, (M), (S), intelligent, insightful, learned, god, sage, teacher, the moon, ★★

Videh, *Vihd-aeh*, (M), (S), formless, involved in divine pursuits, ★★

Vidhav, *Vihdh-uhv*, (M), (S), like the moon, ★★

Vidhi, *Vihdh-ee*, (M), (S), law, order, fate, creed, creation, religious, another name for Brahma, ★★

Vidhi, *Vihdh-ee*, (F), (S), law, order, fate, creed, creation, worship, ★★

Vidhu, *Vihdh-u*, (M), (S), solitary, the moon, another name for Brahma and Vishnu, ★★

Videep, *Vihd-eep*, (M), (S), shining, ★★

Vidisha, *Vihd-eesh-ah*, (F), (S), the Jain heritage centre where the Sanchi stupa is located, a river, ★★

Vidit, *Vihd-iht*, (M), (S), famous, known, ★★

Vidita, *Vihd-iht-ah*, (F), (S), famous, known, ★★

Vidu, *Vihd-u*, (M), (S), wise, ★★

Vidul, *Vihd-ul*, (M), (S), wise, ★★

Vidula, *Vihd-ul-ah*, (F), (S), wise, ★★

Vidur, *Vihd-ur*, (M), (S), wise, talented, ★★

Vidura, *Vihd-ur-ah*, (F), (S), wise, talented, ★★

Vidush, *Vihd-ush*, (M), (S), wise, ★★

Vidushi, *Vihd-ush-ee*, (F), (S), wise, ★★

Vidya, *Vihd-yah*, (F), (S), knowledge, learning, another name for
    Saraswati, ★★

Vidyot, *Vihd-yoat*, (M), (S), brilliant, ★

Vidyota, *Vihd-yoat-ah*, (F), (S), brilliant, an apsara or
    celestial nymph, ★

Vidyul, *Vihd-yul*, (M), (S), lightning, ★

Vidyut, *Vihd-yut*, (M), (S), lightning, ★

Vidyuta, *Vihd-yut-ah*, (F), (S), lightning, dawn, an apsara or
    celestial nymph, ★

Vighan, *Vihg-huhn*, (M), (S), cloudless, attacker, hammer, ★★

Viha, *Vih-hah*, (F), (S), heaven, ★★★

Vihag, *Vih-huhg*, (M), (S), arrow, bird, flying in the sky, the sun,
    the moon, ★★★

Vihan, *Vih-hahn*, (M), (S), dawn, (O) – Pahlavi, cause, ★★★

Vihang, *Vih-huhng*, (M), (S), arrow, bird, the sun, the moon, ★★★

Vihav, *Vih-huhv*, (M), (S), chant, prayer, ★★★

Vihavya, *Vih-huhv-yah*, (F), (S), desired, chanted, ★

Vihavya, *Vih-huhv-yuh*, (M), (S), desired, chanted, ★

Vijay, *Vih-juhy*, (M), (S), victory, another name for Shiva and
    Vishnu, ★★★

Vijaya, *Vih-juhy-ah*, (F), (S), victorious, another name for Durga, ★★

Vijet, *Vihj-aet*, (M), (S), victorious, ★★

Vijeta, *Vihj-aet-ah*, (F), (S), victorious, ★★

Vijna, *Vihj-nuh*, (M), (S), informed, intelligent, ★★★

Vijul, *Vihj-ul*, (M), (S), the silkcotton tree, ★★★

Vijval, *Vihj-vuhl*, (M), (S), blessing of knowledge, ★★

Vik, *Vihk*, (M), (S), bird, wind, ★★★

Vikach, *Vihk-uhch*, (M), (S), hairless, shaven, open, brilliant, ★★★

Vikal, *Vihk-ahl*, (M), (S), twilight, ★★★

Vikam, *Vihk-ahm*, (M), (S), free from attachment or desire, ★★★

Vikas, *Vihk-ahs*, (M), (S), light, brilliance, to appear, development, progress, cheer, calm, ★★★

Vikashini, *Vihk-ahsh-ihn-ee*, (F), (S), brilliant, ★★

Vikram, *Vihk-ruhm*, (M), (S), bravery, power, mettle, best, intensity, another name for Vishnu, ★★★

Vikrant, *Vihk-rahnt*, (M), (S), brave, victorious, ★★

Vikranti, *Vihk-rahnt-ee*, (F), (S), bravery, power, ability, ★★

Viksha, *Veek-shah*, (F), (S), knowledge, intelligence, ★★★

Vikshar, *Vihk-shuhr*, (M), (S), to flow out, another name for Vishnu and Krishna, ★★★

Vilas, *Vihl-ahs*, (M), (S), attractiveness, brilliant, activity, liveliness, enjoyment, play, luxury, appearance, grace, ★★★

Vilasin, *Vihl-ahs-ihn*, (M), (S), brilliant, active, playful, the moon, another name for Krishna, Shiva and the love god Kaama, ★★★

Vilasini, *Vihl-ahs-ihn-ee*, (F), (S), brilliant, active, playful, pleasant, beautiful, another name for Lakshmi, ★★★

Vilohit, *Vihl-oa-hiht*, (M), (S), deep red, another name for Shiva and Agni, ★

Vilok, *Vihl-oak*, (M), (S), to see, view, ★★★

Viloman, *Vihl-oam-uhn*, (M), (S), opposite, reverse, hairless, ★★

Vimad, *Vihm-uhd*, (M), (S), sober, ★★

Vimal, *Vihm-uhl*, (M), (S), pure, white, bright, ★★★

Vimala, *Vihm-uhl-ah*, (F), (S), pure, holy, white, bright, ★★★

Vimarsh, *Vihm-uhrsh*, (M), (S), knowledge, debate, intelligence, investigation, another name for Shiva, ★★★

Vimb, *Vihmb*, (M), (S), brilliant, shining, a ray of the sun, ★★★

Vimuch, *Vihm-uch*, (M), (S), freed, ★★

Vina, *Veen-ah*, (F), (S), lightning, lute, ★★★

Vinay, *Vihn-uhy*, (M), (S), decency, restraint, ★★★

Vinaya, *Vihn-uhy-ah*, (F), (S), decent, modest, restrained, ★★★

Vinayak, *Vihn-ah-yuhk*, (M), (S), remover, leader, controller, teacher,
     lord of prayer, another name for Garuda, ★

Vinayika, *Vihn-ah-yihk-ah*, (F), (S), consort of Garuda, ★

Vind, *Vihnd*, (M), (S), auspicious mahurat or moment especially for
     performing rituals, time when things are recovered, ★★

Vinesh, *Vihn-aesh*, (M), (S), pious, ★★★

Vinit, *Vihn-eet*, (M), (S), polite, modest, educated, handsome, ★★

Vinita, *Vihn-eet-ah*, (F), (S), polite, modest, educated,
     beautiful, ★★

Viniti, *Vihn-eet-ee*, (F), (S), modesty, manners, education, ★★

Vinod, *Vihn-oad*, (M), (S), play, fun, joke, humour, ★★

Vinsh, *Vihnsh*, (M), (S), the number twenty, twentieth, ★★★

Vipa, *Vihp-ah*, (F), (S), speech, ★★★

Vipasha, *Vihp-ahsh-ah*, (F), (S), limitless, another name for the Beas
     river, ★★★

Vipat, *Vihp-aht*, (M), (S), shooting arrows, melting, killing, ★★

Vipin, *Vihp-ihn*, (M), (S), forest, ★★★

Vipra, *Vihp-ruh*, (M), (S), inspired, wise, sage, the moon, a
     Brahmin, ★★★

Vipsa, *Vihp-sah*, (F), (S), succession, repetition, ★★★

Vipul, *Vihp-ul*, (M), (S), substantial, plentiful, brood, ★★★

Vipula, *Vihp-ul-ah*, (F), (S), substantial, plentiful ★★★

Vir, *Veer*, (M), (S), (O) – Pahlavi, brave, hero, ★★★

Vira, *Veer-ah*, (F), (S), (O) – Pahlavi, brave, heroic, wise, ★★★

Viraj, *Vihr-ahj*, (M), (S), ruler, beauty, brilliant, excellence, majesty, the sun, all–pervading, another name for Agni and Buddha, ★★★

Viraj, *Vihr-uhj*, (M), (S), pure, ★★★

Viraja, *Vihr-uhj-ah*, (F), (S), pure, ★★

Virajin, *Vihr-ahj-ihn*, (M), (S), brilliant, ★★

Virajini, *Vihr-ahj-ihn-ee*, (F), (S), brilliant, queen, ★★

Viral, *Vihr-uhl*, (M), (S), precious, ★★★

Virala, *Vihr-uhl-ah*, (F), (S), precious, ★★★

Viranch, *Vihr-uhnch*, (M), (S), divine, another name for Brahma, ★★

Virat, *Vihr-ahtt*, (M), (S), majestic, ★★★

Virav, *Vihr-ahv*, (M), (S), sound, crying, resounding, ★★★

Virik, *Veer-ihk*, (M), (S), brave, ★★★

Virika, *Veer-ihk-ah*, (F), (S), brave, ★★★

Virikt, *Veer-ihkt*, (M), (S), cleansed, purified, ★★

Virikta, *Veer-ihkt-ah*, (F), (S), cleansed, purified, ★

Virochan, *Vihr-oach-uhn*, (M), (S), brilliant, illuminating, the moon, another name for Surya and Vishnu, ★

Virochana, *Vihr-oach-uhn-ah*, (F), (S), brilliant, illuminating, ★

Viroh, *Vihr-oah*, (M), (S), healing, ★★★

Virohan, *Vihr-oah-huhn*, (M), (S), budding, ★★

Virohin, *Vihr-oah-hihn*, (M), (S), budding, ★★

Virok, *Vihr-oak*, (M), (S), shining, ★★★

Viruj, *Vihr-uj*, (M), (S), healthy, ★★

Viruja, *Vihr-uj-ah*, (F), (S), healthy, ★★

Virup, *Vihr-oop*, (M), (S), shapely, diverse, changed, ★★★

Virupa, *Vihr-oop-ah*, (F), (S), shapely, diverse, changed, ★★★

Virya, *Veer-yah*, (F), (S), valour, strength, energy, ★★

Vishad, *Vihsh-uhd*, (M), (S), apparent, calm, gentle, happy, white, brilliant, pure, ★★

Vishakh, *Vihsh-ahkh*, (M), (S), with many branches, another name for Shiva, ★★

Vishakha, *Vihsh-ahkh-ah*, (F), (S), with many branches, constellation, ★★

Vishal, *Vihsh-ahl*, (M), (S), substantial, important, powerful, eminent, ★★★

Vishala, *Vihsh-ahl-ah*, (F), (S), substantial, important, an apsara or celestial nymph, ★★

Vishamp, *Vihsh-uhmp*, (M), (S), guardian, ★★★

Vishan, *Vihsh-ahn*, (M), (S), pinnacle, best, ★★★

Vishank, *Vihsh-uhnk*, (M), (S), fearless, undoubting, ★★★

Vishesh, *Vihsh-aesh*, (M), (S), special, best, ★★★

Vishit, *Vihsh-iht*, (M), (S), released, free, ★★

Vishnu, *Vihsh-nu*, (M), (S), all-pervading, the preserver of the Hindu holy trinity, has ten incarnations including Raam, Krishna and Buddha, ★★

Vishok, *Vihsh-oak*, (M), (S), happy, without grief, ★★★

Vishoka, *Vihsh-oak-ah*, (F), (S), happy, without grief, ★★

Vishram, *Vihsh-ruhm*, (M), (S), calm, rest, ★★★

Vishrant, *Vihsh-rahnt*, (M), (S), rested, ★★

Vishrut, *Vihsh-rut*, (M), (S), famous, happy, ★★

Vishruti, *Vihsh-rut-ee*, (F), (S), fame, ★★

Vishtap, *Vihsh-tuhp*, (M), (S), pinnacle, ★★

Vishuddh, *Vihsh-uddh*, (M), (S), pure, worthy, honest, ★

Vishuddhi, *Vihsh-uddh-ee*, (F), (S), purity, knowledge, genuineness, holiness, ★

Vishup, *Vihsh-up*, (M), (S), the equinox, ★★★

Vishva, *Vihsh-vah*, (F), (S), world, ★★★

Vishva, *Vihsh-vuh*, (M), (S), complete, world, the universe, ★★★

Vishvach, *Vihsh-vahch*, (M), (S), omnipresent, ★★★

Vishvachi, *Vihsh-vahch-ee*, (F), (S), universal, an apsara or celestial nymph, ★★

Vishvag, *Vihsh-vuhg*, (M), (S), going everywhere, another name for Brahma, ★★★

Vishvak, *Vihsh-vuhk*, (M), (S), all-pervading, ★★★

Vishvas, *Vihsh-vahs*, (M), (S), confidence, belief, faith, ★★★

Vishvesh, *Vihsh-vaesh*, (M), (S), lord of the universe, universally desired, another name for Brahma, Vishnu and Shiva, ★★

Vit, *Viht*, (M), (S), prosperity, known, ★★

Vit, *Veet*, (M), (S), desired, pleasant, ★★

Vita, *Veet-ah*, (F), (S), desire, ★★

Vitark, *Viht-uhrk*, (M), (S), imagination, opinion, ★

Vitesh, *Viht-aesh*, (M), (S), lord of riches, ★★

Viti, *Viht-ee*, (F), (S), knowledge, acquisition, ★★

Viti, *Veet-ee*, (F), (S), pleasure, brilliance, fire, ★★

Vitol, *Viht-oal*, (M), (S), calm, ★★

Vitola, *Viht-oal-ah*, (F), (S), calm, river, ★★

Vittak, *Viht-tuhk*, (M), (S), prosperous, celebrated, ★★

Vittap, *Viht-tuhp*, (M), (S), guarding wealth, ★★

Vitul, *Viht-ul*, (M), (S), substantial, loud, ★★

Vivan, *Vihv-ahn*, (M), (S), rays of the morning sun, ★★★

Vivas, *Vihv-ahs*, (M), (S), dawning, exile, ★★★

Vivash, *Vihv-uhsh*, (M), (S), motionless, unrestrained, independent, ★★★

Vivek, *Vihv-aek*, (M), (S), discernment, knowledge, reason, ★★★

Viveka, *Vihv-aek-ah*, (F), (S), discernment, knowledge, reason, ★★★

Vivid, *Vihv-ihd*, (M), (S), knowledgeable, ★★

Vivikt, *Vihv-ihkt*, (M), (S), distinguished, pure, deep, ★

Vivikta, *Vihv-ihkt-ah*, (F), (S), distinguished, pure, deep, ★

Virdhi, *Vrih-dhee*, (F), (S), growth, property, prosperity, joy, development, ★★

Vrij, *Vrihj*, (M), (S), strength, to twist, to leave★★★

Vrind, *Vrihnd*, (M), (S), many, numerous, ★★

Vrinda, *Vrihnd-ah*, (F), (S), many, all, a chorus of singers, Tulsi or sacred Basil, ★★

Vrish, *Rihsh*, (M), (S), male, bull, virile, strong, best, Taurus, ★★★

Vrishabh, *Rihsh-uhbh*, (M), (S), manly, bull, virile, strong, best, excellent, illustrious, ★★

Vrishabha, *Rihsh-uhbh-ah*, (F), (S), strong, best, excellent, illustrious, ★★

Vrishag, *Rihsh-uhg*, (M), (S), travelling on a bull, another name for Shiva, ★★★

Vrishin, *Rihsh-ihn*, (M), (S), peacock, ★★★

Vurna, *Voor-nah*, (F), (S), selected, ★★★

Vyaan, *Vyahn*, (M), (S), life giving, air circulating in the body, ★★★

Vyaapti, *Vyahp-tee*, (F), (S), achievement, omnipresence, permeation, ★★

Vyaas, *Vyahs*, (M), (S), separation, diffusion, name of the compiler of the Puranas, ★★★

Vyakt, *Vyuhkt*, (M), (S), wise, handsome, visible, distinguished, another name for Vishnu, ★★

Vyans, *Vyuhns*, (M), (S), broad shouldered, ★★

Vyansh, *Vyuhn-sh*, (M), (S), broad shouldered, ★★

Vyanshak, *Vyuhn-shuhk*, (M), (S), mountain, ★★

Vyast, *Vyuhst*, (M), (S), separated, individual, ★★

Vyasti, *Vyuhs-tee*, (F), (S), achievement, success, individuality, ★★

Vyush, *Vyuhsh*, (M), (S), dawn, ★★★

Vyushtt, *Vyuh-shtt*, (M), (S), dawned, dawn, clear, ★★★

Vyushti, *Vyuhsh-ttee*, (F), (S), the first light of dawn, elegance, beauty, praise, wealth, ★★★

W

Wafa, *Wuhf-ah*, (F), (A), fulfillment, loyalty, ★★★

Waya, *Wah-yah*, (F), (P), desirable, essential, ★★★

Winona, *Wihn-oan-ah*, (F), (O) – Native American, first born
daughter, ★★★

Y

Yaachan, (M), (S), entreaty, prayer, ★★★

Yaachana, (F), (S), entreaty, prayer, ★★★

Yaadav, *Yah-duhv*, (M), (S), descended from Yadu, another name
for Krishna, ★★

Yaadavi, *Yah-duhv-ee*, (F), (S), of the Yaadav tribe, another name
for Durga, ★★

Yaaj, *Yahj*, (M), (S), worshipper, sacrifice, another name
for Shiva, ★★★

Yaajak, *Yahj-ahk*, (M), (S), religious, sacrificing priest, ★★★

Yaami, *Yahm-ee*, (F), (S), path, progress, an apsara or
celestial nymph, ★★★

Yaamini, *Yahm-ihn-ee*, (F), (S), night, ★★★

Yaamir, *Yahm-eer*, (M), (S), the moon, ★★★

Yaamya, *Yahm-yah*, (F), (S), night, ★★★

Yaamya, *Yahm-yuh*, (M), (S), southern, the right hand, sandalwood,
pertaining to Yama, another name for Shiva and Vishnu, ★★★

Yaana, *Yah-nah*, (F), (O) – Hebrew, Slavic, god is gracious, ★★★

Yaashk, *Yahshk*, (M), (S), desiring heat, exerting, ★★★

Yaasmin, *Yahs-meen*, (F), (A), jasmine, ★★★

Yadva, *Yuhd-vah*, (F), (S), insight, intelligence, mind, ★★

Yahv, *Yuh-hv*, (M), (S), quick, agile, another name for Agni
and Indra, ★★★

Yahva, *Yuh-hv-ah*, (F), (S), heaven and earth, flowing water, ★★★

Yahvi, *Yuh-hv-ee*, (F), (S), the union of heaven and earth, ★★★

Yaja, *Yuhj-ah*, (F), (S), religious, sacrificer, ★★★

Yajak, *Yuhj-ahk*, (M), (S), religious, generous, sacrificing priest, ★★★

Yajan, *Yuhj-uhn*, (M), (S), sacrifice, worship, ★★★

Yajas, (M), (S), worship, ★★★

Yajat, *Yuhj-uht*, (M), (S), sacred, dignified, the moon, another name for Shiva, ★★

Yajata, *Yuhj-uht-ah*, (F), (S), sacred, dignified, ★★

Yajin, *Yuhj-ihn*, (M), (S), religious, sacrifice, ★★★

Yajn, *Yuhjn*, (M), (S), worship, devotion, sacrifice, worshipper, sacrificer, ★★

Yajur, *Yuhj-ur*, (M), (S), a Vedic text, ★★★

Yajvin, *Yuhj-vihn*, (M), (S), religious, ★★★

Yaksh, *Yuhksh*, (M), (S), protecter of forests, speedy, class of demigods, ★★★

Yakshin, *Yuhk-shihn*, (M), (S), alive, ★★★

Yam, *Yuhm*, (M), (A), ocean, ★★★

Yama, *Yuhm-ah*, (F), (O) – Pahlavi, river, stream, ★★★

Yamin, *Yuhm-ihn*, (M), (S), restrained, ★★★

Yamit, *Yuhm-iht*, (M), (S), restrained, ★★

Yash, *Yuhsh*, (M), (S), success, celebrity, reputation, victory, ★★★

Yasha, *Yuhsh-ah*, (F), (S), success, celebrity, victory, ★★★

Yashas, *Yuhsh-uhs*, (M), (S), attractiveness, brilliance, virtue, fame, ★★★

Yashil, *Yuhsh-ihl*, (M), (S), successful, wealthy, popular, ★★★

Yashila, *Yuhsh-ihl-ah*, (F), (S), successful, wealthy, popular, ★★★

Yati, *Yuht-ee*, (F), (S), restraint, ★★

Yati, *Yuht-ee*, (M), (S), ascetic, devotee, one who has subdued his passions, another name for Shiva, ★★

Yatin, *Yuht-ihn*, (M), (S), ascetic, devotee, ★★

Yatna, *Yuht-nuh*, (M), (S), endeavour, labour, performance, energy, ★★

Yatnik, *Yuht-nihk*, (M), (S), making efforts, ★★

Yavan, *Yuhv-uhn*, (M), (S), quick, a Mohammedan, Greeks who
    settled in India before Alexander the Great's invasion in
    326 BC, mingling, keeping aloof, ★★★

Yavana, *Yuhv-uhn-ah*, (F), (S), fast, ★★★

Yodhin, *Yoadh-ihn*, (M), (S), warrior, victor, ★★

Yog, *Yoag*, (M), (S), meditation, concentration, application, energy,
    passion, charm, cure, sum, total, union, ★★★

Yoga, *Yoag-ah*, (F), (S), meditation, energy, ★★★

Yogaj, *Yoag-uhj*, (M), (S), born of meditation, ★★★

Yogaja, *Yoag-uhj-ah*, (F), (S), born of meditation, ★★★

Yogas, *Yoag-uhs*, (M), (S), meditation, ★★★

Yogi, *Yoag-ee*, (M), (S), ascetic, meditative, religious, a Buddha,
    another name for Vishnu and Shiva, ★★★

Yogin, *Yoag-ihn*, (M), (S), ascetic, follower of the Yoga philosophy,
    magician, ★★

Yogini, *Yoag-ihn-ee*, (F), (S), fairy, follower of the Yoga philosophy,
    magician ★★

Yogit, *Yoag-iht*, (M), (S), bewitched, enchanted, ★★

Yogita, *Yoag-iht-ah*, (F), (S), bewitched, enchanted, ★★

Yojak, *Yoaj-uhk*, (M), (S), employer, manager, another name
    for Agni, ★★★

Yosha, *Yoash-ah*, (F), (S), girl, young, ★★★

Yoshan, *Yoash-uhn*, (M), (S), young, ★★★

Yoshana, *Yoash-uhn-ah*, (F), (S), girl, young, ★★★

Yoshit, *Yoash-iht*, (M), (S), young, boy, ★★

Yoshita, *Yoash-iht-ah*, (F), (S), young, girl, wife, ★★

Yotak, *Yoatt-uhk*, (M), (S), constellation, ★★★

Yugal, *Yuhg-uhl*, (M), (S), pair, ★★★

Yugap, *Yuhg-uhp*, (M), (S), best of the era, ★★★

Yuj, *Yuhj*, (M), (S), companion, equal, to restrain, to arrange, to prepare, to concentrate, ★★

Yujya, *Yuhj-yuh*, (M), (S), connected, allied, equal in power, capable, ★★

Yukt, *Yuhkt*, (M), (S), yoked, united, attentive, skilful, clever, proper, of good conduct, prosperous, ★★

Yukta, *Yuhk-tah*, (F), (S), yoked, united, attentive, skilful, clever, proper, of good conduct, prosperous, ★★

Yukti, *Yuk-tee*, (F), (S), tact, skill, argument, ★★

Yupaksh, *Yoo-pahksh*, (M), (S), the eye of victory, ★★

Yuv, *Yuv*, (M), (S), young, vigorous, ★★★

Yuva, *Yuv-ah*, (F), (S), young, vigorous, ★★★

Yuval, *Yu-vuhl*, (M), (O) – Hebrew, stream, ★★★

Yuvan, *Yu-vuhn*, (M), (S), young, healthy, the moon, ★★★

Yuvana, *Yu-vuhn-ah*, (F), (S), young, healthy, ★★★

Yuvraj, *Yuv-rahj*, (M), (S), young, prince, ★★★

Yuvik, *Yuv-ihk*, (M), (S), young, ★★★

Yuvika, *Yuv-ihk-ah*, (F), (S), young, girl, ★★★

Z

Zaaba, *Zahb-ah*, (F), (P), gold, ★★★

Zaahir, *Zah-hihr*, (M), (A), visible, distinct, ★★★

Zaahira, *Zah-hihr-ah*, (F), (A), brilliant, visible, blossoming, dawn, ★★★

Zaara, *Zah-rah*, (F), (A), dawn, brilliance, blossoming flower, ★★★

Zain, Zaen, (F), (A), beauty, elegance, honour, ★★

Zain, Zaen, (M), (A), beauty, elegance, honour, ★★

Zaira, *Za-ee-rah*, (F), (A), brilliance, blossoming flower, ★★★

Zeba, *Zaeb-ah*, (F), (P), beautiful, thankful, ★★★

Zebara, *Zaeb-ahr-ah*, (F), (P), beauty, ★★★

Zahara, *Zuh-hahr-ah*, (F), (A), brilliant, shining, blossoming, ★★★

Zibal, *Zihb-ahl*, (M), (A), majestic, honourable, (P), fast, ★★★

Zoe, *Zoa-yee*, (F), (O) – Greek, life, ★★★

Zohar, *Zoa-huhr*, (M), (O) – Hebrew, lustre, brilliance, ★★★

Zohra, *Zoh-rah*, (F), (A), blooming, ★★★

Zoya, *Zoa-yah*, (F), (O) – Greek, life, ★★★

Zubin, *Zoo-bihnn*, (M), (P), sword, ★★★

Zuhan, *Zu-huhn*, (M), (A), splendour of the world, ★★★

Zulaika, *Zul-aek-ah*, (F), (A), fair, brilliant, well-born, ★★★

Zulfa, *Zul-fah*, (F), (A), first part of the night, ★★★

Further Resources

Books

- Dogra, Ramesh C. and Urmila Dogra, *A Dictionary of Hindu Names*, New Delhi: Aditya Prakashan, 1992.
- Gandhi, Maneka, *The Penguin Book of Hindu Names*, New Delhi: Penguin, 2004.
- Gandhi, Maneka and Ozair Husain, *The Complete Book of Muslim and Parsi Names*, New Delhi, HarperCollins Publishers, 1994.
- Nicholson, Louise, *The Best Baby Name Book*, Canada: Thorsons, 2002.
- Pandey, Uma Prasad, *Sanskrit-Hindi-English Dictionary*, New Delhi: Kamal Prakashan, 2008.
- Parekh, Sachin and Sonal Parekh, *Asian Babies' Names from the Hindu, Muslim and Sikh traditions*, US: Elliot Right Way Books, 2004.
- Patil, Vimla, *Baby Names*, New Delhi: Rupa, 1998.
- Stafford, Diane, *40,001 Best Baby Names*, UK: Vermilion, 2004.
- Tiwari, R.C., R.S. Sharma and Krishna Vikal, *Hindi-English English-Hindi Dictionary*, New Delhi: Jaico, 2006.

Websites

There are countless websites devoted to baby names – and more springing up by the minute – and so, I have given a small selection of those that I have found useful and well-researched. The nature of the internet means that this is by no means a comprehensive list.

www.babynology.com
www.babynames.com
www.babynamespedia.com
www.bachpan.com
www.birthvillage.com
www.desiparenting.com
www.godweb.org/HinduBabyNamesindex.htm
www.iloveindia.com
www.indiaparenting.com
www.nriol.com/babynames/index.asp

Note from the Author
The focus of this work on modern, relevant names means that it will miss some names as they come into use in an ever globalising India. If there are any names that you feel would merit inclusion in future editions of the book, please feel free to email your suggestions to the author at *names@ modernindianbaby.com*.